T0028469

DOWN TO BUSINESS

51 Industry Leaders Share Practical Advice
on How to Become a Young Entrepreneur

DOWN TO BUSINESS

51 Industry Leaders Share Practical Advice on
How to Become a Young Entrepreneur

FENLEY SCURLOCK & JASON LIAW

Random House 🏠 New York

Text copyright © 2024 by Fenley Scurlock and Jason Liaw
Jacket art copyright © 2024 by Loz Ives

Photographs: p. 8: David Yellen (Alina Morse); p. 154: Morgan Hizar (Emma Butler);
p. 254 Dragana Jurisic (Zlata Filipović); p. 310: Anita Barsca Photography (Annabel Chang)

Visit us on the Web! rhcbooks.com

Educators and librarians, for a variety of teaching tools, visit us at RHTeachersLibrarians.com

Library of Congress Cataloging-in-Publication Data is available upon request.
ISBN 978-0-593-65159-9 (trade) — ISBN 978-0-593-65160-5 (lib. bdg.) —
ISBN 978-0-593-65161-2 (ebook)

The text of this book is set in 11.5-point Adobe Garamond Pro.
All interior art used under license from stock.adobe.com
Interior design by Cathy Bobak

Printed in the United States of America
10 9 8 7 6 5 4 3 2 1
First Edition

To my parents, for their worldly advice,
their support of all my goals, and, above all,
their wholehearted love and devotion to my success and joy
—F.S.

To my family for their unconditional love and
unwavering support in everything I do
—J.L.

CONTENTS

Introduction

I'm Fen . . . and I'm Jason. We're lifelong friends—and we're also entrepreneurs.

Fen here! I turned my love of art into a business when I was seven, selling artisanal soaps at farmers markets and business fairs, and eventually fulfilling orders for birthday parties, bridal and baby showers, corporate events, and several Airbnb properties. I was instantly hooked on the thrill of designing and pitching a product, learning the art of negotiation, and earning and investing my own money. I studied business greats such as Warren Buffett, Oprah Winfrey, Bill Gates, Jeff Bezos, Steve Jobs, MacKenzie Scott, Richard Branson, and other famed inventors and investors, while learning to write business plans, market products, maintain customer relations, and absorb other aspects of managing a business. Now I apply this entrepreneurial mindset to everything I do.

Jason chiming in! I am a programmer who learned the basics of coding in school, then taught myself the skills to be a webmaster, and was hired by the Asian Pacific American Chamber of Commerce to establish and maintain their web and social media presence. This ignited my passion to help mission-driven organizations and ultimately bridge cultural understanding in the business world with my bilingual skills.

We both have our sights set high and talk about the power of businesses to change the world all the time. And we're not alone. We are part of one of the most entrepreneurial generations *ever*. We are also a generation questioning everything and thinking outside the box to find solutions that will revolutionize the way we live. But while we have big dreams and drive, we still need to learn some core fundamental skills before we start launching real companies. Unfortunately, business and entrepreneurship aren't taught in most middle and high schools. And although camps, mentorship programs, and extracurricular classes are cropping up in many places, they are still out of reach for most kids.

To try to fill that critical knowledge gap, we decided to gather some very expert advice. We wanted to know: What does it really mean to be an entrepreneur, and what does it take to get there? What can we learn from those who came before us, and from those doing it right now? How do we get up to speed fast, and meld their experience with our ambition, ideas, and instinct? That's what we were set on understanding.

We started by interviewing family friends and local business owners. We asked friends of friends who they knew, cold-called people from LinkedIn, researched businesses we admired, and emailed heads of companies. In most cases, people responded with enthusiasm, and shared their advice and their connections. Some didn't respond, or they told us no, and through that we learned a fundamental entrepreneurial skill: say thank you and move on.

After all, as many of the people in this book told us, when one door closes, another one opens.

We interviewed leaders from diverse fields and industries—indie beauty experts, ice cream makers, bankers, brand experts, military vets, media moguls. They are from both small start-ups and industry giants, and they live all over the world, from Silicon Valley to Washington, DC, Beijing to Boulder, Australia to Ireland. We talked to leaders who went to Ivy League schools and others who dropped out of college. We talked to some who were raised in public housing, some who were raised in privilege, others who were immigrants who chased the American Dream, and many who simply dreamed big. We talked to people across four generations, including some young entrepreneurs who are blazing the way for us and eager to share what they've learned.

Each pop culture reference, funny anecdote, and inspirational story sparked new ideas, and each conversation revealed a new lesson. We often felt like we were getting a master class in entrepreneurship and leadership, learning insights, trade secrets, and advice that would have taken years to learn on our own. And beyond business advice, we asked these entrepreneurs how they suggested we cope with the pressures our generation is facing today and grapple with the challenges before us. We learned their personal stories, what they were like as kids, and how it relates to who they are now.

The lessons from our entrepreneurs are relevant in everything we do today—in school, our businesses, and life. From reminding ourselves not to take rejection personally, to staying authentic to who we are, to putting ourselves out there even when it feels hard, each interviewee had advice to help us grow and reminders for our entrepreneurial journeys: develop grit like Tara, own your ideas like Charles, embrace feedback like Davis, challenge the status quo like Emma. The experts we spoke with are like trusted mentors we can turn to for advice over and over again by reading their words.

Once we finished all the interviews, we selected which parts to include in the book. (We didn't want it to be eight hundred pages long!) What's here is a snapshot of the many hours we spent with these amazing people. We learned that when it comes to entrepreneurship, there's no one-size-fits-all, so in the pages that follow, we grouped our interviewees by some of the qualities we saw in them, and that readers might see in themselves: the Disruptor, the Visionary, the Champion, the Innovator, the Creator, the Investor, and the Strategist. Our hope is that these examples of different mindsets, leadership styles, and personal vibes will bust the myth that entrepreneurship has a strict definition and is a job available to only a few (another piece of advice from one of our experts).

In addition to this framework, we grouped each interviewee by industry, so readers can pick and choose their entrepreneurial path. Inspired by food? We have entrepreneurs for that. Fashion? There are experts there, too. Technology? Check. Media? Yep! The icons at the beginning of the entrepreneur profiles will help readers follow along with their interests and compare leaders' advice by sector. Although we varied our interview questions, we had five questions that we always asked: What hashtag best describes you or your business? Is social media good or bad? Is college worth it? What is your best business advice for young entrepreneurs? And what is your best life advice for our generation? We thought these quick takes would help you get the flavor of someone's personality right away. So you'll see those answers at the beginning of each interview. And at the end of each one, we have listed key takeaways for you to start doing right now, like building resilience, surrounding yourself with the smartest people in the room, testing ideas, and taking risks. All are skills these entrepreneurs said helped them succeed and will help us fill that critical knowledge gap. We also highlighted our favorite quotes from each interview, the ones that really stuck with us and impacted our own entrepreneurial journeys.

Our generation has big problems to solve, from closing the wage gap and leveling out the cost of college to saving the planet and protecting our data. Not only do we want to start now, we have to. This book is a road map to help prepare us, help us develop our entrepreneurial potential, and help us quickly bring the world the next generation of great products, ideas, and solutions. In doing so, we'll be able to make our mark in a world turned upside down, and yet still full of possibility.

Which Type of Leader Inspires You?

The **Disruptor** is a risk taker who challenges the status quo, creating a better way of doing things and blazing a new trail. *You'll meet the cofounder of the e-commerce giant dubbed the Amazon of Latin America, a makeup saint shaking up the beauty industry, the queen of candles, and a sole-minded shoe enthusiast building communities of sneakerheads.*

The **Visionary** is a dreamer who boldly imagines something that few can see: a revolutionary product, service, or idea that could change the world. *You'll read about a serial space entrepreneur who wants to connect everyone on Earth via satellite phone, a filmmaker trying to democratize education, and an app developer bringing authenticity and empathy to the workplace.*

The **Champion** is an advocate or social entrepreneur who is purpose driven and dedicated to a cause or making life better for people. *You will read about a champion of universal sport, a Chief Estrogen Officer imagining an end to period poverty, and a llama-loving outdoor enthusiast on a mission to do well by doing good.*

The **Innovator** is a fixer who sees a specific problem in their own lives, or in the world around them, and actively works to solve it. *You'll meet the inventor of a recycling robot, a sleep whisperer, and an executive bringing more diversity to television.*

The **Creator** is an artist at heart, someone with a unique vibe who uses their extraordinary perspective to design unprecedented products. *You'll meet an ice cream artist, a candy creator, a cookie dough designer, a soap maker harnessing the great outdoors, and kid brothers bringing fun to your feet.*

The **Investor** puts their money behind an idea, product, or service, confident that it will come back to them tenfold. *You'll hear from a venture capitalist who helped launch education companies like Kahoot! and Udemy and an immigrant who is making it easier for more people from other countries to bring their ideas to America.*

The **Strategist** is a master planner who sees the big picture and focuses on aligning vision with goals in order to win. *You'll meet a military veteran improving the lives of his fellow servicemen, a former NPR executive working to end polarized news, and a travel industry expert bringing flying cars to our highways.*

The Disruptor

The Visionary

The Champion

The Innovator

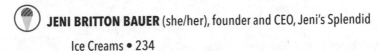
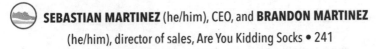

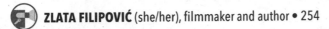
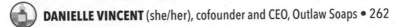
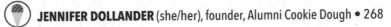
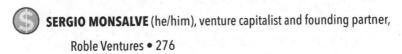

The Strategist

 ANNABEL CHANG (she/her), head of state policy and government relations, Waymo • 310

 KEN STERN (he/him), founder and CEO, Palisades Media Ventures; former CEO, NPR • 317

 ANDREA CLARKE (she/her), founder and CEO, FutureFitCo • 324

 DAN FRANK (he/him), former CEO, Three Wire Systems, LLC • 332

  SEAN PENG (he/him), CEO, Taishan Sports • 337

 JULIE SKAFF (she/her), COO, Viz.ai • 343

 LEE BRENNER (he/him), head of public policy, digital assets, Goldman Sachs • 350

 STEVE DOUTY (he/him), cofounder and CEO, Octopus Software, Smaarts Inc., Scayl Inc. • 357

 JENNIFER SILBERMAN (she/her), chief sustainability officer, Dollar Tree • 363

 ALAN TURLEY (he/him), minister-counselor for commercial affairs, US Embassy, Tokyo • 369

 RICHARD BIRD (he/him), chief product officer, SecZetta • 375

 TIMOTHY KIGHT (he/him), founder and CEO, Focus 3 • 383

The Disruptor

ALINA MORSE (she/her)
Founder and CEO, Zolli Candy

#KeepSmiling

On life: It's about finding your people and finding the people that at the end of the day support you for you.

On business: As long as you can communicate your wants, your vision, and your needs to your team members, confidently delegate tasks, and set up processes in which your team members can succeed, then you've done your job as CEO.

On social: Social media can be a great tool. At the end of the day, it's about how we use it.

 On college: Look for a good fit.

Alina Morse became a chief executive officer (CEO) when she was just nine years old, and she has been defying expectations ever since. She could not have imagined that being offered a lollipop at the bank when she was seven would spark an entrepreneurial journey, and yet that one event inspired her multimillion-dollar idea to create a healthy candy that's good for your teeth. After two years of perfecting her formula and taste testing, Alina came out with Zollipops, the first product in the Zolli Candy line. Today, Zolli confections are sold on Amazon and by more than twenty thousand other retailers in the United States and around the world, and have expanded to caramels, taffy, and peanut butter cups. Now in her late teens, Alina is leading a healthy-candy revolution, challenging a traditional industry filled with legacy brands—and men—to think about candy differently. She even uses her high school experiences in business, applying her theater training to public speaking and media interviews, and lessons from competitive tennis and dance to management and team building. Alina has retained her original vision by creating the Million Smiles Initiative, through which she distributes her candies to schools around the country and simultaneously educates children about the scientific applications in candy making, entrepreneurship, and oral hygiene. She talks to us about how she convinced the industry to take her seriously, challenging the status quo, and being true to yourself.

What is the origin story of Zolli Candy?

I came up with the idea when I was seven years old on a trip to the bank with my dad. The bank teller offered me a lollipop. My dad always told me you shouldn't have candy because sugar is terrible for your teeth. So I asked him, "Why can't we make a healthy lollipop that's good for my teeth?" so that I could eat candy without it being bad for me. And Zollipops were born.

Did you know from the very beginning that you had a hit?

Even from the start, I was surprised by my own idea because it seems like such a simple theory. But I really did think it could be transformational, and something that could fill a niche in the market. Granted, I had no idea to what extent Zolli would grow, and I've been shocked along the way to see an invention that I believed in become a staple at my favorite retailers and in so many households.

It took two years for you to perfect your first product. Could you tell us more about that process?

Those first two years really entailed a lot of trial and error. Initially, it started by purchasing some ingredients from our local supermarket—some sugar substitutes like stevia and other ingredients that I had done some research on—that could act as replacements to the sugary ingredients in a regular lollipop. I learned to make candy by watching YouTube videos, and after attempting to make candy at home in my kitchen, making a huge mess, and having to replace some kitchen appliances, I realized that I needed some help. So we proceeded with researching various manufacturing facilities, taking some tours, and eventually landing on a manufacturing facility that was a perfect fit. They could create sugar-free candy. Then we just got to work with this plant, where we said to the food scientist, we want to start off with six flavors, and let's just try and fail and

"There will always be people in the world who doubt you. For me, it was because of my age and my gender. That's not a great mix in a traditional industry, like candy. I definitely stood out in the room. It always took me a few extra steps to prove that I knew what I was talking about before people stopped doubting me."

try and fail until we come up with something that's really delicious. It felt like over a hundred, but we did upwards of twenty trials per flavor—tweaking the flavor, the color, the texture, and then testing it in various climates to ensure various stability ratings. That process was about a year and a half, and then those other six months entailed formulating the packaging and all the logistics that come with trademarking your taglines and logos and other behind-the-scenes stuff before pitching at the end of that two-year period to our first retailer, Whole Foods in Southern California.

Can you describe that first sale?

Whole Foods is merchandised regionally, so you have to pitch each region. California is a very progressive market littered with early adopters. It's definitely a great place to launch a new and up-and-coming innovation. We traveled to Southern California from Michigan, where I'm from, and I practiced the pitch all the way there. I was super nervous because it was my first time in a real business meeting, and I was also very excited to get this in front of some very powerful people. The meeting went fantastic. At the end of it, they said they would let us know in the next few months if we were in or not, and we waited patiently for an answer. And we got in! It was

> *"When you start embracing what you don't know, embracing what you can learn, embracing your curiosity and kindness and positivity, there's no end to what you can achieve."*

just a very exciting and almost surreal moment, from picturing our items on store shelves to being in a mainstream retailer. From there, we got on Amazon.com and then the business took off after my first media appearance on *Good Morning America*. We were able to reach out to more and more retailers, attend business conferences, and get to where we are now, which is more than twenty thousand retailers across the country.

What are the advantages of being a teen entrepreneur?

There's definitely that shock factor that's played into people's interest in the company. It's also been interesting to see which retailers, brokers, and executives have actually heard of Zolli Candy and heard of my story prior to us meeting with them. That's pretty exciting as well, whether they've seen me on TV, or heard about our story via social media, or word of mouth. There have been several instances where people have already heard of Zolli Candy and have been excited about bringing it into their stores, because it does have that authenticity and that organic family business story that ultimately resonates with their customers. That aspect has been definitely helpful.

Has your age ever hindered you from finding investors or people to partner with?

On the disadvantage end, there's some very traditionalist views in the consumer-packaged goods industry, as well as traditional retail. It is the oldest form of sales. Depending on the retailer, it's definitely an industry that can be pretty stagnant and traditional. Often with those values come the views of "you need a business degree, and you need to go to college before pursuing a business venture." For me, that's been tough to crack because I was starting a company when I was in elementary school. Obviously, I didn't have a degree or real-world experience yet. But being in those situations, and having the mindset of being like a sponge, wanting to soak up all that information, I was luckily able to prove a lot of those traditionalists wrong. Ultimately, it has created a more open-minded market, and has broken down some of those stereotypes.

Does the current education system fail to properly prepare students with skills they need to be an entrepreneur, like public speaking, negotiation, and investing?

Most public schools don't even have personal finance courses that could benefit students going into the real world, whether they're going into entrepreneurship, business, or just looking to take charge of their own financial futures. I'm starting the entrepreneurship club at my school, focused on the behind-the-scenes of building a company, like creating a business plan, how to crowdsource or crowd-fund, and how to analyze sites like the Small Business Administration for loans and programs to help teen entrepreneurs, young entrepreneurs, and women in business. They might not be the most fun parts of business, but they are fundamentals that are important to learn.

What is your day-to-day like in running a business?

My day-to-day is pretty typical. So many teenagers nowadays work. Granted, sometimes I'm feeling like I'm bordering on a heart attack owning a small company. But it really isn't much different than any other typical teenager, juggling school, work, and extra-curriculars. For example, today I woke up, I played tennis, I came home, did some meetings and emails, this interview, and after this, it's going to be some homework. Tonight, I am going on a date with my boyfriend. I like to find the balance between mental health, physical health, and extracurriculars. I'm a dancer—I'm on my school's dance team, as well as on the tennis team. Having that physical outlet and teammates has not only helped me maintain my physical and mental health throughout tough, stressful days, but has also helped me in the team aspects of entrepreneurship. I always like to say business is a team sport. Those team sports and activities where you work together translate into a work setting.

What is your favorite part of the business?

My favorite part is definitely sales and marketing. They inter-twine in a way, doing sales calls, interviews, and communicating with people, whether it's investors, reporters, or team members. That is when my communication skills and relaying my passion, which I would consider my strong suit, shine through. I love to be creative and apply that in fields that I'm knowledgeable about, like social media, and analyzing cash-back advertising services like Google and Instacart. I love marketing, being creative, and applying that in a real-world setting, but above all, I love communicating with people.

What do you find the most challenging?

The most challenging aspect for me is accounting and lo-gistics. Going into a business career with a second grader "math degree"—my math was very low level. Figuring out the finance and logistics has been a game of catch-up my whole career. It has actually provided a lot of real-world insight into what sort of math that I'm learning in high school math class is actually applicable to a real career. I know it's an ongoing comment from generations of students and math classes: "When am I going to use this? Where am I going to apply this? I want to become an oceanographer; when am I going to use Algebra 2?" But it really is applicable even in personal finance. It's been interesting for me to see what's relevant and what's not so relevant in the real world. That's probably the biggest challenge to overcome.

Your Instagram is filled with posts about being a teen entrepreneur. Do you ever experience cyberbullying or get hate comments?

Yes—I've received lots! Either people don't like that I have a Samsung, or they don't like my personality, or they don't like that I'm a girl starting a company—there's always going to be that negative aspect of social media. At the end of the day, it's about how we use it, and how we portray ourselves as a brand, and it has been a great tool to help highlight our essence as a brand. It has also taught me to have thick skin!

What advice would you give to young entrepreneurs who have unique ideas, but don't know how to bring them to market?

My best piece of advice is to write out a plan and do some research. That was the advice that was given to me by my dad when I was seven years old, and it stuck with me. Every time I have an idea, whether it be for a new planning strategy, a new marketing strategy, or a new product, that's the first step. Research if there's anything else like it on the market and research the unique proposition that you provide with an item or an invention. Moving forward, you have to look at your goals. You have to analyze what you want it to be—one item, one **SKU,** a whole brand, a whole line? Where do you want to sell it? Do you want to sell it online? Direct to consumer? In retailers? Set those goals for yourself and outline that business plan. Then it's about finding team members

> SKU: A stock-keeping unit (SKU) is a standardized unit of measure that assigns unique codes to products for effective inventory management and stock control.

and people that not only support what you're doing, but support you, and that you feel that you can trust, and you can delegate work to, because as a CEO, as the founder, you're not going to be able to do it all. That brings me to the next piece of advice, which is find a mission, find a driving passion that's not just making money, whether it's an organization that you start, a **nonprofit** that you'd like to support, or helping people on a day-to-day basis fill that niche in their lives. Find that driving force that's not just monetary, because that's not sustaining. Finally, ask questions. You have

> Nonprofit: A nonprofit is an organization that seeks to have a positive effect on society without prioritizing profit as the primary objective.

to maintain that childlike curiosity and tenacity. You have to stay curious and continue to always look for the next way to improve. You can't do that if you're not asking questions.

What has running a business taught you about not listening when others doubt you?

There will always be people in the world who doubt you. For me, it was because of my age and my gender. That's not a great mix in a traditional industry, like candy, which is full of legacy brands and lots of men. I definitely stood out in the room. It always took me a few extra steps to prove that I knew what I was talking about before people stopped doubting me and started believing that I knew what I was talking about. I think Gen Z has already done a great job of standing out and being confident in themselves and their ideas and being accepting of others. You can't let the limitations of close-minded individuals dictate how you feel about yourself. You have to keep that in the back of your mind, regardless of how high-powered an individual may be. If they are close-minded, that's not going to get them anywhere further. When you start embracing what you don't know, embracing what you can learn, embracing your curiosity and kindness and positivity, there's no end to what you can achieve.

 # Key Takeaways:

- ➔ Set goals and outline a plan.
- ➔ Hire a great team.
- ➔ Embrace what you don't know.
- ➔ Have a childlike curiosity and ask questions.
- ➔ Find a motivation outside of money.

JANE PARK (she/her)
Founder and CEO, Tokki and Julep

#Engagement

On life: What stays with you at the end of the day isn't how much money you made, but how you treated people. Both in terms of moments of pride and regret.

On business: When faced with a challenge, we can choose to engage or disengage. Entrepreneurship is a choice to engage. It's a choice to wake up, to connect, and to try.

Jane Park's first foray into innovative entrepreneurship was as the founder and CEO of Julep, a popular makeup and skin care brand backed by celebrity investors Beyoncé and Jay-Z, Will and Jada Pinkett Smith, and Starbucks CEO Howard Schultz. She now heads her second company, Tokki, which makes reusable gift bags with a technology twist. To launch Tokki, Jane drew on her negotiating skills from law school, her executive experience at Starbucks, and her creative aesthetic. Tokki aims to eliminate the four million tons of gift-wrapping waste that fills landfills each year, while giving people a fun and meaningful experience. Each Tokki gift bag is made with three post-consumer recycled water bottles, and features a recordable QR greeting card so that gift givers can leave digital messages for gift recipients. Jane has deftly navigated the highly competitive landscape of Silicon Valley through sheer drive and dogged determination, and she shares her advice for overcoming mistakes, improving every day, and starting your entrepreneurial journey right away.

What is the main mission of Tokki?

We are about changing the way people gift. I noticed one Christmas that most gift wrap is single use, so if the paper is too color saturated or too coated, you can't recycle it. There are just bags and bags of garbage. I saw an opportunity to reduce waste. I started Tokki in the hopes of making gift wrap more reusable and for gifting to be more fun and engaging. "Tokki" means "rabbit"

> "Don't wait to have an impact. Start by doing the best you can do right now. Take a step. Don't worry if it's the very best impact you could be having. Don't wait until you have everything—all your skills and your credentials—in a row."

in Korean; reusable gift wrap comes from my Korean heritage. But I knew that just wrapping in squares of cloth the way that my grandmother did wasn't going to cut it for Americans. We needed to also make the experience more engaging in order to get them to commit to reusable gift wrap. That's why we created a QR code component, so that people can record messages, with photos and videos right from the phones. The idea is to make reuse not only something obligatory that you should do, but actually more fun.

What values do you try to reflect both in the business and at the office?

One thing that we really try to emphasize is how to learn every day. People like to say there's no such thing as a mistake—there's only learning—but that's actually not true. A mistake stays a mistake unless you are willing to grapple with it, look at it, and think about what you want to do differently next time. In order to turn a failure into a lesson, you'll have to be able to examine it, think about it, and roll around with it a little bit. That's something that we do a lot: try things, then stop and reflect and figure out what we've learned and what worked and what didn't work.

Another huge value for me is assuming positive intent. Understanding that different people have different roles, and if they're not meeting aggressive timelines, it's not because they are out to get you or they're lazy or mean, it's just that they are trying their best, and things are more complicated than you might understand. That idea of assuming positive intent goes beyond just being flexible and trying to understand what the other person is up to. It's a creative endeavor. It also allows you to get curious about what it might be like to be in somebody else's shoes.

What was your most powerful and important experience at either Tokki or Julep?

A lot of the most powerful, enduring lessons are in smaller moments, not in big, huge events. When I sold Julep, the investors that took over moved operations to New York, so all of the people in Seattle I recruited had to find jobs elsewhere. However, an amazing thing was how so many people came back to me to say that the culture that we had at Julep was really unique. The fuel of the camaraderie, collaboration, and transparency was something that they really valued. It's always people-related things that impact us the most. The things people regret the most are moments of character failure; the times that you were unnecessarily mean to somebody or didn't let that person sit at your lunch table in middle school. What stays with you at the end of the day isn't how much money you made, but how you treated people. Both in terms of moments of pride and regret.

What was Julep's secret sauce over the years, attracting investors like Jay-Z and Beyoncé?

I followed every lead that I had for an introduction. It was seven degrees of separation. I had a meeting with the manager of Jay-Z and Beyoncé's investment arm, Roc Nation. I flew in, and the meeting kept being pushed back. I was waiting outside his office, and I got to talk to him for five minutes, but we kept getting interrupted by calls from studio executives, a masseuse, and all these different things. I just kept saying, "Look, I'm going to just sit here until we have a deal." At some point, I was being stubborn and said, "Look, I've been here all day, and you can't just leave when we're in the middle of a conversation." We struck up a friendship because I refused to leave.

What was it like to be a woman entrepreneur in Silicon Valley?

Frankly, the movement to equality is going slower than I'd expected. We only know our own experience, so I can't know what it would have been like to be a man because my leadership, transparency, and vulnerability are rooted in my experience of being a woman. There definitely have been a lot of challenges. Venture capitalists (VCs) only like to fund things that they know and like. A lot of times people don't realize that a venture capitalist will meet with three to five hundred companies a year, and they will only do one deal. The odds are so stacked against you. It's like winning a lottery. When it's such a rarefied thing, it's even harder to pinpoint bias. On one hand, I'm the daughter of immigrants. I didn't speak English when I first came to the country. My parents had a 7-Eleven store. How could somebody like me end up with millions of dollars of investment? That's super, super lucky. On the other hand, you look at the metrics that we were held to, the Silicon Valley "bro" culture, the rewards and bravado, and the companies going public that are run by men that have much weaker financials than those run by women who couldn't get further investment. There's definitely a huge bias. There's no question that it is harder. On the flip side, there's also no question that I'm super lucky to have gotten as far as I did.

Before founding Tokki and Julep, you had experiences in law and as a Starbucks executive. What are some of your most important moments from that part of your career?

It has honestly been about what people have taught me in friendships. My friends from law school are still the ones that I text when things are terrible or celebrate with when things are great. People always want to think that there was something about law school that helped me to understand something, or they think surely that I am a better negotiator. I don't think it's that. If anything, there are things about being a parent that have helped with leadership. I once heard somebody say that if you want to be a good negotiator, you should watch a toddler negotiate bedtime with a parent, because all the rules are coming into play. How you communicate with people, lead, and get them to grow in the same direction really has to do with understanding who they are. I learned that first and foremost by being a parent.

What are the most important personality traits for an entrepreneur?

There are two different kinds of people: there's the kind of person who takes suggestions and feedback as a personal attack, and the kind of person who leans into it and thanks you for pointing

> *"Every critique or disappointment is actually input to help you become stronger."*

out that something can be better. I think that's hard to teach. I haven't found a way yet to change somebody's outlook to make them more open to feedback and to iteration. Managing your strength is essential. Asking "How can I use this experience to become stronger?" is one of the most important questions you can ask yourself every day.

What else do you want our generation to learn from your experiences before we enter the workforce?

You are being left with such a huge mess. I think the biggest piece of advice that I can give is that it doesn't matter if you win or lose. It's really about making meaning every day. If you focus on climate change as an outcome, it can be really depressing if you focus on the fact that we probably aren't going to stop warming in the near future and might never. Regardless of outcome, we cannot stop caring and making meaning. When you start asking "Am I going to solve climate change? Am I actually making a difference?" that's the wrong question. The real questions to ask are: Are you making your life meaningful today? Are you learning things that help you to grow? Are you making joy for yourself and the people you love? And are you trying your best? Thinking in that way is a way to stay mentally strong in the face of all the challenges that lie ahead. There are a lot of challenges ahead, but I also have a lot of belief in your generation's strength and resilience, and you're probably going to have to be stronger and more resilient than any other generation before.

 **Key Takeaways:**

➔ Don't wait to make an impact; start now.

➔ Use the tools you have.

➔ Assume positive intent from others.

➔ Follow every lead.

➔ Treat people well.

DEEPA GANDHI (she/her)
Cofounder and COO, Dagne Dover

#BoundlessEnergy
AndCuriosity

On business: If you are entrepreneurially minded, the earlier you can learn the core fundamentals of strategy and business management, the better.

On social: Make sure it's not all-encompassing, but it's there in the way that you need it to be there.

On college: I built up a lot of grit, resilience, and hard-work ethic while in college, which ended up benefiting me not just as an entrepreneur, but in my career.

Dagne Dover bags are known for function and fashion and, as their TikTok tagline says, are designed "for humans getting the most out of life." **Deepa Gandhi** is one of the three female cofounders of Dagne Dover and, as the chief operating officer (COO), the financial brain behind the brand. She says the leadership trio is always thinking about what people need to make their lives easier and are in constant conversation with their customer base. Dagne Dover has built consumer loyalty by focusing on values like sustainability, eco-friendly products, ethical production, and giving back. Most of their bags are 100 percent vegan, and some styles are made from recycled plastic bottles. They donate bags from previous seasons to charities and women's shelters; support organizations they believe in, like UN Women and Stop AAPI Hate; and offer discounts to teachers, troops, vets, and health-care workers through the Dagne Heroes program. Deepa, who has a master of business administration (MBA) from UPenn's Wharton School and worked in finance before launching Dagne Dover, says she is excited about our generation's entrepreneurial dreams, but urges us to equip ourselves with the core business skills to make them a reality. She suggests developing a business plan, understanding each part of the company, and learning from everyone we meet.

What was your vision in starting Dagne Dover?

We believed that there was an opportunity to provide a product that was more performance focused. Historically, bags were generally either focused on design, like what's fashionable and what's on trend, or on functionality, but nobody was really focusing on both. So our thesis was to build a better brand, a next-gen brand, that was able to keep up with the lives that people are living.

Building on that idea of creating bags that aren't just beautiful but functional as well, what are some of the features you've prioritized in creating your bags?

We surveyed over one thousand men and women, asking what they needed and what wasn't working for them. We started with the "Perfect Work Tote," which was nicely structured, and you could take it to the office, but it also had a place for your laptop, a water bottle, a key strap, pens, lip gloss—whatever you were looking for. We were combating the issue of "the black hole" bag. Over time, we've evolved our assortment to still keep that same smart design ethos in every product that we launch, but we've worked with a lot more innovative material. We're known for our collection that we launched in 2017 that was made out of neoprene, which is like scuba suit material. That's become our hero collection and product, but that still has the same thesis behind it, which is marrying form and function.

What are some of the other decisions or innovations in particular that have helped you stand out?

We think about innovation by pushing the envelope on understanding how people live their lives and then asking what they need. We liked the idea of neoprene because the material hadn't really been used in bags. It held structure, it was insulated, and it was somewhat water resistant. So we thought that this would be really great. It was that time when the casualization of life was starting to happen. We've also thought about how people are living their lives differently. They want more hands-free options. How do we design things like that?

How have you incorporated customer feedback into improving your products?

We really listen to customer feedback. I think that's something that differentiates us from the legacy brands and the heritage brands in our industry. We're in constant conversation. We've always had a dialogue, whether it's through surveys, focus groups, or just on social media. People are very open about what they like and don't like. We use customer feedback for everything. We use it when we're developing new products. We like to make sure they get wear-tested by real customers. We use it to decide whether to bring back new colors. You're able to build so much customer loyalty when you ask the customer what they want and then deliver on it.

How have you built customer loyalty?

Over the past couple of years, we've been working through how to take responsibility as a fashion brand, such as making all of our linings out of recycled water bottles. Any new collection that we launched since 2020 has been made out of eco-friendly, sustainable materials. We're working through revamping our entire supply chain so that we can be an eco-friendly business for the future. At checkout, you can select to donate a percentage of your purchase to a variety of causes. There are some that we keep all the time, but there are some that are more relevant. For example, for Women's Equality Day we worked with an organization called IFund-Women, which helps fund underrepresented female entrepreneurs. We have found that it's important to show up on TikTok and be cool and have the "TikTok made me buy this" vibe, but what's really causing loyalty is that Gen Z is seeing that we're a brand that cares. And Gen Z is really purchasing—they're purchasing much more with their conscience than any other generation.

As a woman in the male-dominated field of retail management, what unique challenges have you faced on your journey?

I would say the challenges we faced were earlier on, and a lot of questions that we received that I don't think men received. More recently, I think we've found the right people to support us. Early on, when we were fundraising and trying to kick-start the brand, there were a lot of questions around whether we were the right team and whether we would be able to execute. I think the most ridiculous question we ever got was "Oh, do fashionable women even care about being organized?" And it was like, "Yes! Yes, they do! They would love that!" Now we've built an entire business around that. In fact, men do as well! Seventy percent of our customers are women and 30 percent are men. Three of

"Being conscientious and responsible is so much more a part of your generation than any other generation, and to see how you will help us start to fix the world is really exciting to me."

us founded the business, and I'm the financially driven one. A lot of times people would ask things like "Is somebody helping you?" "Are your boyfriends or husbands helping you with your fundraising?" And the answer was no. We know what we're doing. People often overlooked the fact that we went to business school. We have MBAs from Wharton. But over time, we also changed the language and the way we presented ourselves to prevent those questions. We are definitely very empowered women, but we also have found some great men who believe that investing in women is a much sounder investment decision. They have large investment portfolios that are heavily dominated by women-founded businesses, because they often have greater returns for investors because of the way that we approach things with patience and resiliency.

You've prioritized social media, online sales, and digital mobility since the inception of Dagne Dover. How successful has this strategy been?

I think being a digital first company is paramount. That's how you build your touchpoint interactions and relationship with your customer. Having said that, people still love to touch and feel, and I think Gen Z actually likes experience. They like to interact, but they are probably finding us first somewhere digitally. For us, from the beginning, it's always been a mix, but there's a heavy slant toward content. What content are we putting out there? What platforms are we on? Where are we connecting? At the same time, being able to walk into a Nordstrom, for example, and find our product is also really important and impactful because you don't know when a customer is shopping with friends or their mom. It's a full matrix, but it is underpinned with a foundation of being digitally native.

What were some of your biggest surprises when first starting out as an entrepreneur?

Everything takes longer than you expect. There's no overnight success. Even the overnight success stories generally had a lot go into it. I think the biggest challenge I foresee Gen Z having is you're coming off a generation of heavy entrepreneurship. When I was graduating college, most people still went to very traditional, finance consulting types of jobs. My first job was in finance. Now there's a lot more fluidity around what people do with their careers, which is great, because I think Gen Z is more intrinsically motivated, but I think one of the biggest challenges is understanding that you still need some core skills to be able to do that. Personally, I'm really happy that I took a couple years in the workforce and learned certain key skills. I worked in the retail industry and was able to understand how a big retail company manages supply chains, operations, inventory planning and management. One of my cofounders, who's our chief creative officer, went to the Parsons School of Design to study design, and then she did some early assistant designer work at large companies to understand how that works. One of my biggest concerns with Gen Z is I think there's sometimes an underestimation of what experience will be helpful versus just diving straight in. Really think about what skills you need to start a business and be successful in the long run, and understand that it's a marathon, not a sprint. You have to have patience, resilience, and grit to get through it. The press has a lot of news about the success stories, but for every success story, there's a lot of unsuccessful stories, and learning from both is really important.

What technology or skills do you think will prove most critical for young entrepreneurs?

If you are entrepreneurially minded, the earlier you can learn the core fundamentals of strategy and business management, the better. I think every founder is better off if they're able to not just speak to their vision, but also speak to how their business runs in the day-to-day. I always tell new founders to put a business plan together, even if it's super scrappy. What is your marketing strategy? Who is your target audience? What is your pricing strategy? Who's your target customer? How are you going to fund this? What's a high-level financial projection process? Make sure you understand all of those key pieces, even if you're not an expert on it. I am much more financially driven than my cofounders; they lean on me for that. But they still have a certain level of understanding of how the company's financials work and why we make certain decisions. I am not a creative by any means, but I understand what the creative process is, what goes into it, how you go about it, what matters, and what you think about. Always making sure you understand at least the high level of each part of your business is important, because that will make you stronger in managing your team and thinking about how everything works together. The founders who take the time to understand all of that generally are stronger.

 # Key Takeaways:

- ➜ Learn the fundamentals of business.
- ➜ Listen to customer feedback.
- ➜ Expand your perspective.
- ➜ Tap into your network.
- ➜ Use data for everything.

STELLEO TOLDA (he/him)
Cofounder, Mercado Libre

#NeverStopLearning

On business: Be willing to take risks, bet on new initiatives, and innovate all the time.

On social: Good because it really takes advantage of the power that technology has to connect people. Bad because data privacy is a big issue and there is tremendous potential to misuse information.

On college: All of my education has benefited me in being an entrepreneur. College is about learning to learn and the relationships you form.

Stelleo Tolda is the cofounder of Mercado Libre, a $50 billion e-commerce giant and rival to Amazon in Latin America. Mercado Libre—"free market" in Spanish—champions a culture of adaptability and risk-taking, which served them well when businesses turned to online commerce during the coronavirus pandemic. Many in Latin America still do not trust online shopping but Mercado Libre is slowly changing that mindset, priding itself on quick and easy delivery that earns the trust of customers. As for Stelleo, here he shares his hopes for our generation, lessons from his entrepreneur father, and his insatiable appetite for learning.

What inspired you to start a business in the e-commerce field?

Our inspiration was eBay, which was founded a few years earlier, initially to launch Mercado Libre as an auction site for our different markets in Latin America. We thought then that technology was going to change people's lives. That was what really inspired us to start a business. We imagined that e-commerce was going to grow, that technology was going to be an integral part of people's everyday lives.

What's your motivation to wake up every day and work on improving your company?

My motivation is to continue impacting people's lives. Within Mercado Libre, we talk about how we have democratized commerce, and how we've made small businesses possible online. We believe there's still a lot more to do. We look at more developed markets, like the United States or China, where e-commerce is now more than 20 percent of retail sales, and think that there's no reason this shouldn't happen in our markets.

What is your perspective on giants like Apple and Amazon?

For the most part, I would say that they have impacted our lives very positively and we buy their services and products because they really cater to our needs as consumers. I admire those companies, and they have been, for the most part, a force for the good. However, there is an issue with big tech corporations and how much data they have accumulated on us over time and the power that they have, given that data. They can use that power in a way that may affect us negatively. We as a society have forfeited so much data and control to these large businesses. It's going to be up to your generation to figure out what to do with the enormous power that these organizations have in our lives.

How did the pandemic open up opportunities for your company?

As people went into lockdowns and businesses closed their doors for foot traffic, they had to turn to online as an alternative to continue selling. Even traditional businesses and brands that are recognized locally in our markets had a very timid presence online. We saw new companies and brands choosing to sell on our marketplace as their doors were closed for consumers. We also saw a significant increase in the number of new consumers.

What is the most important lesson you've learned from running this business?

The most important lesson I've learned is the need to adapt to what is an uncertain market and uncertain world. Most of the time, things don't happen the way we plan, and it's important that we move quickly. It's important that we are agile in changing our plans. As a technology company, we live in an environment that is ever changing. When we began our business twenty-one years ago, there were no smartphones, cell phones were new, and people didn't use them for transactions; they used them to make calls. Adapting is probably the greatest lesson that I've had as a manager of this company.

How did your education benefit you as an entrepreneur?

My education as an undergrad and graduate student at Stanford was formative. Over the years that I've managed this company, I have been in constant learning mode and really tried to build and foster a learning culture in my organization. The other aspect is the relationships I made. My partners, who started the business with me, were colleagues at business school, and the trust that we had from knowing one another there allowed us to become very solid partners, and we're still together after all these years.

How do your personal beliefs carry over to your work?

Mercado Libre is an extremely successful company because of its values. They are values of the company, top management, and my own personal values. One of the main cultural values that we have is to be entrepreneurial and assume risks, which we have done since we started this company and continue to do. We're willing to bet on our new initiatives because

> *"An entrepreneur is someone who looks at a problem from a different angle, who's willing to try things, who's willing to make mistakes, but at the same time is very resilient to come to a solution."*

we live in an ever-changing world, and it's important that we innovate all the time. Another important value is that we execute with excellence, which also comes from our top management. We have high standards of where we want to go and what we want to achieve, and that's something that we try to implement in our everyday work, but also try to transmit to the teams that we lead.

How do you address diversity and environmental friendliness in your company?

Diversity is an important theme for us. We realize, not only is it good for business, but it's also the right thing to do. We're not as diverse a company or a management team as we would like to be, but we'd like to move in that direction, and we have improved. As far as the environment, we are constantly thinking in terms of how to reduce our impact. We have been converting our fleet of vehicles into electric vehicles so that the impact of our trucks and our vans is reduced in the environment. We're also investing in biomes in the different markets where we operate, in order to contribute directly to some of the impact that we as humanity have caused in nature.

Who is your biggest mentor?

My late father. He was an entrepreneur. He started a few businesses in his lifetime, and I didn't realize how much he influenced me until I decided to become an entrepreneur. Unfortunately, he didn't live to see me launch my business. He taught me the value of hard work. He taught me the value of education, even though he didn't go to college. He also taught me how to treat people. A lot of my job as a manager entails interacting with and motivating people. The way that my father treated his employees served as an example for me.

What do you value most in a friend? An employee? Yourself?

One who won't shy away from taking your call, from coming to see you when you really need them and when things aren't going well. I talked a lot about how we are very entrepreneurial, innovative, and a learning organization. I value employees that fit that description. I don't mean that we hire only people who have started businesses previously. That's not our definition of an entrepreneur. An entrepreneur is someone who looks at a problem from a different angle, who's willing to try things, who's willing to make mistakes, but at the same time is very resilient to come to a solution. In myself, it is my willingness to learn. It's not just the time you spend in school under formal education, but it really is a lifetime of learning.

What is your favorite fictional worldview—in a book or movie or TV show—and what can our society learn from it?

One book that I enjoyed is *The Three Musketeers*. It teaches a lot about working as a team, resilience, and persistence in the face of challenge. I like literature from that period of time. *The Count of Monte Cristo* is another one. I like worlds that are our own world, but from a different time and that show people with character and people overcoming obstacles.

 ## Key Takeaways:

- ➔ Adapt, move quickly, and be agile.
- ➔ Take risks and innovate.
- ➔ Execute with excellence.
- ➔ Be in a constant learning mode.
- ➔ Be willing to make mistakes.

CASEY GEORGESON (she/her)
Founder and CEO, Saint Jane Beauty

#Wellness

On life: It's not the happy people who are grateful; it's the grateful people who are happy.

On business: You learn the most when you are doing the work yourself.

On social: Pressures from social media can be confusing, but I think that it's a very powerful platform.

When **Casey Georgeson** launched her luxury clean-beauty skin care line, Saint Jane Beauty, she did it with one hand tied behind her back: Facebook (Meta) had banned her from its site because her brand is one of a growing line of beauty products that contain cannabidiol (CBD), an herb in the same family as marijuana (minus the psychotropic effects). A graduate of the Stanford Graduate School of Business, a former CNN producer, and a wine-industry alumna, she activated her network and got creative. Now Saint Jane Beauty, named after a French saint who helped to heal those in need, is leading the indie beauty industry into a new era that is more compassionate, supportive, and sustainable. Casey talks to us about being authentic and transparent in everything you do, and trusting that it will all work out.

Your career has spanned three different industries—media, wine, and beauty. Has it been hard to start over, and what lessons have you learned by trying so many new things?

I love a good challenge. My job as a CNN producer was one of the hardest jobs I've ever done, because every day was so new, but I loved the challenge. I loved walking into work and not knowing what the day was going to bring. Creating wine brands was a lot of fun, but we didn't know what was going to work; it was a lot of trial and error. I had to have a big appetite for failure. When I went into the beauty industry, I had seen so much already that I felt confident. I was passionate about what I was doing, but knew it was okay to fail if it didn't work out. I was going to learn something from it and move on.

Do you have any regrets?

I regret not having the confidence that I have today earlier on. There's a lot that I didn't do at CNN that I was too nervous to do. They asked me to go on air for some segments, and I was too nervous for that. Today, I'd say, "Why not?" It would be a great adventure. You should try it, and if you fail, that's okay. You get up and you try again.

What is the meaning behind the name Saint Jane?

Saint Jane has two meanings. One is that we're the innocent side of Mary Jane, which is slang for marijuana. We're the innocent side because we use CBD, which is the darling of the herb industry. We are also an homage to Saint Jane, a woman who lived in the 1500s in France and dedicated her life to healing people, specifically women who society wouldn't touch—the very old, very sick, and unwed mothers. It is in her honor that we wanted to create a brand that was dedicated to helping people. Lastly, female empowerment is essential to our brand ethos, as I have three daughters, and I've seen so much inequality in the workforce— like the wage gap—between men and women. Women are paid seventy-three cents on the dollar overall. Our organization is focused on helping empower women as well.

> "Competition is healthy, but I believe that the tide raises all ships . . . so supporting each other is essential."

How do your beliefs give you a competitive advantage over the rest of the sector?

We are a very soulful, authentic brand, and what we stand for resonates with our consumers. I think it's a competitive advantage because it makes us more relatable and more real, and less like a corporate entity.

What is the most important thing you wish everyone understood about CBD in beauty products?

CBD is really an incredible ingredient because it's like a vitamin. It's packed with a lot of nutrients and antioxidants and is non-psychoactive. It's derived from the hemp plant, and the reason why it's controversial is because marijuana is derived from the same source, so CBD and marijuana have been linked and wrongly portrayed as similar ingredients. They're genetically related but that is where the similarities effectively end. The way that Saint Jane looks at CBD is like an active floral, like sunflower or calendula. We are wholly focused on its extraordinary benefits for the skin. It's derived from the whole plant, including the flower, just like any other natural ingredient that's used in skin care or in wellness.

How do you handle the haters and stigma?

We rise above it, and we continue to architect the narrative of CBD for wellness. Education is essential. I believe it will turn the tide against the stigma that can be associated with CBD. I haven't seen a lot of hate and stigma in the CBD category, unlike in the THC (tetrahydrocannabinol) world. I think in the THC world, there's a lot more of it in dispensaries and there are states that still are not legal. CBD is federally legal, so there's nothing stopping CBD from becoming as mainstream as any other supplement. It's why you can find it at Target or CVS or Walgreens.

You were banned from promoting your business on Facebook (Meta) and Instagram, and yet plenty of people lie and bully on social platforms without consequences. How could social media platforms be fairer to business models like yours?

It was extraordinarily frustrating because it felt like we were trying to launch a business with our hands and our feet tied and we couldn't swim to the surface. I still don't totally understand why Facebook (Meta) had that policy. Things have started to change, I think due to brands like ours that were continuously playing it very straight, not trying to promote THC or say anything illegal. We knew that when we started as a brand that included CBD in its formulas, it was going to be a little bit of the Wild West, and it has been.

How do you define your personal brand?

I've just always been who I am. If you let yourself think about your critics or what you're doing wrong, you will never go anywhere. What's important to me is my family, my friends, and doing the right thing. My personal brand has always been about being open, honest, and thoughtful.

What are your core beliefs and how do they guide your decisions every day?

My most core belief is around gratitude and being thankful,

present and grateful for all the blessings that you have on a day-to-day basis. I love the quote "It's not the happy

people who are grateful; it's the grateful people who are happy." One of the biggest tenets of my belief system is seeing the positive in the world. Collaboration among brands and founders is also one of my core tenets. I really believe in lifting each other up. I think competition is healthy, but I believe that the tide raises all ships and it's about more than just brand competition, so supporting each other is essential. Giving back is also very central to not only who I am, but what I've built into the brand.

How do you give back?

We support organizations that we believe are changing the world for the better. We support Girls Crushing It, which fosters entrepreneurship and teaches leadership skills to young girls. We support Loveland Foundation, which is an organization that elevates the experience and cultural change for Black girls and women. We support Lipstick Angels, an organization that goes into hospitals to help transform people who are going through cancer treatment or are facing very severe illnesses, by doing makeup and facials so that they can feel good about themselves in that moment. We support National Bail Out, an organization that helps specifically women but all Black people and minorities who are facing challenges with getting their bail posted. Giving back is a core value to who Saint Jane is as a brand and our way of paying homage to the real Saint Jane's lifework.

What are you doing to promote sustainability?

The beauty industry is a huge offender on landfill and waste with samples and plastic. We're part of a group of brands that are focused on sustainability and making Earth cleaner and safer for future generations. At Saint Jane, we try to use glass wherever we can in our products. We're moving toward post-consumer recycled plastic in any of the acrylic that we have, like in our lip glosses and lipsticks. I think these micro changes ultimately will lead to macro changes down the road. But as a little tiny brand, we are very committed to the big changes.

What would you tell your younger self?

Chill out. It's going to be okay. Go easy on yourself. It doesn't have to be as hard as you make it. Just enjoy the moment. Enjoy the process. It's all going to work out.

 Key Takeaways:

➔ Dive in and learn.
➔ Leave things better than you found them.
➔ Be grateful.
➔ Be authentic.
➔ See the positive in the world.

MICHAEL KRAKARIS (he/him)
Cofounder, Deliverr

#IfOpportunityDoesn't ComeKnocking, BuildTheDoor

On life: Have fun! Make an impact! Do those two things. It's not all dire.

On business: Look for product market fit.

On social: There are huge benefits to having it in our lives, like connecting people, but it can be a big noise machine and force people into certain buckets of thinking, so you have to be careful.

On college: It is not very helpful if you want to be an entrepreneur.

Michael Krakaris's high school yearbook quote reads, "If an opportunity doesn't come knocking, build a door." He didn't know it at the time, but that motto would define his career. After applying to and being rejected from jobs at Facebook and Uber at twenty-two years old, he problem-solved his way to building his own company, Deliverr, an e-commerce fulfillment company that was recently acquired by Shopify for $2.1 billion. Deliverr relies on predictive analytics and demand maps to figure out what customers want to buy and where they want it, and then, as the name says, delivers it to them as fast as possible. Michael was able to take on industry giant Amazon when he saw that there were many retailers outside their network that also wanted fast shipping for their customers. His model soon caught the attention of eBay, then Walmart, and eventually Deliverr's new owner, Shopify. Michael believes Deliverr's technology will only become more in demand as customers measure shipping times in hours, minutes, or even seconds. He shares some of the lessons his journey has taught him, from standing firm in your convictions to the responsibility that comes with being a young boss.

Did you set out to become Amazon's primary competitor when you started Deliverr?

We saw a market that was not serviced by Amazon. There's a big market outside of Amazon, and that market did not have the infrastructure needed to provide a good customer experience.

There's a huge discrepancy between how Amazon does things and how everybody else does things. Amazon is only 20 to 30 percent of the market, so a majority of the market is sitting outside of Amazon in all these fragmented places, and it's on this really antiquated infrastructure. That was ultimately the approach.

Is expecting things instantaneously healthy for our society?

It is definitely positive. I think getting things very fast is going to change how we think about consumer behavior. A lot of times you buy a product to solve a certain problem. I think the slower the delivery times are, the more you're discouraged from purchasing. Going to stores is also inconvenient because perhaps they are not within your route or can't carry a lot of selection. In the online world, you can carry a ton of selection, and I think it's going to open up new opportunities and things you never thought were possible. I think that's what Amazon showed once they got to next-day delivery. It changed consumer behaviors in a lot of ways. I think you're going to see more and more of that. For example, Fridge No More, which unfortunately went out of business, was a company where they would get you groceries in ten minutes. And literally, with the name Fridge No More, they're basically saying you will never need a fridge again. Imagine what your life would look like without a fridge or without some of these other things where you don't need to go to a grocery store every other day. That's interesting. I think it's a good problem to have, and it allows you to focus on experiences and focus on what it is you love to do. You don't need to focus on the day-to-day, TaskRabbit-y type things.

What has running a business taught you about not listening when others doubt you or your ideas?

People are going to obviously doubt you. I think that you need to have a very strong conviction in how you think and your process of thinking. You don't necessarily need conviction in the idea itself because the idea is probably going to evolve over time, whatever it is you're doing. I think you need to have conviction in yourself to solve problems and to think a certain way and say, "I'm going to figure it out because this is how I approach problems and I understand when I'm doing the right thing, and I understand when I'm doing the wrong thing, and I can adapt from that." If you have that understanding, it frankly doesn't matter what other people say. Now you do have to figure out when people are accurate. They might say, "This is never gonna work, you have to rethink your pricing model here, or you rethink XYZ." You should know when to take advice and when not. But that all comes down to your thinking structure. As long as that's clear, you can filter out noise and figure out when to take advice and when to stay firm in your conviction. You'll be just fine.

What is one topic that you think isn't brought up enough when it comes to discussing entrepreneurship?

I think finding product market fit does not get covered enough because it's very hard to do it. It requires a different type of thought process. You'd be shocked at how many companies exist and raised hundreds of millions of dollars, and they never have product market fit. In the end, it always comes out that the product just doesn't fit, but it's a really hard question to ask. I think for an entrepreneur, especially as you start raising more money and having more employees, it's hard to look at the data and admit that it just isn't working. The methodology to get to the point of understanding if you have it or not is very difficult, because it's not always clear or easy to understand.

> "My career has never been waiting for an opportunity to come. I just solved problems, and then opportunities showed up."

Is there any part of business that most people don't realize until actually creating a start-up?

If you're young, the level of responsibility is extremely high. The buck stops with you. If you have a hard decision, it gets floated up the chain. Once you start your own business, you're it. It gets floated to you, and you have to make the decision. Especially once you start raising some money, hiring people, and getting things moving, you're going to feel that weight, and that weight doesn't go away. You just start to understand how to accept it and how to be mature and become an adult.

Is college helpful for a career in entrepreneurship?

It's not very helpful. I think the first year of college is fine, when you are exploring, living on your own for the first time and discovering new things about yourself. As you get into your sophomore, junior, and senior years, especially if you want to go into entrepreneurship and tech, but not in engineering, it's not a whole lot of help. Taking an entrepreneurship class is not very helpful. The way you really learn is either by joining an early-stage start-up or doing it yourself. I went to Johns Hopkins for a year, and then to Northwestern for two and a quarter years. I just did one major in economics, because I was starting to see that I wasn't getting too much value out of it, so I wasn't going to have my parents spend all this money. I did get help from the clubs after school; there were entrepreneurship groups that were fun because you got to hang out with other people who were like-minded and they talked about cool new companies, and what was working or not working. I found that helpful, and I designed apps after school. Generally, I still think going to college and getting a degree is good, but I think a smart approach would be to go to a good public college, get the in-state rate so you're not paying a crazy amount of money, and do a very light major like econ, and then you spend the rest of your day on entrepreneurship. Then you're hedging your bets in a good way, you're not spending a ton of money on it, you're living the best of both worlds, and you get to do some personal exploration, too.

 Key Takeaways:

- ➔ Have conviction in your thinking.
- ➔ Continuously problem-solve.
- ➔ Have fun.
- ➔ Take time to explore.
- ➔ Keep going.

DEJAN PRALICA (he/him)
Cofounder and CEO, SoleSavy

#Resilient

On business: Resiliency in whatever you do is important. You can be wrong and fail, but it doesn't mean you have to stop. You can keep pushing forward.

On social: Social media is a good thing that has grown too fast, that doesn't understand the power it possesses and the impact it can make on people's lives, and in turn, that is a bad thing. There's a lot of work to be done to improve, bring awareness, and make it safer for mental health.

On college: College should be much more specialized and with real-world experiences. I'm not a fan of this education system. I think it is broken.

Dejan Pralica is the cofounder and CEO of SoleSavy, a membership-based online sneaker community and marketplace that has been called one of the fastest growing start-ups in the sneaker industry. He and his cofounder worked for brands like Nike, Jordan, Adidas, Puma, and Under Armour before creating SoleSavy, which has a simple mission: make it easier for people to buy and enjoy sneakers. The "secret sauce," as Dejan calls it, is creating intimate online communities for people to discuss their passion with like-minded sneakerheads. Dejan himself has over five hundred pairs of shoes, so he can relate to his customers—which he says is a big part of the company's success. Dejan imparts his opinions on education, finding yourself, kindness, and whether an entrepreneurial mindset truly is a teachable skill.

What is your favorite part about collecting sneakers?

I have five hundred pairs of shoes now, so I'm a little bit on the extreme scale of the sneaker collector. Obviously, that dictated a lot of what we are doing because I know the customer. I know their experiences, their gripes, their pains, their struggles, their joys, and the whole spectrum of emotions that someone can feel about sneakers. We can tap into that to help us build products because we are our customers. We're not building for a space we don't understand thoroughly, and that's really important for building a business. You should be passionate about what you're doing, because if you're not, you're not gonna have the same drive and conviction as someone who is.

What inspired you to put a different spin on the luxury sneaker industry?

I was frustrated because everything was designed to exploit consumers rather than empower them. It was about making people pay more for the shoes they want versus helping people get the shoes that they want without paying absurd premiums. I did it out of passion and frustration that there were no options for consumers like me.

How big is the sneaker resale market and the sneakerhead community?

The resale industry itself has grown to $6 billion. The sneaker industry is $100 billion on its own. That's a $106 billion market from retail to resell. That's a lot of people.

What are some of the core values that have helped SoleSavy succeed?

The core values are community and culture. It is about bringing together people with like-minded interests who are passionate about something and helping them form relationships and bonds that they currently can't find online.

How do you balance maintaining small, intimate communities with increasing the number of customers?

That is our secret sauce. We believe in cohort communities.

> **Scale/scalable:** Scale represents a range of values used to measure or grade a system, while scalable means the ability of a system to adjust to meet growing demands.

Every community has a max amount of members in it who can bring value to the other users without overwhelming them. There's a balance. You don't **scale** one community to a million; you scale a hundred thousand communities by a thousand.

How did your educational environment affect your development as a leader?

I found college very difficult. I didn't really enjoy it. I spent my high school years designing, developing, and coding. I sold my first website when I was sixteen. When I was in my junior and senior years of high school, I only took courses related to art, development, and film. I'm a self-learner—tutorials, videos, trying, doing, experiencing. When it came to college, I showed up for a yearlong diploma program for graphic design, and I already knew all of it and thought it was super boring. I couldn't believe I was spending ten thousand dollars on it, and I never finished it. I think the education system is a little broken. We all need to know how to read and understand the basics, but there's so much to life and so much to creation. College should be much more specialized and with real-world experiences.

What characteristics do all successful entrepreneurs possess?

Ambition, the drive to succeed and work really hard, and not being afraid to fail. There's no such thing as an overnight success, no matter what you think you read in an article or saw on social media. It doesn't exist. There's no such thing. Clubhouse had a billion-dollar valuation. Their first ten years of developing companies got them nowhere; the tenth year, finally, was a success. There's always blood, sweat, tears, long nights, sleepless nights, or living on a couch—there's always something behind the stories. It's going to be a lot of hard work. You need to be determined, and not ready to give up. No successful company is formed off nine-to-five workdays. You have to be prepared to put your entire life into something to create something special. Otherwise, if you don't have that ambition and drive to work very hard, there's no point in starting. You're not going to succeed because there's gonna be someone out there who's going to want to work harder, faster, and better than you, and they are going to catch up and be better.

Which of those qualities are you born with, and which can be learned? Overall, do you think entrepreneurship is nature or nurture?

It's both. I think some people are inherently born with the drive and the determination that they need, but some people can learn that from their environment. My parents were immigrants to a country that they came to when they were my age, with two kids. They didn't speak English. They did whatever they could to make money, put a roof above us, put food on the table, and take care of us, no matter what. They did anything possible. Nothing could stop them. I grew up around that. Did that influence me? Absolutely.

"You have to be prepared to put your entire life into something to create something special."

> *"Previous experience, failures, and successes can help you save time and iterate faster for what you do next."*

Would I still have that drive and motivation without that? Yes. Are the two of those things coming together really beautiful and helpful to define me as a person? Absolutely. I don't think one way is better than the other or that you can only do it one way.

What is the most important lesson you've learned in your lifetime?

Nothing beats hard work and determination or being a better version of you. I don't think you will read about entrepreneurs who are sixteen, eighteen, or nineteen who start their first company and become billionaires. I don't think that's a very normal path. That's a unicorn situation. As a teenager to young adult, fourteen to twenty-three, you have no idea who you are. You are a fraction of who you will become. You're definitely not as smart as you think you are, and you need life experiences and growth to reach a point where you'll be ready to be an entrepreneur. Patience is probably the biggest thing I've learned; fifteen years of growing up personally and professionally. Different experiences have allowed me to get to the point where I could start and grow a really successful business. To be an entrepreneur, you need to have the attitude that no one can tell you that you are wrong, but when you are wrong, know it, take a step back and reevaluate, then keep working to get better. Resiliency in whatever you do is important. You can be wrong and fail, but it doesn't mean you have to stop. You can keep pushing forward.

What is the best piece of advice you got from your parents growing up?

One of the biggest things my parents ingrained in me was being a good person. In a moment of confrontation and negativity, it's better to walk away and move on than contribute to that energy. Treat people the way you want to be treated. That's something I will pass on to my kids because life is a very wild thing. There's so much to learn, and sometimes the best thing you can do is just be a good person.

What is your best advice?

Your life from ages one to eighteen does not define who you are for the rest of your life. It will help set a foundation, but it's the least important part of your life by the time you grow up. The most important part of life is going to be those adult years as you get closer to thirty. Everyone will have a different trigger point, but don't think that high school defines you as a person. In my opinion, it's just a playground for fun. Take it seriously, but not too seriously.

 Key Takeaways:

➔ Be resilient and patient.
➔ If you are wrong, adjust and keep pushing forward.
➔ Nothing beats hard work and determination.
➔ Treat people well and be honest.
➔ Enjoy your life right now, and take the time to learn who you are.

AVA MCDONALD (she/her)
Founder and CEO, Zfluence

#Real

On business: If businesses want to succeed in the modern economy, they have to make an effort to market to Gen Z.

On social: I've seen so many positive social movements that have been organized on social media.

On college: I am a firm supporter of gaining a college education if you have the opportunity to do so. Going to college allows you to learn so much about yourself, meet incredible people, and have the chance to broaden your mind.

For years, big brands have hired famous influencers with millions of followers to promote their products, hoping to attract new customers and dollars. **Ava McDonald** is flipping the script on that model with her company, Zfluence, a digital platform that pairs companies with their authentic Gen Z fans to endorse their brands. Instead of relying on a follower count to attract new customers, Zfluencers use Gen Z's genuine influence with personal connections to share brands and products they love and are rewarded in free product instead of cash to ensure authenticity. Authentic passion is the secret formula that has attracted big companies like Arctic Zero, Pamprin, Benefit Cosmetics, and Sperry to Zfluence. Now a student at Georgetown University, Ava started Zfluence while in high school and was the youngest member of Ad Age's 40 Under 40 list in 2020. She offers practical advice for businesses looking to market to Gen Z and inspiration for young entrepreneurs who want to pursue a passion for business while still in their teens, telling us age should never be a barrier to success.

Why did you create Zfluence?

I started Zfluence to address the lack of authenticity in influencer marketing that I noticed as a Gen Z consumer and frequent social media user. As Gen Zers and digital natives, we can see through disingenuous, pay-to-say advertisements. I realized that the people who I actually trusted to recommend new brands and products to me were my friends and peers, and that is where the idea for Zfluence came from.

How does Zfluence work?

Zfluence enables brands to turn their Gen Z fans into their best brand ambassadors. We are a digital platform that operates almost like a dating app, allowing brands and the influential Gen Zers who love them to "match" and create authentic and effective brand ambassador relationships. A highly effective and much-needed alternative to the inauthentic "pay-to-say" influencer marketing practices that have defined the last decade, Zfluence addresses the Gen Z demographic's emphasis on authenticity as a core value, enabling companies to leverage the authentic influence of their genuine Gen Z fans to win new Gen Z consumers.

What drove you to target solely lesser-known influencers with under ten thousand followers?

We're really not looking to target "influencers" at all, and that is what makes our network so powerful. We're looking for real members of Generation Z—not professional influencers—who have true influence among their peers from their strong social networks, interests, and passions, and their authentic recommendations speak volumes. Our Zfluencers have followings that range from five hundred all the way up to two million. Zfluencers actually have significantly higher engagement rates than professional influencers—25 percent versus 2 percent. Some companies will ask a lot of questions about our approach because of the way that we are disrupting the traditional "pay-to-say," transactional influencer marketplace and are doing things differently, but once they hear more about our authentic approach, they get on board!

What was behind your decision to pay Zfluencers with products rather than money?

Our product-as-reward model ensures that the relationships between brands and Zfluencers on our platform are motivated by authenticity rather than payment. Unlike marketing networks that are filled with aspiring and professional "cash-for-content" creators, Zfluence only accepts onto its platform members of Gen Z who have earned their influence through campus and community engagement and leadership.

Do you find Gen Z's relative lack of income compared to other generations limits the motivation of businesses to market toward us?

Not only is Gen Z the largest generation, but Gen Z also has tremendous spending power, commanding $360 billion in disposable income—and this figure is only increasing. If businesses want to succeed in the modern economy, they have to make an effort to market to Gen Z. Effectively marketing to Gen Z requires a combination of understanding, effort, and authenticity—Gen Z wants to be marketed *to* and not marketed *at*.

As a digital native and young person with a social media focused business, how valid are claims that social media is unhealthy?

A lot of people immediately assume that social media has only had a negative impact on the lives of young people. While social media can be used in a way that is harmful, social media can also be used for good. I've seen so many positive social movements that have been organized on social media, and social media provides a way for individuals to share things they care about, highlight what they are loving at the moment, and stay in touch with their family and friends during times of isolation, like the COVID-19 pandemic. Social media definitely helped me and my friends stay sane and connected during the pandemic.

What was it like to be named on the 2020 Ad Age 40 Under 40 list?

It was a huge honor! I was especially proud to be the youngest member of the list because I hope that shows other Gen Z entrepreneurs or aspiring Gen Z entrepreneurs that age does not have to be a barrier to entry when it comes to starting a business. Being young can be a huge asset. We as Gen Zers have a perspective that older generations are trying to access and are willing to pay top dollar for.

Was there ever a point in launching your business that you thought you were too young or out of your depth?

I've faced moments of self-doubt, especially when I was first starting out. I sometimes felt compelled to give in to the opinions of naysayers who believed I was too young or too inexperienced to run a successful company. However, being an entrepreneur has provided me with a newfound sense of confidence that I can accomplish anything I set my mind to.

What has the experience of being a female founder been like?

Being a female founder has been an incredibly empowering experience. I'm grateful to have connected with other female entrepreneurs through having started Zfluence. I think that it is super important for young women entering the field to identify strong female role models or mentors to look up to. That is something that was super helpful and inspiring for me as a female founder.

What were your biggest surprises or obstacles when first entering the business world?

I started Zfluence as a junior in high school, so there were a lot of things that I had to learn. I think that the sense of curiosity and willingness to try and learn that comes with being a young person and a member of Gen Z definitely helped me as I was learning the technical aspects of running a company, and it will help other Gen Z entrepreneurs in the same situation.

So many Gen Zers believe they can be the next Steve Jobs or Elon Musk. Do you find Gen Z's widespread ambition admirable or unrealistic?

I think that Gen Z's widespread ambition is awesome, and one of my favorite things about my generation is that we have a strong desire to innovate and create the future we want to see, whether that is through launching a business venture, inventing some revolutionary new technology, or another pursuit.

It is often said that starting a business is far more work than you realize. Do you recommend the field for our generation despite the difficulty?

Starting a business is definitely not easy, but it is incredibly rewarding and worth it when you see your idea come to fruition. I would absolutely recommend starting a business to members of our generation. Starting a business provides you with the ability to make an impact, create a solution to a problem, and learn so much about yourself.

What skills do you think will prove most critical for future entrepreneurs?

I think that having an entrepreneurial mindset is a critical skill for Gen Z entrepreneurs. Being an entrepreneur and a member of Gen Z, you'll face several obstacles, including doubt from others, a lack of experience, and a lack of resources. It is super important to be able to approach these challenges with an open mind and problem-solve. I think teenagers today can prepare themselves by always looking for opportunities in their lives to innovate to build an entrepreneurial mindset.

Has balancing business and college been manageable so far?

I have found that being a student has provided me with countless valuable insights that I have applied to being an entrepreneur and vice versa. It has been a challenge managing my academics with running a business, and it is definitely not for the faint of heart, but with proper planning and a color-coded calendar, anything is possible!

> *"Being an entrepreneur is not easy, but it has been one of the best experiences of my life. I have definitely experienced the highs and lows of entrepreneurship, but every low is worth it when you see the progress that you are making."*

What is one last takeaway from your experiences that you believe will prove useful to entrepreneurs as they enter the workforce?

I am a firm believer that Gen Zers and successful entrepreneurs have a lot of traits in common, such as the willingness to try, the desire to innovate, and the compulsion to take risks. I think that if Gen Z entrepreneurs remember all that they bring to the table, from their unique perspective to their firsthand knowledge of all things technology and social media, they will be able to achieve great things and overcome the doubt of any potential naysayers who might underestimate them based on their age.

 # Key Takeaways:

- ➔ Age is not a barrier to entry.
- ➔ Look for the opportunities in front of you.
- ➔ Don't listen to the naysayers.
- ➔ Approach challenges with an open mind.
- ➔ Innovate.

MEI XU (she/her)

Founder and CEO, Chesapeake Bay Candle,
BlissLiving Home, Yes She May

#PassionToBurn
#CandleLady
#NeverSayNever

On business: If a risk is worth taking, go for it. There's almost no such thing as a 100 percent guarantee in life.

On social: It gives voice to people who otherwise would not be seen or heard, but it's beginning to get monopolized by the wealthy and the powerful who have taken advantage of the situation.

On college: When it's rendered in an open way, education pivots us to new expectations for ourselves to succeed. It's important to learn how to be globally minded.

What does it take to turn candles into a multimillion dollar company? For **Mei Xu**, a successful Chinese American entrepreneur and founder of Chesapeake Bay Candle, it took passion, optimism, and being comfortable with risk. After launching the company in 1994, she used her connections in China and the United States to quickly expand and grow the brand into a candle empire. Mei sold the company in 2017 to Newell Brands, which also owns Yankee Candle and WoodWick Candle, and turned her attention to the luxury bedding industry, launching BlissLiving Home. During the COVID-19 pandemic, Mei created an online platform called Yes She May to support and advocate for women entrepreneurs and their businesses. She is fiercely outspoken about discrimination against Asian Americans and believes cultural diversity builds the strongest teams. Mei shares with us her insights on global entrepreneurship, breaking barriers, and paying it forward.

What first inspired you to create a candle company?

I wasn't inspired by someone making candles. I grew up in China when it was very isolated. Once we opened to the world in 1979, I was able to go to a diplomatic training boarding school, where we were able to watch movies and read books in English—in particular, to really understand a foreign culture. And to me, one of the most inspiring women was Coco Chanel. She was able to create a whole industry, as well as creating what's now known as "ready to wear" for women. Her role in changing the fashion and fragrance industry is profound. Then I was living in New York next to a Bloomingdale's, and every day, I took a trip to see the merchandise. I really loved the fashion floor. I don't like mundane, grandma-ish floral patterns. When I see something that almost looks like menswear, but tailored for women, it's very powerful and empowering. When I went up to the top floors of Bloomingdale's, where they sell furniture and home goods, I realized it was almost like I entered a grandma's home, because it was very ornate, traditional, and dark. I remember thinking someone has to do something in the home goods industry, because it doesn't look as clean and updated as fashion. That's where my calling comes in. I want to close the gap between the fashion business and the home business. I brought a lot of products from China to test in trade shows, and the product that really stood out that retailers bought was the candle. It's about finding a void in the marketplace and creating something people want.

Who was your primary market for Chesapeake Bay Candle Company?

The primary market when we were growing the business was retailers. We started with going to trade shows catering to the mom-and-pop retailers that usually have one store or a few stores in one region. Our product was so innovative and contemporary, and very much what the market was looking for. We started selling to department stores and bigger retailers around the whole country. Eventually, we focused on large box stores like Bed Bath & Beyond, Kohl's, and Target.

"When people like something, sometimes they copy you. It's the biggest form of a compliment."

You have started an online platform for women-owned businesses called Yes She May. What was your inspiration and motivation here?

I sold Chesapeake Bay Candle in 2017, and I stayed on as CEO to help the new owner transition. At the end of 2018, I stepped down, and I became a little restless. I've worked all my life and not having to go to work was a very new experience. At that time, I got a book offer and I started to write my book. I also attended a lot of events for women and women CEOs, and people would ask me how to scale, because most women-owned businesses are much smaller, less than $100,000 to $250,000 a year. I started to realize that I am indeed the exception, not the rule, in the women's business arena. There are a lot of women brands that can use expertise to find new vendors, new sources of funding, and new logistic partners. I was trying to find ways to support them in the back end, and then the pandemic hit. All those companies that used to sell in stores could not ship anymore, because the stores were closed. So I decided to launch Yes She May to showcase what women-owned businesses can do in terms of design and quality, and their understanding of what consumers are looking for. We have more than eighty vendors from five continents and more than thirty countries. We're very proud of being the first e-commerce website with women founders from all over the world.

What is your philosophy on risk and risk-taking?

In Chinese, the word "risk" is written as "danger" and "opportunity." It's two characters: One is danger. And the other one is

> *"Passion ... is probably the most important element that separates an entrepreneur from those who want safety and a good, comfortable job."*

opportunity. Risk is really taking opportunities when there is danger, when there's uncertainty. I'm a big risk-taker. I've done nothing that is considered normal or proven. I have not done many things that are easy, but I do feel if a risk is worth taking, you should go for it.

You have been outspoken about discrimination and stereotyping of Asian Americans and the violence against them. What can be done to stem this tide of racism in America?

Racism has always been here. In the past, we did not seem to be the group of minorities that speak about our experiences, so I do feel that raising the profile and raising the issue is one of the first ways to expose the weaknesses and the problems. Culturally, it's not very easy because Asians are trained not to be so confrontational and not to bring attention to themselves. All these so-called Asian virtues really are against the principles of speaking up and acting on behalf of your community. I feel we must adopt a newer philosophy, which is that we can only have a voice if we speak. If we want to see the change, we have to be the change we want to see and stand up for other people's rights and respect the rights of other minority groups. I always say if our leadership in the business community does not reflect the face of our country, we have another problem. Asians have what we call the bamboo ceiling. We could have the best education and the best record of work, but when it's time for a promotion, somehow, we miss the opportunity. How can we change that? We need to demand, and we need to apply for those jobs so that we can also participate at a very high level. It starts with speaking up and making our voices heard.

What are the most important personality traits for an entrepreneur?

Entrepreneurship is about taking risks, but it's also about being optimistic and positive. It is one of the most important qualities that is almost parallel to immigrants. When you think about immigrants, they abandon what's known, what's arranged, what's familiar, and they want to seek their passion with an entirely different scenario. There is a parallel between immigrants and entrepreneurs in that they can give up comfort, the familiar, and the friendly to make something out of a very uncertain environment. Some of the things I have seen a lot of entrepreneurs have in common are the comfort level with uncertainty, the ability to take risks, and the drive to not give up—also called resilience—passion and drive. They don't count how many hours they worked or how much money they're making. They do it for the fun of it. No successful entrepreneurs in my memory started because they really wanted money, or they wanted to make a lot of money very quickly. They don't stop even once they've made it. They're still trying to prove themselves. They're still trying to give themselves another challenge. Elon Musk and Virgin Galactic founder Richard Branson, who launched into space, don't need to prove themselves. They're "grandpas" already. Why do they still take such risks? Because of their passion. It's the same passion that launched their initial businesses, and now it's launching them into the universe. That is probably the most important element that separates an entrepreneur from those who want safety and a good, comfortable job.

 Key Takeaways:

➔ Be optimistic, positive, and driven.
➔ Take big risks.
➔ Be globally minded and form diverse teams.
➔ Find a void or niche in the marketplace and create something people want.
➔ Never stop challenging yourself.

The Visionary

YEN TAN (they/them)
Cofounder, Kona

#PeopleFirst

On business: You need to have at least seventy-five to a hundred customer conversations before you can confidently say what it is people want and what it is you should be building.

On social: It's essentially a reflection of humanity in its own way, and what it reflects to us may not be something that we expect or something that we like, but it is a reflection.

On college: It's not just what you're studying in school, but people you meet while studying.

Raised by a pair of entrepreneurs, **Yen Tan** was inspired from a young age to follow in their parents' footsteps. In October 2019 while still in college, Yen began working with friends Sid Pandiya and Andrew Zhou on an app named after an Aussie shepherd: Kona is an attachment for the popular messaging platform Slack that allows workers to share how they're feeling and build relationships while working remotely. Little did the creators know that the pandemic would exponentially expand their target audience overnight as more people started working from home and feeling the emotional impact of being separated from colleagues. Since then, Kona has partnered with more than three hundred companies, helping employees build empathy and promote sustainable habits such as taking care of their own health to prevent burnout. This in turn has reduced attrition and boosted employee engagement and productivity. As a queer, gender-fluid, nonbinary member of the LGBTQ+ community, Yen is vocal about equality and entrepreneurial diversity and is working toward a future where more people can feel free to be themselves in the workplace. They are an inspiring example of how young entrepreneurs are using technology to improve traditional work structures and teach us that you don't need to act "okay" to be professional.

What is the premise behind Kona, and how does it work?

Kona is a well-being and people analytics platform for remote teams. It works by slotting into Slack workspaces and allows teams

> *"When we have more diverse entrepreneurs leading the front of innovation, we're gonna get solutions that can serve a lot more people, and that's what the world needs."*

to check in and share with the rest of their teammates how they're feeling and if they need any help, and spark watercooler conversations.

A lot of people work hard to separate work and personal life. But with your app you're bringing a lot of personal feelings into work. How do you draw boundaries?

It's okay to struggle, be vulnerable, and actually be human. If your kids are running in on the Zoom screen and you're struggling to be a parent, I think we should be real about that and talk about it rather than just trying to hide them behind a green screen, essentially. Yes, boundaries are important, especially when it comes to burnout and being able to have work-life balance and focus on life outside of work. I think that's really, really important for overall well-being, but I do think we should be real about being stressed or admitting that work stress is bleeding into life or life stress is bleeding into work.

How do you build empathy and kindness in the workplace?

It really starts with leaders, specifically managers. We shouldn't be thinking at the very, very top or the very, very bottom, but just know that culture actually scales from the middle and from managers that are charged with supporting their teams. When it comes to empathetic leadership, we have studied over a thousand remote managers to this point in building this company, and there's usually a certain type of persona. The goal of a people-first manager is to put their people first and to clear out blockers to really be a supportive figure in that person's life. That is the characteristic of every single major company that we've talked to in tech.

What are some of the most common problems you see in companies today?

The big key problems that we discovered were relationship-building in a remote setting—and with that, isolation and not feeling like you know anybody that you're working with—burnout and well-being. We also heard "How can I make sure that what I'm doing is sustainable, especially in a start-up environment?" Also, just a little bit amorphous, "How do we make sure that people love our company, that they stay, that they retain?" Through "the great resignation," we've seen a lot of issues about this. I would argue all of them are problems that can be addressed by squishy answers, like better leadership, empathetic practices, or being able to support teammates. They're not necessarily something that you can throw money at. You can throw money at it, but you have to be very intentional with the way that you're doing it.

How did the pandemic play into the growth of the company?

The pandemic was a huge accelerating factor. One, everybody overnight became a remote worker, and suddenly, our target audience went from a handful of people to the world. Two, we realized that a lot of the problems that we were starting to investigate were really, really major problems that entire companies were dealing with. Burnout, remote work, transition to remote work, how to lead remote first—all became key issues that every single company worth their weight was focused on. Essentially, it turned this idea into a business.

How do you really measure things like happiness and empathy?

The way we measure empathy is a loaded question because it's something we're still trying to figure out. It's the people analytics part of the app itself. But I can tell you that through internal surveying, trying to understand the data that we've been gathering over time, we can see the company's health at scale, and help leaders visualize that for themselves. Over time, we're able to quantify team happiness by asking the right questions at the right time.

Raising capital is essential to any growing business, and you've been a big success, raising $4 million in seed funding very early. What advice would you share?

Raising capital is essentially a sales process. It has its own pipeline. It has a lot of outreach; you can't expect one email to get you an entire million-dollar raise. From what I've been able to observe, it's all about relationship building. I think that's why for us, the accelerator Techstars was so important. It allowed us to really sink our teeth into getting this kind of network of people and allowed us to have a much easier time fundraising the first time around, and subsequently the next time around. It's a lot about timing, too. There are many factors, but at the end of the day, it's a sales process, and it's very emotional. Folks want to have a deal that really gets them excited, especially at these earlier stages, so trying to position yourself for that is interesting.

Would you advocate skipping college if you were a teenager and had a great idea to bring to the market right now?

I would not have this business had I not gone to UCLA and met Sid and Andrew in college, so I'm heavily biased. Had I not joined certain clubs or gotten involved with certain organizations and groups of people, I wouldn't have made some really key introductions and relationships with people that have literally shaped my life forever. The very fact that you're surrounded by like-minded people, and all having very similar experiences, that alone makes college worth it.

How do you go from a great idea to actually running a business?

When you have an idea, it's just an idea until you talk to customers about it. One of the best pieces of advice we got from the UC launch accelerator, as part of the University of California schools program, is you want to talk to twenty-five customers, fifty, and then a hundred. You can think of it as almost like putting on glasses before you have the glasses—it's a very blurry image. Once you get the right prescription, you start to see it, and then as soon as you talk to enough customers, you see crystal clear what you're trying to chase. They literally said you need at least seventy-five to a hundred customer conversations before you can confidently say what it is people want and what it is you should be building. I think that's some of the best advice ever. It's great to have an idea, and that inspires those conversations, but really pay attention to what customers are

> *"A lot of start-up entrepreneurs paint this very clean, sanitized view of a start-up: that your first idea is the gold, you chase it, and suddenly you're a multimillionaire. It doesn't really work out that way."*

saying, because that's going to inspire the product. Once you have the product, you build it and then the people start to come, based on the conversations that you've had so far.

How did growing up in a traditional Chinese American family shape your development as an entrepreneur?

My upbringing was very untraditional. I'm a sixth-generation Chinese American. We're definitely not your typical tiger parent kind of family. I grew up with two parents who were entrepreneurs in their own right. My dad started a business the year I was born. I have always been so inspired and use them as the model of what an entrepreneur can be and what working for yourself and working remotely looks like. That was always something I wanted for myself, but I wasn't quite sure how to achieve it. My parents have been a huge inspiration and hugely supportive of everything that I've been doing.

You talk openly about being queer, gender-fluid, and nonbinary. What have you learned about being yourself in the workplace?

It sometimes feels like the best time to be queer, and the worst time. I will say that acceptance has been opening up a lot, but that doesn't change the fact that being an authentic person, depending on your industry, can be extremely welcoming, or extremely dangerous. That should not be downplayed. I'm very fortunate to be working in tech in a space where people are very open and celebrate individuality and diversity, but that's not necessarily the case in other more traditional industries. I just want to caveat that my experience is heavily colored by that. I hope that eventually every single industry can welcome people for who they are, and that we might not even have to come out and announce the fact that we are different, and that we can just be accepted and seen for who we are. That is my hope for the future. As far as advice, whether you're closeted or fully out, just be you as much as you can be, and hopefully lift up other people or seek support from other people, because a strong wave lifts all ships.

What are some of your personal qualities that you think have driven your success so far?

I feel like I am very empathetic, and a little humble to a fault. I only say that because I think a lot of my experience as an entrepreneur has been colored by impostor syndrome and feeling like I'm in the wrong space, or maybe that I'm too young to be doing this. I think a healthy level of humility has helped us maintain intellectual honesty, stick with ideas, and really run with what we've been given without being too cocky about it. But I do think that I could work on confidence a little bit, and that's something we're working on every single day.

What has running a business taught you about not listening when others doubt you or your ideas?

Running my own business has taught me that literally, you are your best cheerleader. Self-confidence can get you very, very far. Every time we've heard doubt, we've actually welcomed it. We see it as a data point. We see it as something that can improve our business. We really chase after folks who have negative feedback for us because it informs our product and makes us a lot more flexible. I don't think that it's helpful to go into an echo chamber or only go toward folks who agree with you. I think it's great to be able to have strong opinions weakly held and to go after an idea and to hopefully chase the best answer for as many parties as possible.

What is something that isn't brought up enough when it comes to talking about entrepreneurship?

I think something we need to talk about a lot more is diversity and the fact that Black queer founders get a very, very, very small amount of funding, and how much fundraising and all these different things are established for groups of power. It's wild to me to think that literally less than 1 percent of queer founders have raised a significant amount. There's a lot to be done as far as entrepreneurial diversity. When we have more diverse entrepreneurs leading the front of innovation, we're gonna get solutions that can serve a lot more people, and that's what the world needs.

 Key Takeaways:

- ➡ Self-confidence can get you far.
- ➡ Think about sustainability, not just quick change.
- ➡ Empathize with your customers and users.
- ➡ Be you as much as you can be.
- ➡ Stay humble.

CHARLES MILLER (he/him)
Cofounder and CEO, Lynk Global

#LYNKingTheWorld

On life: Do the thing that nobody thinks is possible.

On social: It brings out some of the worst things in people, but at the same time, it's a great way to learn.

On college: I'm a Caltech dropout. College is not necessarily for everybody, but if you don't set out on a course for a life of learning, then you've set yourself up for failure.

Charles Miller has always been a dreamer with a bias for action. A space entrepreneur, his career has included lobbying for space policy legislation on Capitol Hill, leading commercial space activities at NASA, and founding a consulting firm combining commercial, space, and national security public policy. Today he is CEO of Lynk Global, Inc., whose mission is to connect the world through satellite phones and give access to those typically excluded from Wi-Fi and internet. He has launched six satellites into space and is working with NASA to launch others. All his jobs have had one goal in mind: use space to make things better for people on Earth. He believes that commercial space travel will be common by the time we graduate from college, that mobile phones will function in our earbuds and glasses, that climate change will be radically improved by space exploration, and that the future is very, very bright.

Do you think the recent space launches will become the new normal for how space expeditions will be funded and carried out in the future?

This is the future.

Do you imagine private companies will start overtaking NASA in researching space if that method of funding gains in popularity?

The reason this is critical is it's not just about a few government employees going to space at hundreds of millions or billions of dollars per seat. The critical value of getting private human spaceflight going is that you might get to go, and private industry is the best way to radically drop costs by orders of magnitude. They're going to open the space frontier so each of you get to go, too. It's American common sense. The government doesn't own the railroads or own and design automobiles, or own and operate airplanes and airlines. This is all private industry, and the same thing should be true for spaceflight.

Do you think this will happen in our lifetime?

By the time you get out of college, if you choose to go to college—some entrepreneurs drop out of college and go start businesses—there's going to be some amazing commercial space business opportunities. I have many fellow space entrepreneurs with amazing ideas. Some are a little bit before their time. One of the hardest things to get right for an entrepreneur is timing.

What characteristics or personality traits do you have that have made you a successful entrepreneur?

A successful entrepreneur is very good at is hearing "no." The only way to get to "yes" is to be willing to have somebody tell you "no," and be grateful and say "thank you," and then you move on. Entrepreneurs are persistent. You get knocked down ten times, you get up eleven. You should also think about why you want it. The two of you are totally motivated to be entrepreneurs. It is that motivation that is going to keep you going where other people stop.

You said you believe space travel should be made cheaper and easier. How could this become a reality?

The reason space is expensive is you build a launch vehicle that costs about the same amount as an airplane to build. A 737 might cost $50 million or $100 million to build. Same thing with a launch vehicle, but the 737 flies ten thousand times. You land it, and you refill it, and you take off the same day. Whereas in a launch vehicle, you fly it once and you throw it away. Just imagine if you had an airplane that costs $100 million to build and you flew from Washington National Airport to Los Angeles and you got off, and you threw the airplane away. That's going to be a really expensive airplane to fly. They may have a hundred people on it, it cost them $100 million to build, so just to cover their costs, they have to charge $1 million a ticket. No one's going to buy a flight to Los Angeles for a million dollars for a one-way trip, then spend another million dollars to get home. Launch vehicles that are highly reusable, that you can turn around fast and frequently, are the future and will change everything about going to space. Tens of thousands of people a year will go to space in the not-too-distant future. That's transformational. That's the future you get to be part of if you want to be.

How could space be useful in helping the environment?

In the long term, space is going to solve this problem. The cleanest, almost unlimited source of energy in our solar system is the sun. There has been a concept that's been a little bit ahead of its time called space solar power. The clean energy in space is eight times more powerful per unit area in space than it is on Earth. You can capture the clean energy in space and transmit it to Earth and provide almost unlimited

clean energy to Earth. This will solve the global warming issue. Fully reusable launch vehicles will enable a lot of experimentation in building large satellites in space that can capture this energy and then experiment with sending that clean energy to Earth. You build these satellites in orbit just like you build a big skyscraper in the middle of a downtown of a big city. You take the parts there and assemble them at the site. The only way to protect Earth is by getting off the planet and using the resources of the solar system to move the dirty, polluting things off the planet. We're going to put the dirty industrial stuff into space in the long term, and we're going to use our ability to live and work in space to protect Earth. Because it is the most amazing planet we have found.

How has your current company, Lynk, made a difference in both the space and technology sectors?

We have figured out a way to connect everybody on Earth, with just the phone in your pocket. It's a revolution in technology. We launched our third satellite to orbit in 2019, and in 2020, we transmitted the world's first text message from a satellite in orbit to a standard ordinary mobile phone on Earth. We were the first, and we have done it many times since then. We've proven our technology on thousands of devices, signed commercial contracts covering over thirty-five countries, and are beginning commercial service. Your phone will stay connected everywhere. A couple years ago, people thought it was impossible to connect the satellite to the phone. They were wrong. Conventional wisdom was wrong. If you're doing something that everybody thinks is a good idea, that's probably not a good idea, because you've got a thousand people doing the same thing.

How are you working to ensure equal access for everyone?

About 350 million more men in the world have a smartphone than women. There's a gender gap. More than a billion people don't have a phone just because they don't have affordable connectivity where they live and work.

How do you think that the mobile phone's appearance and functionality will change as technology gets more advanced?

Eventually, they're going to plug the phone in behind your ear and it will disappear. We're going to be integrated with the machines. You'll plug right into the internet and you'll be in constant communication everywhere with a chip that's implanted behind your ear. There's lots of science fiction written on this. With smaller and smaller electronics, you'll see the mobile phone eventually almost disappear.

Were you ever bullied growing up?

Kids said nasty things about me and picked fights with me because I was a nerd. I never understood why. I hated the nicknames that I was called. The main thing you have to remember is you'll get through it. Nerds rule the world, so don't worry about it. Your day will come. Own it. Own that you love science, math, studying, reading, and ideas. The world is full of amazing ideas. That's what's great about you. You love ideas and you love thinking about these things.

 Key Takeaways:

- Just do it.
- Don't be afraid to hear "no."
- Own your ideas and who you are.
- Be persistent.
- Stay motivated.

RICH RILEY (he/him)
Co-CEO, Origin Materials; former CEO, Shazam

#GoGetEm

On business: If you have the right team, you can solve most problems.

On social: Like a lot of things in life, it's all about balance.

On college: For me, it was transformative. It was incredibly helpful to be pushed well out of my comfort zone.

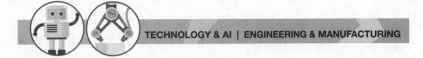

What does it mean to never stop being an entrepreneur? For **Rich Riley**, it meant leaving his Wall Street job to innovate and succeed at company after company. Rich is cofounder of Log-Me-On.com, the company that invented the first internet toolbar (a downloadable browser used for quick internet searches that revolutionized the early internet experience). After his toolbar company was bought by Yahoo!, he worked his way up the ladder to become part of the Yahoo! executive team, and later became the CEO of Shazam Entertainment, which developed one of the world's most popular music identification apps. At Shazam, he also teamed with TV executive Mark Burnett and actor Jamie Foxx to co-produce the hit game show *Beat Shazam,* where contestants challenge the app itself for a chance to win $1 million. After Shazam was acquired by Apple, Rich became CEO of Origin Materials, now the world's leading carbon-negative materials company. Origin partners with companies like Nestlé, PepsiCo, and Ford to help them transition from fossil-based to sustainable materials. Rich teaches us that entrepreneurship exists in every type of business, no matter how big or small.

You have worked at both tiny start-ups and some of the biggest brands in the world. How would you compare those experiences?

I started my career on Wall Street and was an investment banker working in these very fancy offices in New York, wearing a suit and

> *"Courage and optimism are two things you probably need to over-index on if you really want to go the entrepreneurial route."*

a tie, working eighty-plus hours a week, and invented the toolbar with one of my coworkers at the investment bank who was in the IT group. When we realized that we really had made a breakthrough invention, and we went to sell that to—eventually—Yahoo!, it was pretty exciting. It may be hard to imagine, but Yahoo! was one of the first workplaces where there were dogs in the office and people on skateboards and people wearing shorts and that kind of stuff. It was about as big a change as you could have coming from an investment bank in New York to Yahoo! in California. But we always loved the team, loved the energy, loved the product, loved the internet, and it was just getting started at that time. It actually was a pretty easy and smooth transition, even as we moved across the country and went to work at this crazy place with a crazy name like Yahoo!

Why did you decide to sell Shazam to Apple?

Like a lot of start-ups, we had investors who had been invested for a long time, and it was time to find a more permanent home for the company. With Apple, we were able to find that perfect home because they love the brand, and they love the service. They kept it separate, with its own identity, and increased the investment into it, giving it more computing power and resources. When you think about selling a start-up, you want to find that perfect home, where the team and customers are going to be excited, and we really found that with Apple. I know, as a user, the service has only gotten better under their ownership.

The company you now represent, Origin Materials, is heavily focused on the effort toward carbon-zero and even carbon-negative emissions through more sustainable materials. What specifically is Origin Materials doing to help?

Origin is entirely about facilitating the world's transition to sustainable materials. We call it a "once in a planet" transition from fossil-based materials to sustainable ones. Most people don't realize it, but everything around you is pretty much made from oil and gas. That computer you're staring at, the clothes you're wearing—it is all largely from that. So we've got to make a transition to combat climate change. I was one of the earliest investors in Origin over ten years ago. I love the company. I love its incredible technology; we spent ten years developing this highly proprietary technology. It's the only company in the world that can take wood waste and make plastics. For me, it was important to join a company with an incredible mission. We sequester carbon, and we help companies meet their net-zero pledges. It's important to our customers, their employees, their customers, investors, and our team. To me, it's a mega trend. It's one that I care a lot about personally, and I do certainly feel it with the younger generation. For them, this is not a debate. It's a passion with an urgency, and that's great for the world. It's one of the reasons we have so much conviction that we're going to make a dent in the universe, and that companies are going to follow through on these net-zero pledges, and that's what we help them achieve.

What are the most important personality traits for an entrepreneur?

It takes a lot of courage to be an entrepreneur, because you're going to have not just tough times, but you're going to have effectively near-death experiences of your venture where it looks hopeless, it looks like there's no chance, it looks like people are going to lose money, and that you've wasted all this time. That's part of almost every entrepreneurial journey, so you have to prepare yourself for that. Entrepreneurs have to have the courage to believe and know that they're almost certainly going to hit a wall, have to pivot, and figure out what they're going to do, and as part of that have incredible optimism and self-confidence.

How have you developed your leadership style over the years?

I've learned it's really all about the team. If you have the right team, you can solve most problems. I've also learned that it's not just having the right team, but it's empowering that team. When you really get the right person in the right role with the right focus, and then empower them to make decisions and do what they can do, is when you get the best results. Very few leaders are talented enough to truly micromanage and have everything run through them. There are some of those people out there, but they're quite rare. For most of us, it's about finding the right team, setting them up for success, empowering them to make decisions and thrive. That's probably one of my biggest leadership lessons. The other is to be intolerant of dysfunction. As companies grow, they can easily become dysfunctional. People can say they don't like to work with each other, or they want to do things their own way, or they don't agree with the decision, and they don't commit no matter what the decision was. Having a low tolerance for dysfunction is another one of my learnings.

How do you think new technologies will impact entrepreneurship for our generation?

"For some people, being at a start-up makes sense. Some people that can't take that risk, financially or emotionally, can still be an entrepreneur in whatever they're doing."

The cool thing is, it's never been easier to start a company. When I was starting the toolbar, one of the biggest hurdles was you had to raise so much money to buy servers to handle traffic. Now you can just sign up at Amazon Web Services (AWS) and you have computing power on demand, which is an amazing liberator of ideas and talent. Also, I'm on the board of the Wharton School of the University of Pennsylvania Entrepreneurship Department, and entrepreneurship is their most popular field of study. When I got my degree in entrepreneurship, that wasn't the case. It was definitely an emerging field. I think a lot of people are willing to take the risk. I think, also, a lot of us have realized that if somebody takes an entrepreneurial risk and fails, that doesn't mean they're not capable. That doesn't mean they're a failure. That's admired, especially in places like Silicon Valley, where that's somewhat common. That's an awesome change.

Where are the biggest business opportunities and risks in entrepreneurship right now?

I'm very focused on climate change, and through that lens, there are incredible opportunities to come up with decarbonization solutions. So much innovation and investment is needed to attack this problem, and there are enormous opportunities. I think that's one of the big mega trends. It's always nice if you can start a company that's got big, big tailwinds, and I would say environmental businesses would meet that test. It's a great time to be an entrepreneur, for sure.

What positive experiences did you take away from your college experience and how did it help you develop into the leader you are today?

I grew up in Austin, Texas. I really wanted to go to Wall Street. I went to Wharton, which is in Philadelphia. It was an unbelievable education in the field I was passionate about, which was business. I studied finance and entrepreneurial management. It took me totally out of my comfort zone. A lot of my friends went to the state school in town. I was really jealous of how much fun they were having, but I was experiencing a lot of diversity in terms of thought, background, and worldview. That, coupled with a very rigorous academic experience, prepared me for Wall Street, doing business all over the world, and starting companies. For me, it was transformative. It was incredibly helpful to be pushed well out of my comfort zone.

 Key Takeaways:

> Push yourself out of your comfort zone.
> Don't tolerate dysfunction.
> Be courageous.
> Realize that failure doesn't mean you are incapable.
> Take risks.

AARON RASMUSSEN (he/him)
Founder and CEO, Outlier; Cofounder, MasterClass

#Inventor

On business: You get beat up constantly as an entrepreneur, and you have to get back up and keep going.

On social: Social media has had very complex effects, and we don't even know what they are yet. Five or ten years from now, we will look back with better perspective. For all we know, some really good things came from it, or for all we know, everything went off the rails.

On college: College allows you to better understand the world, other people, and other perspectives.

Aaron Rasmussen is the CEO of Outlier, a company devoted to equalizing education by offering accredited college classes at a fraction of the price. Aaron has dabbled in many flavors of entrepreneurship, including creating the survival adventure game *BlindSide,* the *World of Warcraft*–inspired energy drink Mana Potion, an iPhone accessory called Mr. Ghost, and a robotic arm to cut granite, but he has always had a passion for improving education based on his own lackluster experiences as a self-taught student. He brought education to the masses at MasterClass, a cinematic online platform where students can learn everything from cooking to design to sports from celebrity instructors. He used a similar model for Outlier and moved even closer to his ideals. As a mission-driven for-profit company, Outlier offers college fundamentals like calculus and philosophy taught by professors from schools like the Massachusetts Institute of Technology (MIT), Davidson, and Columbia, and offers a full refund if students don't pass, aligning the goals of the company with those of the student. In our conversation, Aaron touches on topics such as what counts as failure, bringing your idea to life, and redefining education.

What lessons did you take from cofounding MasterClass that you used in your new start-up, Outlier?

The most applicable thing that we learned was that consumers care about quality. There is a respect for it, so it's worthwhile to spend your time making something beautiful.

How did your upbringing and education drive you to create Outlier?

I grew up in the middle of the woods in northeastern Oregon, so I actually didn't have access to good education. I was twelve miles outside a town of six hundred people. I was an autodidact, or self-taught. I read a lot of books. I would have loved to have access to a good education. When I went to Boston University—I was one of only a few students in my high school class that went to college—I took community college courses over the summer; then I transferred the credits into BU to make ends meet. That was probably the original inspiration, even though I wasn't thinking about a business at the time. I was just trying to survive and get through college.

Have you always had a passion for improving education?

It was a lack of access to education that made me want to make it accessible for other people. I've always been a curious person. I'm secretly perpetually a student. I used to do YouTube videos about how to make things that became relatively popular. Now I do a similar thing on TikTok, where I'm fixing things around my house, and people seem to like that. I took a year off after Master-Class, and I traveled the world. I went to twenty-eight countries. I learned scuba diving. I flew a glider, which was pretty cool. I also got parasites, and that was less cool. I also ended up finding that my story is not that unusual, and that education can fundamentally change somebody's position in life. What is unusual is

"Many times, failure is a matter of perspective."

having access to it. It's a lot of luck where you end up. Potential and talent are evenly distributed around the world, but opportunity is not. It's our job to make opportunities better distributed.

Outlier is a for-profit company, and yet it also has a clear mission. How does straddling the line between a nonprofit and a for-profit traditional college allow you to do more good?

We say, if you do all the work, and you don't pass, you get a refund. That way, it makes our incentive to teach the students so that they learn, the same as their incentive in passing the course. That's how we can take a for-profit company and have an extreme mission focus. If you solve a massive social problem, there will be monetary value. Getting that balance right is very important but it also allows for incredible new heights for opportunity and access.

Do students get the same education as if they were in a brick-and-mortar school?

We have success rates that are even with or better than a brick-and-mortar school. These assessments are overseen by the University of Pittsburgh and a number of other universities. We know the students are learning the information well, which is extremely exciting. There are additional benefits to being in a brick-and-mortar classroom. You're around students your age, make friends, and ask questions. But for a lot of people, that's just not a reasonable thing to ask them to do. What if they're taking care of a sick parent? What if they need to work a job and the job doesn't have static hours? They need to be able to take courses on their own time. That means we would actually be a far better scenario than a brick-and-mortar. Some students are more willing to communicate in a virtual setting. It's easier for some people to just type something than speak up in class. I was a very shy kid, so I struggled with that. I think this probably would have been easier for me. Everybody learns in their own way. Different people are comfortable with different things online. It accommodates for a lot of different learning styles and comfort for students.

What do you say to someone questioning the value of college?

I understand why the next generation is questioning the value of college, because when you charge a huge amount for something, you really have to question the value of it. Take a roller coaster ride. Let's say you don't know how good the roller coaster is going to be. If somebody says it's a thousand dollars to ride this, you're going to question how valuable it is to go on that roller coaster ride, but if it's four bucks to ride it, it's worth a shot. College can be like that. College is an incredibly valuable experience, and I've had a huge amount of value from my own undergraduate college experience. I have a BS and a BA. I have degrees in computer science and advertising. People always asked me what I would use it for. For me, college is to understand the world better. It's to understand other people and understand their perspectives better. That doesn't sound like something that makes a ton of money, but it does, because we all work on this planet and we have to work with different types of people. You want to understand and respect

> *"It's all about taking an idea and making it real."*

them, understand other people's perspectives and the way they're interacting with the world.

How might your cheaper courses with similar results win back our interest?

The way Outlier makes it accessible is it allows somebody to take two years of school with us, as opposed to a university charging classic rates. Right now, it would be about $6,400 or $3,200 a year. One of my big concerns right now is people are making decisions on their majors going into college, because they know it's so expensive, but coming out of college, they have student debt, and they start making decisions on what job they take based on that. If you come out with student debt and an economics degree, you could go into finance and make a lot of money, or you could go work at a nongovernmental organization (NGO) that figures out trade disputes in a war zone where you're doing really incredible humanitarian work. The problem is you don't make any money going to the NGO. If you have tons of student debt, you simply can't make that decision. However, if somebody takes half their degree through Outlier, my hope is it reduces enough debt that it gives them that option. When people question the value of college, they are questioning time and money. The time is absolutely well worth it. There's plenty of stats that say it will increase your overall life earnings. As the enrichment of a human being, learning the way our species thinks and views things is incredibly valuable. But the money? That's a huge and completely fair question!

Did you have any failures before you saw such great success?

I've had plenty of failures. Sometimes it's hard to classify what's a failure and what's not. Everything includes some failure in it, even the successes. You'll have these crazy setbacks that really are failures. When MasterClass launched, everybody said it was an overnight success. We launched the company, people loved the classes, they bought a lot of them, it became popular, and it was well reviewed. We'd been working on it for a harrowing eighteen months before that. My cofounder and I spent the first seven months in a borrowed office space, hoping somebody would work with us. There was no reason that a celebrity should work with us. We didn't have a track record. I had been in different industries. Yet things are sometimes ultimately successful. There's usually failure along the way, and sometimes companies can also fail after they've been successful. Many times, determining the difference between success and failure is just the moment in time that you're looking at something. It's important to remember that because sometimes you have something that's successful, and then it stops being successful.

Is entrepreneurship nature or nurture?

Entrepreneurship definitely can be learned. It's probably a combination of nature and nurture as most psychological traits are. For some people, it's the only thing they can do. They have a hard time working for anyone else. I'm one of those people. I don't have a lot of choice about being an entrepreneur.

Key Takeaways:

→ Do things you are interested in.
→ Learn to work with different kinds of people.
→ Make something beautiful.
→ Be resilient and keep going.
→ Learn subjects that will give you perspective.

The Champion

DAVIS SMITH (he/him)
Founder and Board Chair, Cotopaxi

#DoGood

On business: If you want to be an entrepreneur, be as disciplined and as diligent in coming up with your idea as you are in running the idea.

On social: I'm a big believer in social media. It's a great way to build brands, both as individuals and as a company. It is an opportunity for business leaders to use their voice to effect positive change.

On college: Some of the biggest lessons I learned were around surrounding myself with really good people.

Davis Smith is all about using his business and his life to do good. As the founder, chairman of the board, and former CEO of the outdoor adventure gear and social impact brand Cotopaxi, his goal is to leverage his life experience, creativity, and success to make the world a better place. Cotopaxi donates a percentage of every vibrantly colored, instantly recognizable backpack, jacket, and fanny pack toward poverty alleviation, primarily in South America, where Davis spent much of his childhood. He became an entrepreneur after a mentor suggested it would be a career where his ideas and values would matter and where he could bring to life his vision of making a difference. At Cotopaxi, Davis has fostered a culture of innovation, kindness, and generosity—from that commitment to give back to a company structure that encourages creativity and discovery from every employee. He talks with us about building purpose into business, learning to test your ideas, and using feedback to improve everything you do.

What was your vision in creating Cotopaxi?

My vision and dream for the business was something that I'd been working on since I was your age, where I started thinking about what I wanted to do with my life. I didn't know I wanted to be an entrepreneur at that point. I didn't really know that many entrepreneurs, but I knew I wanted to help people and I knew I wanted to make a difference in the world. As I finished college, a mentor recommended that I consider entrepreneurship as a career path, and he suggested that I might be able to make a difference in the world as an entrepreneur. I spent ten years building a couple of different businesses. Honestly, after ten years, I was feeling a little discouraged that I was building businesses, but they weren't having any kind of social impact. I was feeling frustrated that I hadn't quite figured that out, but in 2013, I started having some ideas around building a business and a brand that was all about giving back, and I really connected deeply with the mission and within the brand. I launched the business a year later, in 2014. We now have around three hundred employees, and it's just been amazing. Last year, we helped 1.3 million people living in poverty. It's fulfilling every dream that I had.

Let's talk a bit about those humanitarian causes and giving back. Why is promising to do good, and delivering on that promise, a core value to you and your company?

We donate a minimum of 1 percent, although historically it's been closer to 2 percent. We commit to a minimum amount, and we try to do more. In 2020, we actually gave 2.9 percent. The point of us giving is not to make a commitment and give as little as we can, it's really trying to be as generous as we possibly can.

Why is that important to you and to Cotopaxi?

It's a passion and a value that I really care about. I think I have a responsibility to use my life to help others. I think as leaders in business, we have a responsibility to look out for the people that are most vulnerable among us, and to look for opportunities to lift others. I'm a big believer that people want to support businesses that are doing good in the world. If you have strong values that align with the values of your consumers, then they're going to support you. We built values into the business, but we also tried to make a really strong case with our investors that businesses that do good in the world are going to do better. I also think one of the reasons that matters is because we will do better as a business, the better we do at doing good. I believe you can do well and do good at the same time. Those two things aren't mutually exclusive.

What do customers get when they buy your product, and what is your brand promise?

Our slogan is "gear for good." It's a two-part commitment. It's a promise that our gear is going to last for good, and they're gonna get a great quality product for what they paid us for. The second part of that is a commitment that our gear is going to do good in the world; that we're going to use our brand and our business to make a positive impact. We specifically focus on poverty alleviation. That's our core issue, and within that are three key pillars, which are health care, education, and livelihood training.

Can you tell us the story behind the llama logo?

When I was eleven or twelve years old, my family lived in Ecuador. We were camping at the base of a mountain called Cotopaxi—a big volcano—and a herd of wild llamas ran through our camp. My mind was blown. I thought these are the weirdest animals, they have these long legs and these long necks, and they're super fuzzy and furry and just really unique, and they stood out to me. What I loved about these animals is they were really rugged. They could live in high altitude and the cold. They are pack animals and they love being together. You'd never see a llama by itself. Llamas are always in groups of other llamas. I thought they were a good mascot for the brand. It's memorable. It's a little bit quirky and different. They are these tough animals that can live in harsh conditions, but that love lifting each other and being together. I thought it was a great representation of our brand.

Are there any tactics you use to stay creative with your products?

Innovation is one of our three core values. We've tried to create processes that encourage innovation within the team. Every quarter or so, we run an innovation tournament, where we give everyone in the company a challenge. I'll email everyone a week ahead of time and ask them to brainstorm a solution to the challenge on their own. Then everyone comes together, we break into teams of five to six people, they all share their favorite ideas with each other, and pick their favorite one or two ideas. Then they put together a pitch deck and have one minute to present their favorite idea to the whole company. We end up with thousands of ideas and we filter it down to a few. It's a really fun process. At one of our last innovation tournaments, one of our distribution center workers, who works in our warehouse picking and pulling product and putting it in boxes, won the best idea. She came up with a product idea that was awesome. By creating this process where we let everyone in the business be part of innovating and solving problems, it encourages people to think differently, think outside the box, and think outside of their own responsibilities.

What is your best advice in the face of rejection, especially when first starting out?

I've been rejected thousands of times. When I started Cotopaxi in my first round, I pitched over a hundred different investors to raise the money for the business. At this point I've pitched the business probably one thousand times to different investors. I've gotten a lot more noes than yeses. The way that I see it is that rejection is just feedback, and feedback is awesome. It allows you to get better and to improve. When I get rejected, I ask what I learned from that experience and what things I could have done better. I find if I look at it that way, then it gives me encouragement to go out and do it again and try to do it better the next time, versus thinking there's not anything good here, I'm going to quit, or I'm going to move on. Sometimes that is what you need to do. Sometimes you go pitch and you have an idea that just is not working and sometimes you need to abandon it and go try something new. There's a fine balance. I learned a lot about rejection when I was nineteen. I moved to South America and was a Mormon missionary for my church for two years. I got rejected every single day. It helps you build resilience. It helps you understand that it's okay to be rejected and your message or your idea isn't for everyone. There will be some people who love it and other people who don't. And that's okay.

What did you learn from your experiences at Brigham Young University (BYU), Wharton, and Stanford that you apply to your work today?

I learned different things at different places. They were at different stages of my life, too. I think some of the biggest lessons I learned were around surrounding myself with really good people. When I was at Wharton, my classmates started some amazing businesses and brands, like Warby Parker, Allbirds, and Harry's, the shaving company. I saw these great, ambitious entrepreneurs who were thinking differently about how to build purpose into business, and that was really inspiring to me.

What makes our generation different from other generations and how can we effectively make use of our uniqueness?

Your generation is thinking about our planet and people in a way that my generation never thought about. You guys are very driven by purpose. You want to be part of a cause. I think that's inspiring and important. It gives me a lot of hope that we can build a better world because we're going to be led by people who really care about these things. That's the big opportunity with your generation.

What is one topic that isn't brought up enough when discussing entrepreneurship?

One of the things that I think is just not discussed enough is the process of coming up with great ideas. A lot of people talk about how you are going to be an entrepreneur, you come up with an idea, and then never give up and work really hard on that idea. People are willing to give up years of their time and all their savings, and take all these risks for an idea, but I don't think they spend enough time coming up with the idea. I'm a believer that you should run a process. If you want to be an entrepreneur, be as disciplined and as diligent in coming up with your idea as you are in running the idea. A lot of times I've seen entrepreneurs pick an idea and it's not a good idea, but they're willing to put everything into it to try to make it work. They would have been better served just spending three months or six months making sure that was the very best idea. Come up with fifty or a hundred ideas over six months. At the end of the six months, test the ideas, vet them, put a little bit of money behind your favorite ideas, and try to narrow them, just like we do with that innovation tournament in our company. Take all those ideas and pitch the best ones and see how people respond to them. See if people are willing to buy it. Once you run that process, you're going to have a much higher likelihood of success than if you just come up with three ideas and you choose the favorite idea and run with it. The likelihood of that idea being really great is low.

 Key Takeaways:

➔ Make time to be creative.
➔ Take risks while you are young.
➔ Use social media to effect positive change.
➔ Bake innovation into your work.
➔ Test your idea before running with it.

DANIEL SCHARFF (he/him)

CEO, Machu Picchu Energy; Founder, Startup CPG

#GoodEnergy

 On business: The people who learn how to tap into a network have a huge advantage.

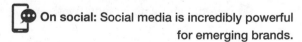 **On social:** Social media is incredibly powerful for emerging brands.

 On college: It was a really important experience for me.

Daniel Scharff brings the power of good energy to everything he does in his life and career. It is fitting, then, that his company's motto is "Energy to Feel Good, a Mission to Do Good." Machu Picchu is an organic energy drink company designed to fuel your body, taste delicious, and give you a boost of energy to go out into the world and make it better. Daniel believes that while energy drinks are one of the fastest-growing sectors of the food and beverage industry, Machu Picchu Energy towers over other brands. It couples organic flavor technology and zero-sugar organic sweeteners with organic green coffee beans, organic maca, and B vitamins, all infused with refreshing natural flavors like pineapple, blueberry, ginger peach, and blood orange. From supporting NGOs in Brazil and Peru working with children in underserved communities to leading socially conscious entrepreneurship simulators in US public schools, Daniel lives his company's values and proves that businesses can and should do much more than sell products. Daniel brings his experience working at big brands like the candymaker Mars to Machu Picchu Energy, and he's helping other emerging companies via Startup CPG, a networking hub he founded for emerging food and beverage businesses working toward a better food system. Drawing upon the company's twin missions of feeling good and doing good, he shares with us some of the lessons he has learned as a do-good entrepreneur, from speaking from the heart to the potential for his industry to improve the food system, to the link between business and helping others.

More and more beverage companies are investing in zero sugar and low-calorie alternative drinks. Are these products as genuine as they seem?

Most of the stuff that's out there uses artificial sweeteners like sucralose that taste fake and too sweet, and combined with their artificial flavors, colors, synthetic caffeine, and preservatives, the overall product is not good. Then there are drinks on market that use high-quality ingredients and are zero sugar, but aren't winning on taste. We're going for both—high-quality organic ingredients and winning taste, to meet consumers' demand for healthy energy drinks.

What is your process to make your product taste so good?

We use the most sophisticated organic flavor technology and smooth organic sweeteners—delicious, refreshing, natural-tasting, and with no aftertaste. It's a craft approach to zero sugar, rather than using fake sweeteners that just register on our taste buds as overpoweringly sweet. If you taste one of those products, and then ours, you will immediately understand the difference.

Where does the energy fit into the formula?

Our organic energy drinks have 120 milligrams of organic natural caffeine that comes from organic green coffee beans (a water extraction), as well as yerba maté, in the case of our craft organic yerba maté

"Business is a language as much as Spanish or programming. When you learn it, you start understanding and having a frame of reference when people are talking."

drinks. They also feature organic Peruvian maca, an adaptogen traditionally used for energy and stamina.

What meaning does the name Machu Picchu Energy hold for you?

Machu Picchu is one of the most inspirational outdoors sites on the planet—and a place of incredible, almost mystical energy. If I'm sitting here at my computer, drinking a Machu Picchu, maybe it'll remind me that after work or this weekend, I should get outside and go for a walk in nature, or get to the beach and swim in the ocean. For me, I need that to reset so that I have good energy coming back into the week and feel balanced. We're really proud to provide support to the mountain itself and cultural initiatives through our partnership with UNESCO in Peru—we're founding members of a ten-year cultural pact, providing badly needed financial support.

Machu Picchu Energy's slogan is "Energy to Feel Good. A Mission to Do Good." What specifically is Machu Picchu Energy doing to help kids?

The work that we're doing is aimed at helping kids and underserved communities. We work with two NGOs in Latin America. One is in Lima, Peru, in a neighborhood called Chorrillos, that works with kids and offers outdoor education opportunities like surf therapy. We want to help them grow their operations and help as many kids as possible. We do the same with an NGO in Rio de Janeiro called Favela Radical, meaning "radical," as in they're really trying for big change, and trying to better the lives of kids who have it pretty tough. We also have created BevLaunch, a program that will teach kids all over the United States the fundamentals of being a do-good entrepreneur. We create a hands-on simulator where kids learn to launch a beverage company—from creating a liquid, to sales and marketing strategy, and even pitching VCs—as a way to demystify entrepreneurship. We've piloted our curriculum through two semesters in Miami Public Schools and will expand to schools across the country through a partnership with NAF, a leading education NGO.

Why is it so important to you personally?

I love education, and I love sharing what I'm excited about and what I'm working on. It gives me a special kind of energy, so it felt natural to go into schools that could really use this kind of exposure. When I was twelve, somebody's father came to my school and did a stock market simulation with us. And I thought, "That's cool, that's exciting. I'm gonna do business." Then I went on and got internships and found a career in business that has been incredibly fulfilling. If someone hadn't done that for me and created a spark, who knows where I would have ended up going. We're looking to do that same thing for kids and communities that probably don't get that chance as much. We would love to expose them to role models and careers in business and entrepreneurship, and really get them excited about what we do, which is do-good entrepreneurship.

What are the steps of entrepreneurship?

Come up with a mission: Why are you doing this in the first

place? Same with you guys for your book: I know you have a mission of really explaining this to your generation, which is great. That gives you your guiding principle. Now it makes it a lot easier to come up with your target customer; then come up with the qualities of the drink that you're going to create. That's getting to product development, and then you do branding, you actually draw up cans, but all of that is the same no matter what kind of company it is. Product development, branding, design, marketing strategy, sales strategy, and pitch—you have to know all these things.

What is a word or phrase that would summarize your career?

Good energy, which of course fits pretty well with this company. I try to bring good energy to everything I do, and to all my relationships. Even when things get tough, I aspire to bring good, positive energy.

What advantages and disadvantages does social media have for small businesses without big budgets?

Social media is incredibly powerful for emerging brands. It gives you an opportunity that a lot of brands wouldn't have had before. Consumer products like the food and beverage industry, like many industries, was dominated by big incumbents, who I think a lot of people would say weren't really doing enough to try to improve the food system. For all of us who are trying to bring better food and beverage, the obstacles are a little lower when you have tools like social media. I've seen many brands that showed a lot of heart and authenticity on social media and were able to carve out a space for themselves, and capture share from bigger brands. I also think some brands could rely too much on it. The costs of advertising and marketing through social media are going up. There are still tried-and-true tactics that are going to be important, like how to get people to try your product in the market and in stores, that people need to understand and pay attention to, rather than only relying on clever videos.

How did your time in college affect your development as a leader?

I didn't have the maturity to have a successful career right out of high school. I got some amazing things out of my college experience—a very good, well-rounded education. I did a liberal arts degree. What I learned about critical thinking and writing is what got me to the next level. I would have been just fine to a certain point in my career, but I can't tell you how many times the thing that mattered was being able to critically problem-solve something, an ops nightmare or a marketing challenge, where having the experience from a lot of psychology classes or study designs was the thing that helped me break down a problem and come up with creative solutions. I don't think everybody needs to go, but for me, where I was and where I wanted to get to, those were really important experiences for me.

What did you learn in business school at Wharton that you use every day in running your company?

Business school was a wonderful way for me to reset my career, meet a lot of people, explore a lot of different potential career paths, and just try to figure out what I wanted to learn and what I could do, and start to speak the language. Business is a language as much as Spanish or programming. When you learn it, you start understanding and having a frame of reference when people are talking. Business school really helped me with that. One course that has paid dividends was learning about negotiations—it ingrained in me the importance of building relationships and doing the hard work to find optimal mutually beneficial outcomes.

How did your earlier experiences at Mars, Morningstar, and Deloitte lead you to where you are today?

I took a path where I started at big companies, and then went smaller and smaller and smaller until I was able to meet the founder of Machu Picchu and come in to start it as the CEO from day one. All the experiences that I had in school, at big companies, at progressively smaller companies, and having the attitude of wanting to always learn, try anything, and take on any opportunity at the company so I could learn new things positioned me to be much more successful when I eventually went the real start-up route.

Learning how to pitch an idea and being an engaging presenter is so important in today's business world. How did you learn and refine this skill?

I think expertise and authenticity are what makes you a good public speaker. At my first job out of college, they brought in a public speaking expert to teach us, and he just made us get up and present, and then watch it on video. It was horrifying for all of us.

I remember this out-of-body experience when you're up in front of a room of people and your mind is a little blank, and you're just trying to remember the things you've memorized. Over the course of my career, that feeling just got less and less as I knew what I was talking about more. I got better at talking to people from the heart and from my experience instead of talking from my brain.

What advice would you give to people who find the idea of public speaking intimidating?

The most compelling speakers are people who speak from their heart and talk to you like a person. They're doing it because they're telling you about a company that they're passionate about and it comes from a mission that they are on personally, and you can feel it. It makes a complete difference. When you speak to somebody who is a passionate mission-driven founder versus a CEO who is a tactician and doesn't connect with the values of the company, it's night and day. Everybody in the room feels it when somebody is speaking from the heart.

What's one thing that you commonly notice small businesses can improve on?

If anything, I would say the thing that they get wrong is not using that network enough, not just grabbing people who are in the same situation that they're in and asking them questions and asking for help—because they will give it to you. I've seen some pretty amazing examples, even from people who are in the same kind of competitive category, helping each other out just because they really sympathized and wanted to share their resources and connections and feel the same entrepreneurial spirit. The people who learn how to tap into that have a huge advantage.

 ## Key Takeaways:

- → Tap into a network.
- → Ask for advice.
- → Be authentic.
- → Speak from your heart.
- → Learn constantly.

SEMHAR ARAIA (she/her)
CEO, Diaspora African Women's Network (DAWN)

#CreateTheSpaces

 On life: The world is yours.

 On business: It isn't the idea that makes you a successful entrepreneur, it is your ability to do any and all of the work required.

 On social: Everything in modération.

 On college: If you aspire to be in a highly competitive industry, degrees are still the benchmarks.

Eritrean American lawyer **Semhar Araia** says her life's work is helping marginalized and underrepresented groups create the spaces they need to be heard. She is the CEO of the Diaspora African Women's Network (DAWN), a global network supporting African diaspora professional women, and throughout her career she has advised more than one hundred African, Asian, European, and Arab diaspora communities, governments, and organizations. Her achievements caught the eye of Facebook (Meta), and executives asked her to institutionalize her impact there as head of diaspora policy for the Africa, Middle East, and Turkey public policy team. She has also worked in Congress and at nonprofits such as the United Nations International Children's Emergency Fund (UNICEF) and the Oxford Committee for Famine Relief (Oxfam), and Nelson Mandela's organization The Elders. President Barack Obama named her a White House Champion of Change, and she is profiled in the Smithsonian National Museum of African American History and Culture's *Next-Generation Voices* exhibit. Semhar shares with us her thoughts on social entrepreneurship, women's leadership, cultural competence, and the power of role modeling.

You are the CEO of the Diaspora African Women's Network. What problem are you trying to solve?

I started the Diaspora African Women's Network because, when I was working in Congress, I was responsible for issues related to

Africa and US foreign policy, and I found that there were very few women of color—in particular, Black women and women of African descent—working on Africa. I started to find many other women like myself who had similar portfolios. I realized that we needed a support system and that there were serious gaps to support women's leadership in the workplace. The organization was built to address that gap. It really helps create a space for networking, professional development, peer-to-peer learning, as well as learning about opportunities in different careers.

How would you explain the work you did at Facebook (Meta) to someone who isn't familiar with your field?

At Facebook (Meta), I worked on the public policy team for Africa, the Middle East, and Turkey. I was the head of diaspora policy, looking at the ways that communities and users rely on Facebook (Meta), Instagram, and social media to stay connected with family, relatives, and developments in their homelands.

What are the most important lessons you've learned at each job—from Congress to nonprofits like UNICEF and Oxfam to big corporations like Facebook (Meta)?

The most important lesson I've learned is to trust that you are skilled and the right fit for the job, and to be comfortable with asking for advice and learning. Sometimes you feel like you have to work your hardest, prove that you can solve a problem, and bring results all on your own. When in truth, so much of the work in almost every industry is collaborative. It's team-based, and it relies on constant learning and improvement.

How did being raised in an immigrant family give you a competitive advantage over your peers?

It helped me pick up nuance in context of what was being said. When you are the son or daughter of immigrants, you not only know the language of your parents' ancestral homeland, but you also know English. Your mind is working in two languages. Whenever a message is being sent, I'm always interpreting it. How will it be received by non-native English speakers? Conversely, how can I help non-native English speakers communicate their message in English? It gave me dexterity to read between the lines, emphasize nonverbal cues of communication, and understand that cultures have different types of communication. In some cultures, it's inappropriate to look someone directly in the eye. In other cultures, age is a determining factor in who leads meetings and conversations. Cultural competence has really been helpful.

When I travel or work abroad, I'm able to also connect with communities, whether they're African, Arab, or Asian. My family's immigrant background helps me bond and connect with them. I also have more patience for an outcome. One thing that leaders who come from immigrant backgrounds may struggle with is in the American pace of doing business. We move very fast. Time is of the essence because time is money. For people who have come from an immigrant background, time is so valued, you take your time, and it is incremental.

What does it take to be a successful entrepreneur?

It isn't the idea that makes you a successful entrepreneur, it is your ability to do any and all of the work required. An entrepreneur's first step is being willing to learn and learn how to do every aspect of a business. If you plan on creating a business that you want to grow and have employees, your best bet is to own the idea, but also learn how to build the idea, grow it, market it, communicate it, manage the finances, generate interest, and find the right people for your business. It means late hours; it means that your social life, your friends, and your relationships have to be reconsidered. At the same time, you need to be very prepared for failure and rejection.

Also, financial instability is not spoken about enough for people who don't come from generational wealth, or don't have the chance to obtain a major investment for their idea. You are putting a lot of your financial vulnerabilities on the line. That becomes a really personal journey, and finding ways to learn how to handle it, finding allies, supporters, financial advisers, and friends, is key because entrepreneurs, particularly from Black, brown, and immigrant communities, are increasingly challenged.

Is it harder for immigrants to become entrepreneurs?

I don't know that it's harder for immigrants. You can find loads of successful major companies and organizations founded by immigrants, so I think immigrants are even more equipped to start a business because of the agility and the ability to see what's missing.

What business advice would you give to young entrepreneurs?

Really focus on your plan and your **value proposition**. What do you think makes you unique, and is that already there in the market? That value prop argument is so important.

Value proposition: A value proposition identifies a niche and communicates the unique benefits of a product to a target audience.

Sometimes the value prop can be as simple as "It's just easier. It shaves off time from your day. It gives you back the time that you needed." But there are some powerful value props staring right at us. And sometimes entrepreneurs just don't grab them. They love their idea so much, but they're not able to turn the value prop. The other thing is to be ready to test, test, test, fail, fail, fail. Sometimes entrepreneurs are led to believe that it's super quick and super easy. You could do a business which is successful for a year, and then you might pivot and realize that this isn't actually the business model you want, and that's okay. Even in success, you have to keep testing and modifying. A good business leader isn't afraid to make changes.

You worked at the United States Agency for International Development (USAID), the US agency that helps with development around the world. How can you get Americans to care more about the rest of the world?

There are a lot of misperceptions about how much the United States does for the rest of the world, as if it's a charity, philanthropy, or donor relationship. When you ask an average American how much of the US budget goes to foreign aid, the average answer is 20 percent. In truth, it's 1 percent of the entire budget. And this 1 percent covers our dues to the United Nations. It covers the humanitarian assistance that is provided for emergencies. It covers global initiatives like girls' education, HIV/AIDS, and fighting climate change. It also supports countries rebuilding after a war. There's also human development and the peer-to-peer track of diplomacy and development, where you have cultural exchange programs and educational exchange programs that support diplomacy.

There are so many different programs that we're able to invest in with a fraction of what most people think.

How can those of us who already care get everyone else on board?

The thing that really influences people to think differently is watching people they know think differently. The power of role modeling is huge. That means showing a window to the world, a new way of thinking, or your daily life as global. Making that an opportunity for your friends, followers, or your broader networks to see it really does help change sentiment. There was a time where it used to be about celebrities and what famous people were saying, and people would follow them. That still works, but over time, it has really become about who you trust. You trust your friends, your family, people that you see at school, people you see at work. Getting to show why the rest of the world matters and being that lens is incredibly influential.

Do you think social media is a good thing or bad thing?

I ultimately believe social media can be a good thing. When you think of what the power of social media is globally, what kind of tool and access it's giving to people who hadn't otherwise been able to connect countries and regions where there is no electricity or no power grid, where they can't afford a telephone. Then they find a Wi-Fi signal in their village, and they can now make a call or video. If they've been lucky enough to go to school, they can do classes online. The power of social media on a global scale is truly incredible. I think it has more potential to do good. I think what we should be asking ourselves is how do we do things in moderation? As Americans, we're a very insatiable culture. Social media, I think, is another example of that.

What is one thing that exists today that you would never have imagined existed when you were a kid?

The country my family is from (Eritrea) wasn't independent when I was a kid. When I was born, the country was fighting for independence. It wasn't yet a country, and it took thirty years. By the time I was a teenager, it had just become independent. That's something we always wished for, and when it happened, we were thrilled. The other thing I couldn't have imagined is how you can send a text, WhatsApp chat, or video and just check in with someone halfway around the world in India, China, or Mexico. It has made my life richer.

What types of people do you like to be around and why?

I'm an extrovert, so I feed off people's energy. I like people who are optimistic, curious, authentic, and genuine. There are a lot of people in this world who seek to build a relationship for false motives. I really value mission-driven people, who feel that they have a calling or a purpose in life, and that they need to use their time for good.

What movie, literary or TV character are you most like?

There is a nineties sitcom called *Living Single.* It's got four African American women and two African American men. They all live in the same building and it's about their friendship. My favorite character is named

> "I am 100 percent certain the jobs you're going to be doing have not been created yet."

Maxine Shaw. She is an attorney. She is very outspoken. She is an extrovert. She also does too much. I love that character. Sometimes it scares me how much I'm like her. I don't know what character I would want to be like, because honestly, Black women represented on TV are kind of an anomaly. There's very limited representation. For me, so much of this is about my experience as a Black woman and as a daughter of African immigrants that sometimes I can love a character, but I may not feel that it speaks to me because it misses a core part of my identity.

What type of art form do you like the best and how does it influence your work?

I love music and singing. I go across genres. I love rhythm and blues, soul, classical, and New Age. My brain responds very positively to singing and to classical music. You can almost feel your neurons firing or relaxing because of the sound. That's always something I need.

 Key Takeaways:

➔ Be willing to do it all.
➔ Don't be afraid to make changes.
➔ Use your time for good.
➔ Model global understanding.
➔ Be collaborative.

CLAIRE CODER (she/her)

Founder and CEO (Chief Estrogen Officer),
Aunt Flow

#PersistencePays

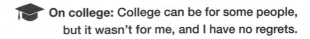 **On life:** If you believe in a mission that is critical and will change the world, you will make a difference.

On business: Focus on solving the problem and not just passing it along.

On social: I only like LinkedIn. LinkedIn is really powerful for expressing the brand, growing our user base, and building business relationships.

On college: College can be for some people, but it wasn't for me, and I have no regrets.

Claire Coder's success can be summed up in a word: persistence. It took eighty-six noes before she finally got the yes that would pave the way for her to start her company, Aunt Flow, a for-profit with a mission to end period poverty. Since launching in 2016, Aunt Flow has designed and installed smart tampon and pad dispensers in bathrooms for businesses like Apple, Google, and Netflix—as well as State Farm Stadium in Arizona, home to the 2023 Super Bowl. Claire was so passionate about starting Aunt Flow that she dropped out of college to chase her vision and become an entrepreneur, a career path she never imagined while growing up in Toledo, Ohio. Today, the twenty-six-year-old is not only leading her own company, but she's also unabashedly leading a movement to destigmatize period care and ensure that everyone who menstruates has access to quality products. Aunt Flow donates one tampon or pad for every ten sold, and distributes products to libraries, schools, and nonprofits across the country. Claire credits Gen Z with supercharging the menstrual movement and urges more students to help by writing emails to their school principals and legislators. Though still a young entrepreneur, Claire has plenty to share about what it takes to turn passion into business.

What is period poverty? And how did your passion to solve it lead you to start Aunt Flow?

Period poverty refers to the lack of access to period products. According to the State of the Period 2021 study, 23 percent of students in the United States struggled to afford period products, and according to their 2019 study, 84 percent of students have either missed class or know someone who has missed class because of lack of access to tampons and pads. Period products aren't covered by the Special Supplemental Nutrition Program for Women, Infants, and Children (WIC) or food stamps in most states, so that is a direct implication of not having access. That's what period poverty means and what it refers to—the lack of access to period products.

At Aunt Flow we're really trying to solve this issue through ensuring access to period products just like toilet paper. We created a tampon and pad dispensing system to ensure that period products can be offered for free in bathrooms across the United States, Canada, and the United Kingdom. We are a for-profit company, and our dispensers are designed with both the janitor as well as the end users in mind.

Is it more about affordability or just being able to find and have these products when you need them?

Affordability is obviously a concern, and that's why we stock middle schools, high schools, libraries, and nonprofit organizations across the country. But sometimes you get your period unexpectedly in public and you don't have access to the product that you need. Maybe you're using a menstrual cup or sustainable period underwear, but you're not wearing it that day and you just start your period. What we know about menstruation is that everything is an average. When we talk about a menstrual cycle, a standard average menstrual cycle is twenty-eight days, but that can really vary from twenty-five days to thirty-four days, which means that you can unexpectedly get your period in public, and that's why Aunt Flow exists—to make sure that no one ever has to worry about getting their period in public.

You have been extremely successful at fundraising for Aunt Flow. How do you effectively pitch to partners and investors, especially men who may not have considered the issue of period poverty?

I grew up in Toledo, Ohio, and entrepreneurship or venture capital were not career paths. They were definitely not in the dictionary that I was reading as a girl from Ohio. I eventually learned about venture capital and growing enterprises in 2018 when I went through a program called Techstars. That is when I first raised our seed round of financing. Back then, there really wasn't a market for **business-to-business (B2B)** period care. Remember, that was a moment where no states had passed legislation regarding access to period care or even access from a tax perspective, so I was really charged with convincing investors who don't menstruate that, one, there was a market for this, and two, that I was going to be successful in dominating the market for this. That was a pretty hard bar from a scrutiny perspective. Thankfully, I was able to convince a few folks early on that there was going to be a market for this, and today it's very clear that there is a market for B2B period care access. To date, Aunt Flow has raised $11 million from publicly traded companies like Jones Lang LaSalle, all the

> B2B: Business-to-business (B2B) describes a commercial transaction between companies selling or purchasing goods or services.

way to traditional venture capitalists like Harlem Capital and Precursor Ventures.

How did you come up with the prototypes and designs for your dispensers and other products?

It is constantly changing because we really want to make sure that we're improving our products every single day. From a dispenser and product perspective, I wanted to make sure that our period products were sustainable for your body and for the environment. That's why all of Aunt Flow products are made with organic cotton. In addition, they're designed with integrity to support and ensure that our world is going to be around for generations to come. That's how we designed our period care products. From a dispenser perspective, I spent a lot of time in the bathrooms following around janitors, understanding their workflow, because our janitors are responsible for restocking those dispensers.

How have your passions for social issues, such as the environmental concerns that you mentioned, underpinned Aunt Flow's core beliefs of giving back to the community and using those sustainable 100 percent cotton products?

I personally care about tons of things. As a company, it's our mission to ensure that we can make the world better for people with periods. That's a pretty lofty goal in itself. We focus our efforts on doing just that. What that looks like day-to-day is that for every ten period products we sell, we donate one to a menstruator in need. From an environmental perspective, at the end of the day, it's corporations that can really save the world. That's why business owners, especially Generation Z business owners, have to take it into their own hands and improve packaging in every single way. That's why we incorporate that into our business.

What would you say are some of those ways that our generation can get involved in the menstrual movement at our own schools and workplaces?

The menstrual movement changes by students. In fact, most of the programming that we have at schools today is because a student said, "It is important to me that period products are offered in the bathroom." Not in the nurse's office, because you go to the nurse when you're sick; you don't go to the nurse when you're having a natural bodily function. We have resources on our website for students who want to get involved. They can start by sending an email or talking to their principal and asking to implement Aunt Flow at their school. A step further is to write to legislators to pass legislation in your state requiring schools to offer free period products. Every state that has passed legislation has had some form of support from students. Those are two ways that we've already seen such phenomenal change in the menstrual movement based on students and Gen Z.

You're very vocal about using "period," "tampons," "pads," and similar words openly rather than dancing around them. What is your best advice for talking about difficult topics?

We know that language matters. Aunt Flow was the first company to eliminate the words "feminine hygiene" from all our packaging, referring to the products as period products or menstrual products instead. We did that because "feminine hygiene" is not a clear term. What is

feminine hygiene? It literally could be deodorant; it could be a boob cleaner—it could be anything. It's so unclear. By describing the product as it actually is, a period product, that also reduces the taboo nature of the topic.

When I founded Aunt Flow in 2016, it was very clear that people are so concerned to talk about periods, which is a natural bodily function. Everyone knows somebody who menstruates. So the way that I approached the topic was adding humor. I found that when you add humor to really challenging conversations, it lessens that burden of trying to have a formal conversation when you're squirming inside. First, I add a layer of humor, and then I add the layer of facts—it's a fact that 86 percent of women have started their period in public without a tampon or pad—and then I go for the sale. That's how we really have changed the conversation around access to period care.

You've worked with a lot of big companies, including Apple, Google, and Netflix, as well as universities like Princeton. How did you land some of these partnerships?

We are so lucky to support more than five hundred companies, ranging from NFL stadiums to schools, to Fortune 500 and 100 companies. Each of them chose Aunt Flow as their provider for period products in all of their bathrooms because of our mission, because of our brand, because of our inclusivity, and because of our commitment to the environment. It's not just another SKU that they purchase. They're really buying into the menstrual movement.

You've written that "no" is not the end of the conversation, but the beginning. What do you mean by that?

I have gotten so many noes. I had to have eighty-six conversations with different venture capitalists to raise our first $1.5 million. It took eighty-six people saying no before I finally got my yes. I think that that is so important when we consider how companies become successful. It's really perseverance and persistence. Persistently showing up and persevering when so many folks are saying "No, that's not a market" or "No, you'll never be successful."

Do you ever regret dropping out of college to focus on Aunt Flow?

College was not for me, and it's not for everyone, but it is for some people. For me, I knew that I wanted to build my company, and I knew that I learned best from trial and error. The universities back in 2016 really didn't offer that. There weren't necessarily entrepreneurial programs like there are today. I think it's important to remember that holistically, college can be for some people, but it wasn't for me, and I have no regrets in the decision that I made. That said, I am going back to college, to Columbia University, for some finance management and training. But once again, not a traditional degree as we've known it.

What skills do you think are most important for business?

Perseverance and persistence are critical to any successful business. The other thing that is really important is to focus on solving the problem and not passing it along. School today teaches us to just get something done, but not always to solve the real problem or complete the entire project. When I was in school, I was so good at getting the thing done and turning in the assignment and then moving along to something else. But in business, as the CEO, finishing an assignment does not suffice. You have to get the whole project done, and you have to see it to completion. I think that is a fundamental change that we would have to see in school for us to be able to build the next generation of entrepreneurial CEOs.

What kind of people do you tend to surround yourself with?

I love surrounding myself with people that force me to level up, challenge me, inspire me. I don't like hanging around with people who just want to hang around with me because I have a company. And I don't like hanging around people who sugarcoat things because I do really want to improve, and I know that the only way for me to do that is by having a circle of friends who will challenge me to be better.

What is one piece of customer feedback that you found surprising or useful?

At Aunt Flow, we know that the only way to make real change is to include everyone in the conversation. We call our guys that support menstrual equity our Flow Bros. The piece of feedback that was really surprising to me came from one of our men who support Aunt Flow. He said, "Claire, for the first time I felt empowered at my organization to stand up for a woman's issue." Often, men feel nervous about getting involved or unclear about how to get involved. They don't want to say the wrong thing and then have women come after them. So the piece of feedback that was really powerful to me was that we've designed a movement that includes everybody in the conversation because we know we need everyone to make real change. That's inspired us to continue to include Flow Bros and uplift messages of all genders.

 ## Key Takeaways:

- ➔ Develop perseverance and persistence.
- ➔ Understand the people using and working with your products.
- ➔ Include everyone in the conversation.
- ➔ Surround yourself with people who challenge you.
- ➔ Take action.

LOU LAURIA (he/him)
Chief of Sport and Competition, Special Olympics

#Happened

On life: If people only have one singular perspective, it can be hard to see around it. There's a ton of value in being that person to see other perspectives.

On business: Empower people to do what they do best and remove obstacles as a leader.

On social: It has accelerated divisiveness and the spread of misinformation that has ruined people's lives and destroyed organizations.

On college: One of the most valuable things for me was meeting people from diverse backgrounds. College was as much for my social development as it was academic.

Growing up in the Bronx, New York, **Lou Lauria** loved to organize neighborhood baseball and football games. He uses those same skills today as chief of sport and competition at the Special Olympics, overseeing programs in two hundred countries. Having celebrated their fifty-second year in 2020, the Special Olympics has led the way to inclusive sports events revolving around opportunities for athletes with intellectual disabilities of all levels of sport ability. Lou shares with us his stories of working in disability and his experience at previous organizations such as the International Olympic Committee and International Paralympic Committee. We talk about the many lessons he believes sport can bring to the business world.

What has working in disability sport taught you?

I have worked directly in or alongside disability sport my entire career, and if you believe in sport, then sport is sport, and athletes are athletes. The transformative power of sport has the potential to work across all sport and this includes disability sport.

How could that transformative power be applied to business and leadership?

Sport has broken barriers for as long as it has been around, and for business and leaders, I think the lesson is that talent exists everywhere, and access has historically been the challenge. I think as the world embraces learning differences and neurodiversity, you're seeing people value people who think differently. Your generation is going to be more accepting of people learning in different ways. You have to look no further than Silicon

> *"I tend to see the good in people. I tend to give people the benefit of the doubt. I'm an optimist by nature. Maybe that's what has drawn me to disability sport."*

Valley to see people who are looking at things in a different way. In businesses, I think this is becoming something that people are seeking out.

What revelations have you had about human nature through your experiences in sport and leadership?

The ability to travel around the world has exposed me to a lot of experiences. I think people are generally good and resilient. People can set aside differences and enjoy sport. It's a cross-cultural common language. When I travel to a country, I read up on their football league or Olympic sport; then when we are at dinner, I ask people which team they support or about an upcoming Olympic Games. I let people talk and they want to talk about sports. If you show interest and listen, there's a lot you can learn.

Mentality is a key part of sport and is the core of a competitive spirit. What does this mean to you and the athletes you work with?

It's all about your personal best. The competition is just an evaluation of your training, in reality. If you put the work in, you will see the results as it relates to achieving your best. This is true in sports, school, workplace, and family. This is the lesson

> *"Enjoy what you do, put the time in, and keep a balance in your life."*

that sport can teach us and the impact it can have on an athlete. When people think of Special Olympics athletes, they perhaps think of a lower-ability-level athlete, but it is our job to prepare the athletes and build a stage for them to deliver their personal best, whether they are a lower-ability athlete playing bocce or a higher-ability athlete in a triathlon. I think of a story about a Motor Activity Training Program (MATP) athlete, which is for athletes that have high support needs. There was an athlete who was trying to put a ring on top of a traffic cone. It took him eighteen minutes to complete the task. People were in tears; they were standing on their feet cheering and were inspired. That athlete was operating at the best of his ability, and he achieved something that was every bit as important and worth celebrating as a triathlete crossing the finish line. In sport you learn leadership, you learn how to work with other people, and you learn a lot about yourself. I would love to see the focus drift toward sport for the good that sport can provide, like leadership, self-confidence, self-esteem, and independence, rather than talking about people's contracts, sponsorships, or brand.

Many businesses are trying to better incorporate diversity, equity, and inclusion into their core values. This is something the Special Olympics has long understood. What can the Special Olympics as an organization teach other companies?

We have a sport model called Unified Sports, which was started decades ago in Connecticut. It is athletes with intellectual disabilities being on teams with athletes (partners) without intellectual disabilities. It is a model where people can build relationships through sport. We're doing a lot of great work in schools around this. We've got a Unified Champion Schools program that's very big in the United States and growing internationally. A lot of our corporate partners are looking for inclusive workplaces. We're working with companies where we provide expertise, connect athletes that could be employees, and then set up an environment where people can succeed. Kerry is a dairy company in Ireland, a family-owned farm that grew into a big global brand. They were introduced to our movement and met our athletes and rethought how they worked. They have since employed many people with intellectual disabilities, and it's been great for their whole organization.

What makes you an effective leader?

They call it emotional intelligence this decade; I'm not sure what they will call it in the next decade, but I have always been good with people and relationships. I can connect with people and am pretty well-rounded. At this point in my career, the professional development of people on our team is one of my favorite things about my role. Empower people to do what they do best and remove obstacles as a leader. You have to love leading and can develop skills around that love.

Is social media good, bad, or both?

It has accelerated divisiveness and the spread of misinformation that has real consequences and has ruined people's lives and destroyed organizations. It also glorifies the individual, and we are raising a generation that grew up on selfies and being told how great they are. While different from traditional media, the end game is the same, and that is to drive revenue.

What was your biggest challenge in school and your greatest challenge today?

My biggest challenge in school was more social than academic. My high school was the first time that I had any interaction with some people from another socioeconomic demographic. This was even more pronounced in moving from high school to college and was challenging to deal with back then. This challenge has likely contributed to one of my challenges today, which is my lack of formality and perhaps a bit of a chip on my shoulder. I have never been a person who is formal or enjoys protocol, and at times the small talk that accompanies it. I think it comes down to believing that no one is fundamentally better or more valuable than anyone else.

Did you think you'd have this occupation when you were our age?

I knew that I love sports. I thought I would be a broadcaster. When I went to school, I found that it was not a fit for me, nor was I really interested in what those roles entailed day-to-day. Also, sport industry was tiny compared to where it is today, so there were limited roles and broadcast was the largest sector.

What hashtag best describes your career?

#Happened. I was the first person in my family to graduate high school. There was no playbook for once I graduated high school or college and no role model to follow or seek advice from. Honestly, looking back, this took a lot of pressure off and allowed me to grow up and mature at my own pace and pursue my passion.

 Key Takeaways:

- ➔ Be your personal best.
- ➔ Be confident.
- ➔ Lead by example.
- ➔ Listen to others' stories.
- ➔ Look for diverse perspectives.

EMMA BUTLER (she/her)
Founder and CEO, Liberare

#InclusionRevolution

 On business: Be fearless in your pursuit of fundraising and introduce yourself to everybody you can.

 On social: Social media does a lot of good in connecting people, especially those in the vulnerable populations.

 On college: It allows you to exercise your critical thinking muscle.

Emma Butler envisions a world where beautiful clothing is easy, functional, and made for everyone. She is the twenty-four-year-old founder and CEO of Liberare, an adaptive clothing line specializing in undergarments for women. After witnessing her chronically ill mother struggle to put on clothes and find limited choices in the market, Emma decided to fix the problem herself, making it her mission to empower women with adaptive apparel that would look and feel beautiful. She launched her company in her dorm room at Brown University and networked with everyone she could find, ultimately landing in the fashion capital of the world with a million-dollar investment and partnerships with some of the biggest names in the intimates industry. She talks to us about breaking down ableist barriers, building an inclusive workforce, working fourteen-hour days, and leaning on people who care about you.

What is your founder's story?

My founder's story started when I was about ten, and my mom was diagnosed with a few different chronic illnesses, which left her with limited head dexterity. It was very hard for her to put things on over her head and clasp things. Watching her get dressed was really hard. When we looked for new clothing that met her new functionality, the only things we could find were ugly and medical. I watched my mom's confidence plummet, and I thought, "Nobody should have to get dressed like that." Everybody should be able to have beautiful clothing that's empowering and easy to get on. By the time I got to college at Brown University, nobody had done anything specifically in bras and underwear, which can be really difficult to put on, especially the hook on the back of a bra.

I didn't know the first thing about starting a business—I was an art and French student—but I just began interviewing people. I started my company from my dorm room and read a lot of books. I had an idea about the vision of the future where everybody felt included in the fashion industry, and everybody could find clothing that was easy to get on, including disabled people. I started this idea in 2018, incorporated in 2019 while still in college, and in 2022 we launched and raised a million dollars.

You're based in Paris, the fashion capital of the world. How has the fashion industry embraced you—or not?

I originally went to Silicon Valley for a tech job, and I floated the idea about disability fashion, and it wasn't as well received. I had studied abroad in Europe, and I knew that there was a lot of money around fashion in Europe. I also wanted to make sure that our products were the most beautiful and close to our supply chain and manufacturers, so I decided to move to Paris. There are pros and cons to both markets. All our partnerships with companies, influencers, and press are in the United States. We're doing a launch with Aerie, which is a billion-dollar corporation for intimates in the United States. I see a lot more disability inclusion in the US market, but ultimately, I raised the majority of my money from French and UK investors.

How did you fundraise effectively for your company?

There are so many other businesses that don't have or don't need VC money to be profitable and become giant corporations. There need to be more resources for female founders, underrepresented founders, and disabled founders. My advice to people that are about to fundraise is to read absolutely everything you can. Ask as many questions as you can. Make sure that you understand everything from pre-seed to seed funding rounds to convertible notes to priced equity rounds. Ask questions before you start fundraising, and then start building your network. You need to build your network years in advance before you really start fundraising. Ultimately, **warm intros** are the most important thing in fundraising. Even if investors claim that they don't need a warm

> Warm intro: This is a referral from a mutual connection to establish a personal connection to a client.

intro, they really do. Make sure that you use your connections. Be fearless in your pursuit of fundraising and introduce yourself to everybody you can.

The employees at Liberare are also the clients you want to sell to. Why was that business model important to you?

It was really important for me to hire a disabled team because we create adaptive products. It's important to have customer-focused design and disabled people who are experts in their disability experience. But disabled people are also experts in things beyond disability. My team is not only amazing in informing on the products and content to reach our target audience, but separate from that, they're brilliant, talented strategists, creatives, and everything else.

I believe that to truly have an inclusion revolution and be a forward nation, we need to have people with disabilities in every level of every single company, not

> C-suite: The C-suite encompasses the top executives in a company, typically denoted by job titles beginning with the letter C, for "chief."

just companies like mine that create products for folks with disabilities. Every corporation all over the world should have disabled people, from their board members to their **C-suite** to their employees and interns.

Are there other brands that are doing well in adaptive clothing?

There are a few other players, but our products are far superior to any other adaptive products on the market. I don't think that it's enough to slap Velcro on a few things; you really need to be intuitive about your design. I also don't think any of them employ disabled people the way that we do or have the community that we're building; no other brand has this type of community of thousands of disabled people who inform us on products, but also come together to talk about topics like sex, beauty, dating, and other things in relation to disability.

What is one piece of customer feedback that you've found surprising?

Our community is always telling us about more ways to continue to be accessible, and whether it's through our font choices, or colors, or different product ideas. We're always implementing those and always listening to our community. I think that our community has always had the same needs, but we're just willing to be open and listen and update products and create new products with all their feedback.

Where do you plan on going next?

I always hear the word "niche" referring to folks with disabilities, but the global adaptive apparel market—meaning clothing for folks with disabilities—is projected to be worth $400 billion by 2026. That's larger than the teen market. And people with disabilities have over $500 trillion in disposable income and buying and spending power, so it's not really a niche market. Also, the products that we design are for everybody. They are perfect for disabled people, but I still have to fiddle with my bra and hook it in the front. We still get dressed like it's 1906. This is a way of dressing for the future. Ultimately, the market is everybody. It's just getting dressed easier. We do want to expand out of intimates into regular clothing, focusing on women with disabilities, because we believe it's a strong community, but I can definitely see men's clothing in our future one day.

How do people react when you say that you're a CEO at your age?

I feel like every founder has impostor syndrome, especially at a young age, and I definitely do. However, it's a strength because my goal is to take down an ableist fashion industry that's been operating this way for as long as the fashion industry has operated, especially within the last hundred years. Never ever have they included disabled people the way that we have. I think that the naivete it takes to think that we can tear down an ableist structural system is needed, and that only comes with my young age and ambition, and the fresh eyes to think about new ways to do it. I have not had twenty years in the fashion industry knowing exactly how it works, so I'm willing to challenge all the status quo about how things work and how things need to be done. That's how I see it. I think that other people are learning to take us seriously. Maybe not when I started, when we didn't have capital or real products. I was just a girl and an idea in a dorm room. But now I think people are taking me seriously and taking our company seriously because we've shown the world what we're worth.

While entrepreneurship seems glamorous, it is hard work. How have you fared in this regard, and do you recommend the field for others, despite the difficulty?

I work fourteen-hour days most days. You're not working a nine-to-five. It's your heart and your soul. You sacrifice a lot of your relationships and friendships because your business is a marriage. It's not for everybody, especially with start-ups. There's a lot of privilege that comes with being able to go without health care or a reliable source of income. If you have a problem that you want to solve and a good solution, and you're one of those people who is like me, who can't live another day seeing it unsolved, then absolutely it's worth it. It's going to be a long haul. It's going to be an emotional journey. As a solo founder, I was in this alone. I have a wonderful team, but for many years it was just me. If this is your battle, it's gonna be the battle of a lifetime, but to me, it's worth it.

Learning how to effectively pitch an idea is critical for an entrepreneur. How did you learn and refine that skill, and what advice would you give to people who are terrified of public speaking?

I was never a good public speaker. I have an identical twin sister who is a really good public speaker. She has won awards for poetry recitation on a national level, but I was always in the back seats. I was nervous. I fiddled with my hands a lot. I took one class at Brown University with Professor Barbara Tannenbaum that changed my life and allowed me to speak more eloquently and get rid of a lot of "likes" and "ums." The best advice I can give is that it takes a lot of practice. I remember the first time I pitched in front of people was at the summer program at Brown, and I couldn't put my thoughts together and I was so embarrassed afterward. I took my sneakers out that night and I walked around the track probably a hundred times and just recited the same pitch. It was just a five-minute pitch, and I recited it a million times. The next week they asked me to pitch again, and I did it wonderfully, and people were shocked. Practice really does make perfect. Practice in front of your friends. Practice for anybody. For people like me who are painfully shy, a coach is a good idea.

How did you balance starting a business with getting an education?

The best thing you can do is go to a liberal arts college and learn to think. In high school there's a lot of busy work, but when you go to a liberal arts college, you read and think critically and exercise that muscle. That is a really strong piece of what's needed to create a business. You might not learn things like accounting at a liberal arts college, which would also be beneficial, but you can learn that on your own. The most important piece about college is critical thinking.

I know that college is not an option for a lot of people, and if you can't afford college, or you don't want to go into student debt, and you'd rather start your business, I think that's a wonderful thing. You still need to find a way to learn how to think critically, whether that is through talking to people much more advanced in their life journeys and asking them to mentor you—and not just some, like, random Instagram mentor but someone credible in their thinking process—or reading all types of books. Whether it's related to business or Tolstoy or something else, you need to learn how to think critically.

What skills do you think will prove most critical for current and future entrepreneurs?

One of the most important things that you can do is focus on relationships in your life. There's gonna be a lot of hard times. It's going to be a lot of grit and hard work. Sometimes you just want to get off work on Fridays at a reasonable hour, and go out with your friends, but you're stuck at your computer trying to fix something, and then you work Saturdays and Sundays, and you haven't taken a break. It's that grit and work ethic that you need to keep going and get it done. If you don't have good relationships around you, whether it's with your team, friends, family, or a mentor, it's gonna fall through the cracks, because you need that emotional support. It's amazing to work with a company and solve a problem, but from an emotional-health standpoint, you need to be with people who you love and care about. Focus on those strong ties and those connections, because you'll need them.

As we enter the workforce, this generation has been redesigning jobs in the office. What do we bring to the table that you think everyone should adopt?

In my section of Gen Z, which is very liberal, open-minded thinkers, there's no tolerance for sexual harassment, no tolerance for discrimination, no tolerance for inaccessibility. I think that all generations need to keep that in mind. For example, the #MeToo movement came from the generation above us speaking out. I think that Gen Z is even more vocal, and I think that we need to continue being vocal and changing workplace standards. We're not snowflakes asking for special accessibility accommodations. We truly have a new standard that is the best standard.

What final lessons from your experiences as a young female founder do you want to pass on?

If you are a female founder, people will underestimate you. There is limited access to capital, especially for underrepresented founders. You need to keep in mind all of these barriers and know that we need to work harder to get it than the other folks, and it's not fair, but I hope that

"If this is your battle, it's gonna be the battle of a lifetime."

Gen Z can change that landscape. We've got a big world and a lot of problems, and we've got to solve them.

 Key Takeaways:

- Learn to think critically.
- Network.
- Challenge the status quo.
- Read everything.
- Don't let anyone underestimate you.

MARK HANIS (he/him)

Cofounder, Inclusive America, United to End Genocide, Progressive Shopper

#Inclusion

On business: Be strategic to get the change you want to see.

On social: We need to figure out how to make sure social media is a tool for positive, constructive change and not negative, destructive change.

On college: A college degree is really important for your life, career, and health. If you are able to go to college, you should do it, hands down. But colleges need to provide better value for that amount of money to get a degree.

Mark Hanis is a serial social entrepreneur dedicated to making change in the world—even though he knows he's playing a long game, and a very difficult one at that. He grew up in Quito, Ecuador, in a small Jewish community, the grandson of four Holocaust survivors. This background set the stage for him to become a champion for social change and to never stand by in the face of injustice. He has fought for causes such as anti-genocide, organ donation, asylum access, and representative government, and he worked as a White House fellow and national security affairs special adviser for South America, Africa, and human rights. His newest venture is the nonprofit Inclusive America, which works to increase diversity, equity, and inclusion within the government by holding officials accountable in their hiring practices. He encourages young people to agitate for change with the causes they care about, starting now. He shares with us his remarkable experiences in helping to make a difference.

How did your background spark your passion for change?

I am the grandson of four Holocaust survivors. My mom was born and raised in Scotland. My dad was born and raised in Ecuador. They met in the United States and decided to start a family and raise us in Ecuador, so both the cultural and the religious side were very much intertwined on being a global citizen and being an upstander for social change.

How has meeting people from different backgrounds who have also faced oppression and inequality driven you to want to make an impact?

There was a genocide in Darfur that was declared when I was a senior in college, and that was the first time in the twenty-first century that a crisis was given that label. One of my classmates was from Rwanda and her family were victims of the Rwandan genocide, and combined with my background as a grandson of Holocaust survivors, when we were confronted with the first genocide of the twenty-first century, it didn't feel like a huge leap to say, "What are we going to do about it? How are we going to take action?"

What have been the most defining moments of your work around the world that have made you a successful force of change?

Social change is hard. I wouldn't say that I have been overwhelmingly successful. We saw some milestones in response to the genocide in Darfur. Unlike in Rwanda, where most of the world did nothing, or in some cases withdrew some of the humanitarian aid or the peacekeepers to protect people, on Darfur we did do more. We were able to see more peacekeepers and more humanitarian aid, but the genocide is not over. There are still people who are being targeted for who they are. In the other areas that I have worked on, like organ donation, there are still people who are dying as they wait to get a kidney, liver, or other organs. I'm trying to move the ball forward. On most social justice issues, if anything is really easy, most people would have done it already.

Every effort I've done has been a team effort. Some of it has also been luck. When we got involved in Darfur, we had famous people like George Clooney and Angelina Jolie, and journalists like Nick Kristof, who were already passionate about this issue. When we started organizing, it was helpful to have people willing to write about it in publications like the *New York Times* or have celebrities tweet on social media. Some of it has been timing. When I was a senior in college, Facebook (Meta) came out. We had one thousand student chapters working on Darfur, and there was no way we would have been able to reach that many people were it not for Facebook (Meta).

You have talked about the three Ps: protection, political will, and permanency. How do those strategic focus areas relate to your own core values and why are they important for making change?

Sometimes we need to change the way we look at the problem to help us address it. Instead of treating genocide as a natural disaster and throwing humanitarian aid at it, treating it like a protection problem might allow us to get better at addressing it if we can't solve it outright. Political will and permanence are two values I feel passionate about on any problem that I'm working on. When young people think about how to solve a problem, they often think of a nonprofit or a business solution. They don't think of politics because they can't play an active role, or because governments have been so dysfunctional. It makes sense that they want to give up on the government being part of the solution. I think that's a disservice. When they look at the ways we can solve problems, politics and government need to be part of that. Permanence depends on the social issues that you're working on. A vaccine for COVID-19 can solve it like we did with polio or smallpox. In cases like hunger

"On most social justice issues, if anything is really easy, most people would have done it already."

or climate change, I don't know if there's a permanent solution. Putting solar panels on your roof is not the only solution to solving climate change. We need to reduce carbon, single use plastics, and other things. You need to think about where and how to have a permanent solution depending on the problem that you're trying to solve.

Another one of your start-ups, Progressive Shopper, helps consumers identify whether companies like Lego, Charlotte Russe, Hershey, Sephora, and many others are donating to Democratic or Republican causes. Why was this nonprofit needed?

I started Progressive Shopper to help make conscious consumption more user friendly. We have over twenty thousand users and hope that when we have between five hundred thousand and one million, it will be a large enough group of users that companies will change and improve their behavior on one or more topics or issues.

Has your mindset or perspective on any of the issues you are fighting for changed over time?

I'm still very passionate about politics and governments playing a role in any social issue I have taken on. I've become a little bit more strategic about the message, the messenger, and the timing of the message. There's a playbook for how you get change. I've become more strategic and thoughtful about how to achieve the change that I want to see. Yelling at the president to do something, like in police reform, is helpful, but if you want to get a bill passed, you need to target your senators and your House member first so that they can introduce the bill and get it passed, and then yell at the president to sign that bill. It's how you put it in which order that matters more and more.

How does technology help?

Technology is unbelievably helpful to accelerate the change we want to see. At the same time, no matter how many smartphones, computers, drones, or other technology solutions, most social injustices are human. They are either caused by humans, like genocide, or they require humans to change their behavior, like climate change. Having more smartphones is not going to solve the problem if people keep driving their cars, which is an old technology, or getting on planes, a little older technology, if we don't figure out how to change human behavior. I don't think technology by itself is going to help that, but I think technology can persuade, engage, and target in a much, much more powerful way than ever before.

What Instagram filter would you use to spread your message and motivate the people around you?

My worry is a lot of young people are taught that, to do change, you have to have a lot of money or power, and I don't think that's true. You don't need to become LeBron James, a president, a famous CEO, or a philanthropist like Bill Gates. Whatever filter would motivate people to say "You don't have to wait," that's the filter I want.

Who was your biggest mentor, and what did they teach you?

My grandmother has encouraged me to aspire to do the social change I want to see, but she's also very pragmatic. When I told her that we'd been able to engage young people around the country on anti-genocide work, to pressure their parents, their pastors, rabbis, and Congress members to do things, she said, "Yes, but what did it do for the people in Darfur?" Sometimes we get distracted with how many Instagram or TikTok followers we have. We look at those metrics and feedback loops, which is important because more people are paying attention, but it doesn't always lead to reform. I've loved that my grandmother applauds me but forces me to think whether it is actually delivering results to the people who need it. And if the answer is no, then who cares?

 Key Takeaways:

- ➔ Be an upstander for social change.
- ➔ You don't have to be famous to start making a difference.
- ➔ Surround yourself with people with different perspectives.
- ➔ Ask yourself what action you can take to make change.
- ➔ Be a global citizen.

The Innovator

WONYA LUCAS (she/her)
President and CEO, Hallmark Media

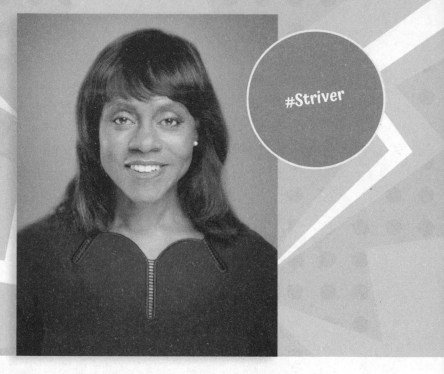

#Striver

On business: You get buy-in by inviting leaders to sit in on focus groups, hear consumer insights, and build a vision together, understanding who we are and who we can be.

On social: It's a good thing. It is a way to interact with our fan base and get their feedback.

On college: I use what I learned in marketing, finance, and engineering in grad school and undergrad every day.

Wonya Lucas is using her background as an engineer and a marketer to innovate at Hallmark Channel, part of the century-old Hallmark company that—like their cards—is a beloved brand with a vocal fan base. Founded in 1910 by teenage entrepreneur J. C. Hall, Hallmark's portfolio of businesses includes Hallmark Cards, Gold Crown stores, Hallmark Media, and Crayola. Wonya was hired at Hallmark not only for her skills but for her reputation as being kind and graceful even in the face of adversity—lessons she learned from her famous uncle, baseball legend Hank Aaron. Wonya has worked for NPR, Turner Broadcasting System, and Discovery Communications, and talks to us about the biggest opportunities in the media industry, and competing with companies like Netflix, Apple TV+, and the Disney Channel.

The Hallmark brand has been adapting for over a century. Beyond cards and movies, what do you plan to offer in the future to maintain momentum and growth?

The Hallmark brand is a storytelling brand. It started as postcards, then moved to the greeting cards we know today, then Crown Media. We're known primarily for movies, but we also have series on our air. Moving forward, you'll see us broaden and evolve our brand in the movie space, and we'll lean a lot more into series, not only for our linear networks—Hallmark Channel, Hallmark Movies & Mysteries, and Hallmark Drama—but also our direct-to-consumer subscription streaming service, Hallmark Movies

Now. Netflix and Apple+ services are driven by series, and we plan to increase our focus on serial storytelling.

What are you doing to change who and what we see on TV?

We just launched Mahogany—a content initiative based on the Hallmark Card line—which offers storytelling by, for, and about African American women. Mahogany cards have been around for over thirty-five years, and they are a beloved brand for the target audience. African American women, a demographic we haven't attracted, watch more television than any other demographic, so we saw an incredible opportunity to marry the strength of a brand like Mahogany with Hallmark Media to create movies, series, and podcasts. We're looking at other Hallmark intellectual property, too. There are so many powerful brands under the Hallmark umbrella, including Crayola and Vida, a Hispanic-targeted brand, and we are exploring which ones make sense to bring alive as storytelling and programming vehicles.

How do you bring people along with your vision?

My perspective and the way I approach every single brand that I work on, whether I'm leading it as a CEO or working as a marketer, is that I start with the consumers first. I started my career at Clorox and Coca-Cola, as a brand manager at both. We did a quantitative psychographic segmentation study; we did a lot of qualitative research, we identified our current audience, but also identified opportunity audiences. The bottom line is you create a vision that is consumer focused, that's data driven. Through focus groups, you get the emotional side of things, which helps you understand what elements are core to that brand and the business that you must maintain, but also what is missing, and how to expand the brand. By inviting leaders to sit in on focus groups, hear consumer insights, and build a vision together about understanding who we are and who we can be—that's how you get people to buy into it.

Since you became CEO of Hallmark Media, you have focused on diversity, equity, and inclusion (DEI). How have you changed the company to better reflect these values, and what more do you plan to do?

I joined Hallmark Media in 2020, in the year of the summer of social justice. The world was different than it was in any of my other jobs. People were attuned to what was happening to people of color. The Hallmark brand is a big tent brand, and by that, I mean it's for everybody. Whether it's Latinos, African Americans, the LGBTQ+ community, or different religions or faiths—there are cards for everyone. The grandson of the founder used this term—and I think about it every day—our cards have to be: "universally specific." When you walk into a card store, you have to see a card that is perfect for that person you're getting it for. But a whole lot of people have to feel that way, so it's specific to you, but it's universal. In the midst of the environment I just mentioned, Hallmark Media was not as diverse as we could have been, and we have an opportunity, because of our brand and the very wide brand aperture, to invite more people into the tent, to have stories that show that there are commonalities between people regardless of race, gender, or age. We can create content that's universally specific, where people can see common themes that relate to anyone, but it's specific enough to an audience that you can say, "They see me."

Do you have any examples of how you are doing that?

I love the movie *Christmas in My Heart*. It has a biracial daughter. She has a white father, and her African American mother had passed away. She has an African American grandmother and the love interest for the father is a biracial woman. That story has got a whole lot of diversity! There was one very brief conversation about the daughter's hair, and the grandmother came in to do the daughter's hair. If you're African American, hair is a big deal because it's not always easy to do. That's what everybody talked about on social media. It just lit up. That's a conversation happening in Black households every day. Every parent has to do a daughter's hair, but if you're an African American person, that brief dialogue said, "You see me." To me, that is what real DEI is. It is universally specific. It is talking to a group of people—a wide swath of people—who can see commonalities and shared values. We are a brand about kindness and caring, and that is a shared value across any demographic or socioeconomic status. That is why I love this brand.

How did your educational environment affect your development as a leader?

I am an industrial systems engineer. I went to Georgia Tech. I studied engineering, then I got my MBA at Wharton in finance and marketing. I am left and right brain. I went to a high school for performing arts. I have my engineer's pad of paper that I use every day. I am a process engineer at heart. I'm hyper-focused on how we get things done and making sure that we do it in a transparent way so that we can bring people along. My

> "It took me a year and a half and thirty-seven first interviews—not including the second ones—to cut my salary in half and get a job in this business. I'm a striver. I took a chance on myself."

training as an engineer taught me discipline and process. It taught me how to turn my natural curiosity into action. The creative side of me taught me how to work with creatives. They're very different from the engineers. I understand how to relate to creatives and how to draw out creativity in non-creatives. I believe that creativity happens everywhere, and I engage people in the process.

You have written that your famous uncle, Hank Aaron, helped guide your career. How so?

In some expected and in some unexpected ways. My father was also in baseball. He worked for the Braves. We were at every game. I was lucky enough to be with my cousins. They lived around the corner, and I could walk to their house. I watched my uncle chase his dream of breaking Babe Ruth's record in the South. I read the hate mail. I saw the police cars show up in front of his home. I was young, and I was fearful. Baseball was his job. What I learned from him about what was going on in his life was the importance of focus, the importance of knowing who you are, and the importance of overcoming obstacles with dignity and grace. I've had some bad things happen in places I've worked—everybody does—and when I face obstacles, I think about that. I think about how he taught me to always do the right thing, and to be kind to people no matter what. I work in a highly competitive space, and at times, people are unkind. I never go there. I walk in grace and kindness. Our brand is about kindness, which is one of the reasons I'm the CEO. They were looking for a brand builder who was kind, and people brought up my name. I learned from him to really keep your eye on the ball, focus, work with dignity, and that quiet will to win. He was fiercely competitive. Pete Rose was another big player back in the day, and he was visibly competitive. My uncle was very quietly competitive. I am incredibly competitive, but my spirit and the way that I operate is much more measured, and filled with grace, and all the lessons learned from him.

 Key Takeaways:

- ⮞ Be kind no matter what.
- ⮞ Overcome obstacles with dignity.
- ⮞ Take a chance on yourself.
- ⮞ Invite people in.
- ⮞ Be transparent.

REBECCA HU (she/her)
Cofounder, Glacier

#StayCurious

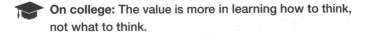 **On business:** Starting a company is pretty easily broken down into a lot of tiny little decisions or little steps that individually might not be all that difficult.

On social: The path forward for responsible social media usage is certainly not to restrict people's access to it; it has to be used very thoughtfully.

On college: The value is more in learning how to think, not what to think.

Rebecca Hu and Areeb Malik started their recycling tech company, Glacier, with an empty tub of Greek yogurt, a ball of string, and a bag of rice. They used them to build a prototype of a robot that would sort through and recycle mountains of trash. After many iterations, Glacier's robots are now working inside recycling facilities 24/7, increasing the pace of a job that has been hard to find humans to fill. Relying on their diverse backgrounds in artificial intelligence (AI) and business—Areeb hailing from Facebook, and Rebecca from consulting firm Bain & Company—they created Glacier in the hopes they could make an impact *right now* as the world waits for bigger climate-mitigating technologies to be created and tested. Rebecca talks to us about what people and companies can do to become better at recycling, the importance of curiosity in all you do, and the future of robotics in working alongside humans to improve the planet.

What was your vision when cofounding Glacier?

The main goal was to feel like I was spending my time working on a meaningful pursuit that would ultimately benefit everyone on the planet. I really was passionate about social impact, and in my opinion, there's no more valuable thing to be working on right now than helping to reduce the effects of our climate crisis. Being able to start a company that has a meaningful impact on climate change was very important to me.

Out of all the products, services, or application of robotics, why did you choose recycling in particular?

When we were deciding to start Glacier, my cofounder and I were looking at a variety of different subdomains within sustainability or climate tech. We chose to work on recycling, in part, because it's a very interesting application where existing technology like artificial intelligence and robotics can step in to improve existing infrastructure and make a very rapid improvement to the sustainability goals we have in mind. A lot of the other technologies and development within climate tech are moon shots—technology that has not fully been developed or commercialized yet. We're really taking these big bets to see if we can build a new type of technology we've never seen before to decarbonize our planet. I think that those moon shots are incredibly valuable and are going to be a lot of what gets us out of this current climate predicament. But at the same time, we need a lot of technologies that can buy us more time or improve the situation effectively and immediately.

Can you quantify the impact of Glacier's "ending waste"?

One statistic that comes to mind is when you think about the amount of material that's currently not being brought back into circulation, something that still has value, like a plastic bottle or an aluminum can, that ends up in the landfill or in our oceans; the estimated value of that is $123 billion every single year. That's basically straight value that we're throwing away, not to mention the negative impact that it has on our planet. In a lot of ways, there is both a simultaneous environmental and economic argument to be made to massively improve our recycling infrastructure. One of the reasons I was really excited to start a recycling technology company is because it is a space where it perfectly aligns financial incentives with environmental incentives. The more your business grows, and the more successful it is, that necessarily means that you're creating more climate impact.

In your opinion, why don't more people choose to try to make an impact?

Two reasons come to mind for why people might not recycle perfectly. A lot of people wonder if recycling actually helps climate change, especially when you distill it down into each individual action. To them, the impact is not clear. They wonder if they can really move the needle, and if they don't think they can, there is perhaps some apathy toward recycling. My response to that is to say it absolutely makes a difference. I can quote many numbers to you. For example, the amount of energy required to recycle an aluminum can is 95 percent less energy than it takes to produce an entirely new one. When you think about the fact that I drink multiple LaCroix sparkling water cans a day, and then you multiply that across a year or across a lifetime, not to mention all the plastic that I consume or the other materials, it is a lot. Then when you think about your ability to impact those around you, to get your family, your friends, and other people in your network to also improve recycling, you as an individual can have a massive impact on our ability to recycle effectively. The second reason why people might not recycle as well, which is a harder one to solve in some ways, is that it's actually very difficult to know how to recycle something properly. This is where I would put a little bit more onus or burden on manufacturers and brands to improve the recyclability of their products.

How did you turn a simple idea of a robot that could identify recyclable materials into the innovative machines they are today?

When I met my cofounder, he had literally built a contraption off an extremely inexpensive Raspberry Pi, a webcam that he bought on Amazon, and a spooling mechanism that he built from an empty Greek yogurt tub, a bunch of string, and a bag of rice to demonstrate that it was possible to create a machine that could pick something up off a moving conveyor belt. That was the very first robot prototype just to prove that, scientifically, it could be done. Beyond that, it evolved in its product development cycle. At each stage, the goal was to look at the riskiest parts of our robot that we were not sure would work and figure out the fastest and most inexpensive way to prove that it does work. If you look at photos of our robots over the years, you'll see that it started as a bag of rice and a Greek yogurt tub; then it evolved into actual mechanical components in our tiny garage lab space, and then it evolved into something that was robust enough to actually put inside a recycling facility and understand what breaks and what is working.

Would you say the majority of the responsibility to really solve—or at the very least contribute to solving—climate change would fall to the government, companies, or personal decisions?

Maybe a bit of a cop-out answer is certainly to say all three. Without cooperation from all three of those pillars, this isn't going to work. It really is a collaborative effort. The way that I see it playing out is similar to the chasing triangles of a recycling logo, where each stage informs the other. The government in recent years has released a lot of legislation that is encouraging the health of the recycling markets, like minimum recycled content and more responsible instructions on packaging for how things should be recycled. Of course, the government can put a lot of pressure on companies to enact those product decisions. At the same time, each individual should ask what they can do to impact recycling legislation or climate change as a whole. The answer is that it all starts with people. People are putting pressure on both the government to actually do something to mandate change, and putting pressure—either literally, through social media, outreach, or with their wallets and what they're buying—on companies to produce more responsible packaging, or to show that they care about sustainability. A lot of manufacturers and brands now have climate or sustainability commitments that they've issued as a direct result of understanding that the consumers they're selling to care about this, and it's better for their business to care about sustainability.

Do you feel it's possible in the future that robots will replace most human jobs altogether?

Based on what I know from leading a robotics company, I

would say that if a future does arise where robots can do many jobs that humans currently perform, that future is a very, very long way off. I don't see it as an immediate risk because I think that not only do you have to develop the technology quite a bit further, but there also has to be a lot of social movement in that direction. I don't necessarily see robots as being able to perform a lot of the more nuanced and complex things that humans can do. That said, I do think that robots give us a really good safety net for certain things. For example, in the recycling industry, and in many other industries where automation is taking place, there is actually a huge labor shortage currently. People sometimes talk about robots as replacing humans, but in many of these applications, the people that we think we're replacing already don't exist. Working at a recycling facility is a really dirty job. You're literally picking things out of the trash stream. A lot of recycling facilities we speak to have said they've had a lot of difficulty recruiting workers, and they're running at partial shifts and have been for years. In that regard, automation, like robotics and AI, might be our only way to solve those problems in the near term. The robots that are coming online are allowing the human labor in the workforce to move on to more interesting or rewarding things.

You're a very young founder. How has that impacted your ability to find investors and interested partners?

I don't feel like I've experienced any explicit headwinds in terms of my age. I think that people respond to your level of conviction and your depth of expertise. I'm not able to change the fact that I am the age I am, but what I can do is convey to people how much knowledge, conviction, and passion I have about a topic. I choose to focus my attention and my energy on the things that are in my control. When it comes to pitching customers or investors, I want to make sure that I walk in really equipped to answer any question they could throw at me. The depth of my knowledge and my conviction about the company and the product we're building goes a long way.

What is your best advice for teenagers as they prepare to enter the workforce?

One useful lesson for me in my career has been not letting perfection get in the way of progress, or said another way, perfect is the enemy of done. For people who are hard on themselves and expect a lot of themselves, it can be difficult and very daunting to feel like you're taking on a huge challenge like starting a new company, but in fact, the effort of starting a company is pretty easily broken down into a lot of tiny little decisions or little steps that individually might not be all that difficult. I spent a long time feeling a little bit intimidated at the idea of starting a new robotics and AI company, but I got over it and said, "I'm going to start taking baby steps in that direction. If it ever gets too scary at any point, maybe I'll reevaluate." In breaking it down into tiny, manageable steps, I found myself in the current position I am in, and I would not choose to be anywhere else.

Is there anything you have learned that you believe would be helpful for young women entering the field?

My advice to young female founders is in some ways similar to the advice I would give to anyone who's trying to be an entrepreneur: have a really good and realistic handle on what you are capable of and don't be too worried about what others are telling you that you can and can't do. You know yourself, your own limitations, and your own potential best. While it's always good to take in feedback from others, at the end of the day, being a successful entrepreneur is so much about just trusting yourself and your own decision-making ability, and just letting that play out.

 ## Key Takeaways:

- ➡ Know yourself and your capabilities.
- ➡ Break things down into small steps.
- ➡ Be prepared and passionate.
- ➡ Don't let perfection get in the way of progress.
- ➡ Ask why.

EYAL LEVY (he/him)
Cofounder and CEO, Yogibo

#DiscoverTheField

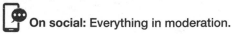 **On business:** It's all about persistence, hustling, and working hard for what you want. It's a very long journey.

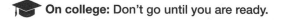 **On social:** Everything in moderation.

On college: Don't go until you are ready.

Yogibo CEO **Eyal Levy** is making the world a more comfortable place, one colorful beanbag at a time. He first had the idea for the product when his wife needed a comfortable chair during her pregnancy. After hearing positive feedback from her, and soon from his friends, Eyal dove headfirst into the beanbag industry. He tells us that Yogibo beanbags have many benefits beyond comfort, such as relieving back pain, stress, and anxiety and providing sensory input for children on the autism spectrum and with attention deficit hyperactivity disorder (ADHD). Yogibo has already partnered with Disney, Star Wars, and Pokémon to bring beloved characters to the line, and Eyal says there are more partnerships on the horizon. A people person who loves to travel and adapts easily to new cultures, Eyal's ultimate goal is to make people feel good—and his beanbags are doing just that.

How would you explain your company to someone who has no knowledge of what you are doing?

Yogibo makes people feel better and more in tune with themselves. And we believe that when people feel more in tune with themselves, they feel happier. And we started with the new generation of beanbags, and then developed into other comfort things.

How did you come up with this idea?

The Yogibo idea came about more than fifteen years ago. My wife was pregnant, and we were looking for something where she could sleep on her belly. I discovered this stretchy fabric, and we filled it with beads. Our friends tried the product, and we realized it's not just pregnant women who want to be super comfy. We started it out of the basement and sold it to just friends and friends of friends. People kept asking for more, so we started the company.

What kind of health benefits, other than comfort, do your beanbags have?

Since they conform to your body with no pressure points, they are great for people with physical disabilities, people who have a hard time moving, and people with chronic pains in their back, neck, or other parts of the body. They are also super beneficial for people with sensory processing disorder, kids with autism or on the spectrum. They provide a safe space with a lot of positive feedback for sensory integration. We've been partnering with organizations for kids on the spectrum. We've built sensory rooms in overwhelming environments like NBA and NFL arenas, and we're very active with this community.

What is your creative process?

We have focus groups with customers, staff, and influencers, and we follow the trends. Our product team looks at ideas and as many perspectives as possible. We like to launch products, test them out, get feedback and make changes or improvements, and then scale.

What types of people do you like to hire, and why?

People who hustle. "Hustle" doesn't mean overwork or work too many hours. "Hustle" means doing anything to achieve your goals. I also like people who are open to criticism and willing to learn, and people who improve from feedback and mistakes. Those are probably the three most important things. Of course, I also like people who are fun to be with and have good interpersonal skills.

How do you make your product more eco-friendly?

We recycle everything. When people want to throw away their product, they can bring it to us. We recycle it. We don't throw away any beads. We work with recycling companies and the beads are repurposed. We look constantly at changing the fill for something organic or biodegradable, but that will make the product more expensive and it's not something that customers will be willing to buy at that price. We are making the product as light as possible using the least amount of filling that we can. We focus on recycling, repurposing, and not wasting too much on materials or packaging.

How has your experience creating and leading Yogibo changed you as a person?

I learned that if you jump into the water and just swim with the current, you see that you can do it, and there's nothing you can't do. The idea is to face challenges and be able to overcome them. Everything becomes easier.

What advice would you give to young entrepreneurs?

One of the things that built me up to be the person that I am today is all the milestones and stages in my life that I had before Yogibo. Whether it was working as a kid at my dad's company or later working as an engineer in a big company or being a manager in different companies—all those things made me ready. It is important to experience different industries and different positions. Nothing replaces personal touch. Interpersonal relationships are key. A lot of great ideas don't succeed, not because they're not good, but because of the management or the leadership.

What new ideas do you think our generation will bring to the workforce when we join it?

I'm constantly learning from younger people about new trends and new tools to make work and life more efficient.

How did your college experience affect your personal development as a leader?

As someone who grew up in Israel, the regular path is we go for military service for at least three years, then travel the world for another year, and then we start college. One of the things I see here is people start college when they're eighteen and they don't know what they want to study. I think that is a mistake because those are precious years in your life and you should start college

194

when you're really ready for it. Not when you're ready for partying, but when you're ready to study. To go to college at the age of eighteen before really experiencing anything is something that for some people may not be the right thing to do. It's a lot of money, especially in America. I think one of the things that helped me during my undergrad years studying engineering was working while I was studying and seeing how to implement what I studied into real life. Combining the two is the key.

If you could tell your past self from ten years ago one thing, what would it be?

We grew too fast and didn't anticipate some market changes, so I might slow down the growth.

What is something you find unique about yourself?

I'm comfortable anywhere. I visit many different countries, and I always adapt quickly to the culture.

 Key Takeaways:

➔ Hustle.
➔ Be open to criticism.
➔ Face challenges head-on.
➔ Plan and go slowly.
➔ Work on interpersonal skills.

ARIEL KAYE (she/her)
Founder and CEO, Parachute

#DreamBig

On life: Being honest, transparent, clear, and communicating well goes a really long way.

On business: Building a strong team around you at all levels of the business is critical for success.

On social: It can be an amazing place to share stories and learn from others. It can also be incredibly soul crushing, isolating, and very "highlight reel-ish," which can have lasting implications on our self-worth and how we view the world.

On college: There are a lot of ways to get educated outside of a traditional education environment.

Ariel Kaye is the founder and CEO of Parachute, a luxury home lifestyle brand specializing in high-quality—and super-comfy—bedding. Ariel says she has always had a passion for design, and she often decorated the homes of friends and family. But it was a trip to the teeming markets of Italy and Portugal that helped her identify a gap in the market and inspired her to launch her own brand. Her instincts were right—the products were so popular that she sold out of inventory almost immediately and has since cultivated a devoted fan base both online and in her retail stores. She continues to find inspiration through traveling the world: in mountains, beaches, and desert landscapes, even in the sprinkles in her ice cream bowl. She talks to us about facing the skeptics as a young entrepreneur, the importance of mentorship, and prioritizing diversity.

Why did you start Parachute?

I was spending a lot of time helping friends decorate their apartments and was very enthusiastic and passionate about the home space. In my shopping for myself, friends, and family, I realized that there was a lot to be desired. The retail experience was basically products wrapped in plastic, stacked floor to ceiling. There was a lot of misinformation about things like thread count, and different marketing gimmicks. I talked to friends and realized that no one could tell me what brand of sheets they had on their bed; they could just tell me what stores they went to.

I saw this huge opportunity to build a brand to connect with customers, to inspire and educate around what really matters in terms of quality and create a better shopping experience.

As a young CEO, did you have trouble persuading venture capitalists to come on board?

Absolutely. I had people ask me all the time why I was a solo founder and why I couldn't find anyone who would want to work with me on this project. When I first went out to raise money, I didn't have a team yet. I was a first-time founder. I had a lot of people push back and question my ability to get this business off the ground. I had a lot of people saying I should come back later when I had more traction, which is tricky when you need capital in order to get traction. . . .

What was the best feedback you got when you first looked for funding?

I tried to play it cool. I was low-key in meetings, and part of what I kept hearing was that I might not have enough passion, drive, or hustle to get this done. It wasn't until I put myself out there and showed a little bit of my intensity, that I really was going to stop at nothing—moving mountains was not out of the question for me—that I started seeing a positive reaction from investors.

Many young brands keep costs down by sticking to online sales, but you are doing the opposite, expanding in-person retail. Why?

We are very bullish on retail. We think there's a lot of potential to do retail creatively and differently, and one of the things that allows us to do retail profitably is that our store footprints are not so large. They are getting bigger, but they're manageable, and we're able to create this experience. One of the things that we did before COVID-19 that we're excited to bring back is having a number of events, workshops, and speaker series—things that really helped build the relationship with our customer as a whole and as a brand. Certainly, in retail the primary purpose of our stores is to build that relationship; the transaction is secondary. We have not been swayed by COVID-19. We are taking advantage of the opportunity.

What is Parachute doing to contribute to causes like sustainability and racial equality?

We have a sustainability task force that launched in 2019. We are very focused on sustainable practices for our products, packaging, office, and the way that we're thinking about growth. We are putting together what will be a very compelling and thorough action plan for the next few years, but there's been a lot that we've been doing behind the scenes to really put our planet and our world first. Likewise, we have a diversity and inclusion committee at our company. We prioritize diversity in everything that we do, from our team to our marketing efforts to our models that we use in all our shoots. That's diversity in age, ethnicity, and size. We also founded an initiative called the "Homes for Dream Initiative," which is an accelerator program for Black-owned businesses that are product focused to accelerate their growth, where we provide capital and mentorship to help businesses that may otherwise have a harder time getting capital.

Please tell us more about your mentorship program and why it is so important to you.

I actually got started in an accelerator program myself, called Launchpad, in 2013. I attribute so much of my early success to that program. It gave me a community of people to work with, a group of mentors and investors, and people to practice my pitch with. I was around other founders. It gave me access to so much information that I otherwise would have had such a hard time getting. I've been really excited to figure out a way for us to give back and to replicate as much as we could of that experience and bring it full circle, so we decided to launch our mentorship program in 2020. We've now had one participant. Her name is Taylor Long, and she has a company called Nomads, which is a size-inclusive swim line. We provide a grant and access to our entire team, so she gets conversations with our finance, marketing, site development, and B2B teams, and I spend a ton of time with the recipients as well. I think it's just a tremendous way to make a real impact on a business that has so much potential and gives them an insight to what we've experienced. There's a whole reciprocal aspect of it, too, where our team is getting the opportunity to mentor someone outside of our space and use what they've learned through their experience at Parachute in a really positive way.

How much of an advantage does college truly provide?

I absolutely think questioning college is the right thing to do. I don't think it's for everyone. I look back

> *"I love to be wrong. I love when other people say there's a new way to do this. I'm 100 percent game for that."*

at my college experience and think that my mentorships and my internships were really what gave me an advantage when I went to the workplace. There's a lot of ways to get educated, to get experience, and build connections and a network outside of a traditional education environment. Certainly, we're not looking at where people went to school when we're hiring. We're looking for experience, drive, and passion.

You mentioned that you hire for passion and drive. Can you tell us a little bit more about what other qualities you look for?

I look for curiosity. I look for people who are endlessly curious, who love to solve problems and view challenges as opportunities. I look for people with a really positive attitude, who are truly kind. We look for good, kind people to join us at Parachute. People who are positive, have great energy, and are team players and very collaborative. Resilience is key. There are a lot of highs and a lot of lows to entrepreneurship and being able to push forward even when things seem impossible has been critical to my success. The other thing that I often refer to as my superpower is a real self-awareness of what my strengths and weaknesses are and where I can allow other people to take control and lead, and I can take a back seat. Building a strong team around you at all levels of the business is critical for success. Being able to delegate, give people confidence, and empower people to learn, grow, and do more is better and best for everyone involved. I love to be wrong. I love when other people say there's a new way to do this. I'm 100 percent game for that. It's easy to want to do it all, but it's not scalable. Get a good team.

What is one flaw or common roadblock that you see in entrepreneurship today?

It's easy to be in the weeds when you're growing a business and to think about the near term, three to six months. It's hard to plan twelve to eighteen months ahead, but I think pushing yourself to think big picture, get out of the immediate future, and look at longer-term strategy can help you plan ahead so that you're not always chasing opportunity or responding, but you can be really proactive to seek what's best for the organization.

As a young business owner, what's your best advice for entrepreneurs who might be faced with skepticism for wanting to start their business now rather than as an adult?

You're always going to get skepticism, whether it's today or tomorrow, so politely tell people that they can send that skepticism elsewhere. Honestly, do it, follow your passions, fail, have fun. Don't take yourself too seriously. Get creative and explore and know that it's hard and it's the most rewarding and enjoyable experience as well, and that you can do anything that you put your mind to.

Key Takeaways:

➔ Be aware of your strengths and weaknesses.

➔ Get creative and be curious.

➔ View problems and challenges as opportunities.

➔ Be proactive rather than reactive.

➔ Be honest, transparent, and clear.

VIVIAN SHEN (she/her)
Cofounder and CEO, Juni Learning

#DevelopsLeaders

On business: Your first boss is very important. They end up having a really big influence on how you work and how you interact with people.

On social: Bring it back to creating connections between people instead of polarizing people.

On college: You meet other great people who inspire you and challenge you.

Vivian Shen believes that computer science is more than just memorizing lines of code—it is a mindset. She didn't start learning programming until college, when she realized that there is a relative lack of coding curriculum for children. She set out to fix that problem, and soon after graduating from Stanford, she started Juni Learning. Juni hires university computer science majors who are passionate about coding to teach kids online anywhere in the world, helping them spark an interest in coding through real-world applications. Vivian believes that coding will soon be a skill that is taught in schools as readily as reading and writing, and necessary in everyday life. Juni is also creating a pipeline of diverse talent, which is critical in an industry where there are far more men than women, hoping to make a lasting impact on the future of technology.

When you learned to code in college, you realized that there were few coding opportunities for kids in middle and high school. What is Juni Learning doing to fix that?

Most of the time, kids get really inspired by a teacher who shows a passion for a subject and gets them excited about what potential is out there, what kinds of careers there are, what kinds of projects they can build. We brought those together and thought about how we could create something that got the best teacher for anybody anywhere in the world. That's why we started Juni.

How will Juni Learning help prepare students for later in life?

The main goal is not only to teach the actual subject to students, but also to inspire them to be self-motivated. How can they be self-directed, get excited about a topic, and run it themselves?

How would your life be different if you had had access to Juni Learning as a child?

Growing up, you end up role modeling a lot of the people who are around you. If you don't have an engineer in your life, you might not ever see that as a viable option. Our goal is to surface as many mentors and role models to students as possible so they can see what's out there. Actually, the reason I got into coding was because I accidentally sat in the wrong lecture in college. That was where I got started. If serendipitous things like that didn't happen, then you might be down a very different path.

How do you ensure the best-quality instruction?

At the Juni headquarters, we try to be role models for the junior instructors, and then the junior instructors in turn for junior students. That has really helped create an environment of role modeling for the next generation. We try as much as possible to emphasize what our instructors do outside of their major in college, an extracurricular like soccer, for example, and how they can relate to people that way. The other piece of our instructor recruiting is that we don't look as much at GPA or grades as their teaching skills. Obviously, we look for a minimum of technical expertise, but then we look at tutoring or teaching experience. We do a live session where they teach us a mock class, and we look at how they can connect with students and explain things very clearly.

Your business model is unique. How has it helped you to have relatively little competition in what you do?

When we founded the company in 2017, having parents and students trust a new online option was definitely a challenge. The way that we overcame that was through one-on-one sessions to simulate meeting somebody in person. That was challenging in that there was no exact product replica of what we were doing. That also gave us an opportunity to create an entirely new experience and build trust with our customers. Now it's different because everybody is online. We've become a category leader in our space. When we first started, it was hard because we were creating a new product and a new category. Now we're at the forefront of that today.

As technology grows more advanced, do you think coding will become a necessary skill for everyone?

Even if you're not specifically an engineer, increasingly you either work for a tech company or you work on a technical team. There's also a way of thinking and analytical problem-solving that engineering teaches you, thinking about how to break things down into pieces and how to test for **edge cases,** where you might not have assumed something would happen, but you're trying to be thorough. Those things are increasingly

> Edge cases: Edge cases are problems or situations that occur at the limits of a system's normal operating parameters and often present unique challenges.

> *"Surround yourself with good people and people that you're happy to spend every day with and work with because nothing else really matters outside of love."*

important. In the future, maybe we will have such sophisticated AI that you won't have to program everything from scratch yourself, but it is the new frontier of thinking, problem-solving, and approaching things. That will not go away, and it will probably become more and more important. Even doctors and lawyers are getting more tools, software, and data to make those jobs more elevated. There are people who go into those professions who need this training as well.

There are many more men working in computer science than women. How are you helping to close this gap?

There are obviously a lot more role models now. There's a big push to bring more girls into computer science to make it more accessible. Instead of just focusing computer programming around video games, there are options around art, graphic design, and animation—a lot more options for the applications of programming.

What are you doing to increase racial diversity in both your workforce and students?

For a long time, we focused a lot on gender diversity. Over 50 percent of our instructors are female and we try to keep the student base at 40 to 50 percent female as well. My cofounder and I are both female. We've also thought about racial equality as a different lens and how we can refocus there. With our instructor recruiting, we've always had a good mix of diversity and inclusion. We've started to think more about how we can accelerate our timeline for building scholarships to expand access, which is really important for us, but it is not an overnight fix, unfortunately.

How can you integrate social issues into your curriculum?

We've been building more and more real-world applications into our curriculum and into our events. For example, we ran a hackathon on Earth Day, and we had a lot of entries that were related to global warming. Some folks analyzed weather temperatures in different areas and how it's changed over the years. We did another hackathon focused on health care, very much related to COVID-19. We've revised our curriculum over time to be paired with the timeliness of events, and it also helps students see tangible ways that they could work on these issues. That also set us apart. Having a curriculum where you just memorize things is not exciting. If you can work on things that have a real-world application or inspire somebody to go into a certain career, that's where we want to focus.

You went to Stanford. What can you learn from going to an Ivy League or similarly respected school that you can't replicate anywhere else?

It has benefited me, but I think there are also a lot of very successful people who go to other great universities. They just need to help students think in a way that enables them to build things from the ground up, to be entrepreneurial, and to take advantage of opportunities. That's more important than the brand name of the school. Then it comes down to the people that you surround yourself with.

Who was your biggest mentor?

When I was in high school, it was my college counselor. She inspired a lot of what we do at Juni, which is enabling kids to be independent, think for themselves, and develop their own passions. Sometimes parents can be very involved in your college decisions, and she never let my parents get involved. It helped me create my own opinions and be happy with the path that I chose for myself. Another mentor was my first boss. He was really great in showing me how to care for people's well-being and how to work with people.

What was your greatest challenge in school? And what is your greatest challenge today? Are they related in any way?

One of my biggest challenges in school that I've worked on for a long time to try to get over is I held myself to a very high standard, and I still do, but that's very tiring if you peg that to certain goals. For example, if you're always trying to get an A in a class, and then you do achieve it, the feeling good about getting an A goes away very fast. Then getting a B plus or an A minus will feel bad for a long time. It's really about resiliency and picking yourself up every time you don't necessarily get what you want. When you do get something that you want, spend the time to celebrate that, but also think about what's next

> "You have to be flexible. That's what will get you through life, because you can never predict anything."

and stay grounded. I've been working on that over the years. That's why I think when you're working on a company, it's important to surround yourself with people who make you happy, and work with good people, because that's what sustains you.

What movie character are you most like?

I always wish I was like Mulan because she was really independent, and she took things into her own hands.

 Key Takeaways:

➔ Think about how to break things down.
➔ Test for edge cases.
➔ Be flexible and resilient.
➔ Explore a lot of subjects.
➔ Surround yourself with the best people.

CINDY SOO (she/her)

Global Innovation and Co-Creation Matrix Manager, IKEA

#EverythingIsUnknown
#WithCrisisComes Innovation

On life: If you haven't come across challenges, you've not achieved anything.

On business: Because our needs as people change so frequently, the only way to understand results is by testing possible solutions.

On social: We get a false sense of reality from social media, but it has brought the world a bit closer to each one of us.

On college: University taught me a lot of soft skills like scheduling, social cues, respect, persistence, patience, communication skills, and to be diligent.

Cindy Soo's job is to predict the future. She thinks about the coming years in unexpected ways in her role as global innovation and co-creation matrix manager for the Swedish home furnishing company IKEA. Cindy manages innovation and co-creation teams in twenty-five countries and regions, helping them solve today's problems and any problems we might encounter in the future, particularly around the definition of "home" in an era of remote work. Cindy's training in applied sciences, computer science, design, art, and communication has made her a gifted fusionist, someone who builds bridges between people who think and work very differently. She believes we need more fusionists in our generation to help solve the world's biggest problems, like climate change, war, food security, and health. Cindy introduces us to her strategies for redefining the future of business and products in our conversation about understanding different communication styles, using emotions as a point of strength, and learning from mistakes.

Can you describe what you do as the global innovation and co-creation matrix manager at IKEA?

IKEA is in twenty-five regions and countries around the world. In each of these countries and regions, we have an innovation and co-creation team. They're responsible for looking at what problems we have here and now, what problems we will have in the future, and how we bring about solutions to meet those problems or those needs of our consumers. That team is responsible for that, and I am responsible for those teams. I manage all of those countries and all of those individuals who lead their own innovation team in those countries. I am based in Sweden, in Malmö, which is in the southern part of Sweden.

What does it mean to you to "Enable the Future of Home"?

We now know that the home is changing, and for some people, home is where Wi-Fi is, which means that they're constantly traveling. Now that the world is more open, they're able to go anywhere they want and work wherever they would like, so the meaning of home is evolving. If that's the case, how do we enable them to feel at home, to feel comfortable, to feel safe, so they can feel comfortable in their own space, even though they're going to different places? Those needs are changing. For some, it is still one location. For some, it's three. For some, it's ten or twelve. So, what do we need? What resources do we need? What people do we need? What kind of finances do we need? What skills and tools do we need to enable us to figure out what solutions we can offer to the many people?

What is a fusionist?

To me, a fusionist is somebody who is the bridge between multiple things. My major was in communications. It was in the applied science department, which was a bit odd at the time, but it makes sense now because you do have a process that you must go through in order to put together a communication package or a strategy. There is some science behind it. I was quite good at computer science and programming. I was also an interactive designer, and I designed for engaging experiences. I understand the computer side of things. I understand science. I understand technology. I also understand design and art. I understand process and research. These are very different and quite polarizing areas. How do we bridge the gap between these areas with people? Because when it comes to science, or design and art, we have very different languages and very different cultures. We move, we speak, and we interact very differently. Oftentimes, there are disconnects between these individuals when they're working in one company. I found that I really enjoy meeting and speaking with people from all walks of life, and I'm able to take what they say and what they mean from one side and translate it so that others can understand. It creates an environment and an atmosphere for a much easier way of working. That is the definition of a fusionist—to be that bridge. It requires somebody who's very empathetic, who is a listener and not a speaker, and who cares about the feelings of others. That has been a very touchy topic in business. It's almost like, if you feel, you're weak, and I want to change it so that if you feel, if you are empathic, then you are strong. You become the strength behind the team because you're able to gather those around you who have the same vision as you, who know that they're safe in that environment.

Would you say that our current education system is failing students, in the sense that they separate subjects so strictly

in standardized teaching and tests, so that it is harder to make these fusionist connections?

I did not realize that I learn quite differently, and I honestly think every one of us learns in different ways. Some are very visual learners, some need structure, and they need a process, and they need tests. And some learn by doing. I think we're on the way, but we haven't really developed an educational system that allows for these different types of learners to learn well. We are failing those who have a lot of potential to do good in this world.

How did your educational environment affect your personal development as a leader?

University taught me not only about the topics that I learned, but it taught me to be diligent. It taught me about scheduling. It taught me about social cues, respect, persistence, patience, and how to communicate. Those soft skills are so important now.

What skills and processes do you use when developing new strategies for business?

Empathy, research, critical thinking, open-mindedness, curiosity, and being courageous. That's a very difficult thing to do when you're working for a company that wants to see very tangible results, because oftentimes being curious does not result in a tangible result. Not being afraid to question the status quo or to question your manager is quite difficult to do when you're new and green, in a new job or in a junior role. You want to make everyone happy, obviously, and do well and get promoted. But I also think that we need leaders who allow for juniors to do what they feel is correct and to experiment and explore. We need to learn what makes you all tick and what makes you excited and passionate about what you do every day.

What are the biggest problems our generation will have to solve?

In the short term, we know there will be some fallout with COVID-19. Health is a huge issue. We know that many of us will have some mental health concerns, and that's not a bad thing. It shouldn't be a taboo thing. We need more individuals who want to work in the mental health-care industry. We know that there's going to be a food crisis, if we're not in one already, because of what's happening in Ukraine, and because of climate change, which is a huge red flag. Could there be more development in new food sources? Is there a way that we can normalize growing our own food? Is there a way that we can empower and provide support to our local farmers? I don't mean just throwing money at them, but educational support and support in infrastructure. Can we uplift our local community in terms of creating more locally produced items and not just food or crafts? We need to improve our methods of recycling and refurbishing. Many companies, including IKEA, have way too much stock, way too much product. Not only is it confusing for consumers, but it makes it very difficult for us

"In business, if you are one to feel and have emotions, you are considered weak, and I want to change this perception. If you are capable of feeling, of having empathy, you should be considered strong."

to refurbish and recycle. I think companies should be more focused on creating products that will last a long time and have multiple uses. Can the young generation identify what those big problems are, and from those big problems, identify areas where we can be innovative and disruptive? We have some crises that affect us every day. Focus on those, and then we can start creating solutions for them.

As a leader of teams in twenty-five different countries, do you tailor your management style for different cultures to be more effective?

Some people in my team communicate by giving others their support, help, advice, or training. We have a meeting every month, and multiple meetings between them, to support different projects. I tend to not say much in our meetings. I often let them tell me what's happening. I'll ask questions, but that's it. We find a solution together. It is a discussion, a brainstorm, and sometimes a workshop. I don't speak to people from certain countries in a certain way. There are some who live in a country but are from a different culture. For example, they live in the United States, but they come from Italy, or they live in Italy but are from China. It's really about the person, and I look at them individually and see what they need. Sometimes those people don't like to use the camera during meetings, and it is totally fine to turn it off. Some like to communicate via email, some via text, and I adapt accordingly. I tend to be very observant, and I try to be as empathetic as possible to understand what makes them click, and what makes them engaged.

Learning how to pitch an idea and being an engaging presenter is critical in today's business world. How did you learn and refine the skill in yourself?

I'll tell you something that's very close to me: I used to have a stutter. When I was in high school, I was so afraid to speak, and I would always hide at the back of the classroom. I hated presentations. I hated raising my hand. I only would do it if I knew that I only had to say one word, and that was in math class where there was one answer. I had a stutter, and I'm not quite sure how I overcame that, but now, because I'm a designer by heart, I use slides, I use pictures, two or three words maximum, or one ten-word sentence to communicate what I want to say to an audience. I love telling stories and I love using visuals to tell stories. It takes practice, and it took a lot of failures. I have frozen onstage for a few minutes, and I even cried in the bathroom after a presentation, but it was all in my head. Over time, you gain confidence.

What advice would you give to people who find the idea of public speaking intimidating?

My advice is to think about what you want to say and think about your facial expressions and your body language. If you really believe in what you want to say, you will never have a problem, it will always come out. That is my trick—to feel honest and passionate about what you want to say when you want to communicate. It's okay if you make a mistake. That just means you're human, and people will be eager to connect with you. You also must practice. Practice in front of your dog, in front of the mirror, in front of your friends, or in front of your mother, even though she might criticize you. That is always a good thing.

 Key Takeaways:

➔ Don't be afraid to be curious.
➔ Understand different communication styles.
➔ Identify smaller areas of larger problems to solve.
➔ Shoot for the stars, but don't hurt anyone around you.
➔ Develop your creative side.

TRAVIS ROSBACH
Founder, Hydro Flask

#JustDoing
TheTravisThing

On business: Believe in what you're doing, act boldly, and unseen forces will come to your aid.

On social: Many Americans are deeply asleep and heavily entrenched in the modern world. Social and mainstream media places the masses in a collective amnesia. Like when we see a cute kitten video and forget about the negative ramifications of having that app on our phone. Or watching the TV and blindly believing what the current "crisis" is.

On college: You can be one thousand times more effective running toward what you're passionate about than spending four years doing something you're only mildly interested in. There's no reason to be there if you're not passionate about college.

Growing up, **Travis Rosbach** didn't plan to become a water-bottle guru—but the company he founded, Hydro Flask, has developed a cultlike following and is now synonymous with cool hydration. The BPA-free, 100 percent recyclable, double-wall, vacuum-insulated stainless-steel water bottles keep liquids hot or cold for hours. Like many start-ups, Hydro Flask's early days were plagued by problems: rust and non-insulating bottles in early shipments, difficulty keeping up with demand from manufacturers, and the increasing need for more significant funding as the company grew at unprecedented rates. Instead of taking shortcuts, Travis and his team found creative ways to problem-solve while sticking to their values and their mission of hydrating the planet. Travis shares his story about his goal to create the number one water bottle in the world and his journey from selling the product at the Portland Saturday Market to selling the company for $210 million. He proves that, with hard work and confidence, even the most straightforward ideas can have a major global impact.

What was your vision when you created Hydro Flask?

I was basically bestowed with the vision. It was to create the number one water bottle in the world and hydrate as many people as possible. I wasn't in the outdoor industry looking to create a better water bottle; I was just thirsty and looking for a bottle that wasn't going to end up in the ocean when I was done with it.

What was it like starting Hydro Flask?

I had many sleepless nights and early mornings working in the warehouse laser engraving, packing, shipping, and constantly stressed about how we would make payroll. In the early days, traveling to the factories and trade shows started to wear on me as well. I was learning so much and receiving so many positive feedback stories, and it began to make it worth it after a while.

You started selling Hydro Flask at a farmers market— the Portland Saturday Market. What are your best tips for transitioning from a place like a farmers market to mass production?

The Portland Saturday Market in Oregon was a terrific place for us to learn about our new product and experiment with the emerging category. We were fortunate to be able to ask the customers and other vendors questions about their likes, dislikes, preferences, wants, and needs—this was all invaluable. We then took this newfound knowledge, returned to the factory, and made all the improvements and dropped the negative aspects. That was huge; it allowed us to be super nimble and able to change things quickly. For example, things as simple as the color of the bottle was best left up to the customer. In addition to the market, we were doing as many local "pop-up" events as possible. The Oregon fairs, evenings in parks, art festivals—we would hawk our goods wherever they would let us. The money was great, as there was very little overhead in these events, plus they would fund more orders and more events. At one of these events, our first sales rep approached us and said he'd seen us in the local newspaper. Not only was he able to get us into major retail locations, but he also had a phenomenal Rolodex (you guys may need to look that one up) of other sales reps, who then went on to find more retail locations across the country. Hydro Flask just sort of blew up from there.

What advice do you give entrepreneurs starting out who have to push through rough spots?

You are not alone. It will get easier. And look for the "why." Why are you doing this? What is your desired outcome? What's your exit strategy? Can you focus on that? What can you do to improve the business/brand and grow in the meantime? Or is it time to say "I'm out"? You always have options.

You created a large worldwide community centered around Hydro Flask. How did you cultivate this community?

We started by building a high-quality product that became an everyday carry device. This meant the little "H Guy" was constantly seen by whoever was in the customer's unique "tribe." I knew we needed to grow those tribes by getting more bottles in more hands. That was always the biggest goal—to get more bottles out on the streets and help people hydrate because they'll feel better, think better, and be better suited to share that story with more and more people. The brand then gained traction, and along with the marketing we were doing, the cultlike following started to gain traction, too.

"You have to be bold and confident and believe in what you're doing."

You've reportedly said that you were ready for a change when you sold the company and spent time traveling. Was it hard to let go?

It wasn't easy walking away, but it was the right time. I was ready for some personal time away from the stress and constant 600 percent a quarter growth we were experiencing. I don't do well in a suit and tie or a stuffy office environment. I was comfortable and confident in the investors that were buying the company and was satisfied that they were going to uphold their promise to keep (within reason) all the employees, keep the company in Bend, Oregon, and maintain the integrity and ethos of the company after I was gone. That made it easier, knowing that Hydro Flask would still be the same rad company.

We read a quote where you said, "When we start thinking in boxes and categories, we don't see what's on the other side of the box or category; we don't see the rest of the picture." What is the best way to practice this kind of outside-of-the-box thinking?

Be very cautious of the boxes and categories people want to put you in. Be very careful about who is telling you what and how to think. Do your own research, experiment, and try things out, especially while you're young. Learn what you do like and do not like, try new things, explore, get out of

"You need to have drive and perseverance because it will get hard. People will tell you no and tell you it can't be done. If you give up or think those people are right, you'll never make it as an entrepreneur."

town, and travel! Experience new cultures and meet new people. Talk to them, go into their homes, share food and stories, and meet their families and pets. All of those little experiences add up. A lot of my confidence today came from my international travel and experiences when I was younger. I really can't recommend international travel enough, solo when possible, and when safety permits, of course.

What is your newest idea, and how do you plan to capitalize on it?

I probably have about 150 ideas a month. When these ideas come, I first (and foremost) look at how they can help the greatest number of people and the planet. Then I ask, do I have a passion for this, am I interested in the category, and is it something I don't mind working eighty plus hours a week toward? You need to have drive and perseverance because it will get hard. People will tell you no and tell you it can't be done. If you give up or think those people are right, you'll never make it as an entrepreneur.

What are the most important personality traits for an entrepreneur?

Tenacity, endurance, and perseverance. Entrepreneurs need to be a little bit cocky. Not arrogant, but confident. You have to be bold and confident and believe in what you're doing. You have to believe in yourself, your team, and your manufacturers. You don't want to be arrogant or rude, but you do want to be self-confident.

Growing up, who were some of your biggest inspirations in the art, design, or literary worlds?

At the age of twelve, I was fortunate enough to inherit a good-sized book collection from my neighbor who had a lot of business and success books by authors like Brian Tracy, Zig Ziglar, Jim Rohn, Napoleon Hill, Wayne Dyer, and a lot of those old-school business self-help gurus, and now legends. I dove in and spent a lot of time in that business and motivational genre. That has continued throughout most of my life.

 Key Takeaways:

➔ Be confident.
➔ Focus on human contact.
➔ Don't cut corners.
➔ Be honest.
➔ Get out and see the world.

ANN CRADY WEISS (she/her)

Cofounder and CEO, Hatch

#Authentic

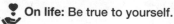 **On life:** Be true to yourself.

 **On business:** Develop a thick skin.

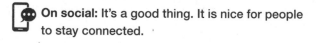 **On social:** It's a good thing. It is nice for people to stay connected.

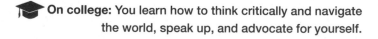 **On college:** You learn how to think critically and navigate the world, speak up, and advocate for yourself.

Ann Crady Weiss is the cofounder and CEO of Hatch, a company focused on helping people fall asleep, stay asleep, and wake up feeling rested and energized. Hatch was launched on *Shark Tank,* where Ann used sheer determination to convince the Sharks to back her company at the last minute. Hatch began as Hatch Baby, whose aim was to help struggling parents with young children by utilizing smart technology to help them sleep soundly, but it has evolved into restful sleep products like night-lights and sound machines for all ages. Ann previously ran the company Maya's Mom before selling to industry giant Johnson & Johnson, an experience she carried into her successful second go at entrepreneurship. On a more personal level, Ann talks about her tips for self-care, being authentic, and ignoring the naysayers.

How did your start on *Shark Tank* benefit your company in the long term?

Shark Tank helped us meet America and introduce America to our company. At the time we did it, *Shark Tank* had fourteen million weekly viewers. It was scary to do because they love to rip you apart. But as I always tell my kids: if you're not doing things that scare you, you're not challenging yourself, you're not learning.

Did having to logically and rationally explain your business philosophy to a team of experts at *Shark Tank* help you solidify what you wanted to do?

We already had a vision, a mission, and a culture in place before

> *"There are going to be some things that other people think are weird, silly, or great. What other people think should not be your yardstick. Your yardstick should be what fills you up and what makes you happy."*

we went to *Shark Tank*. *Shark Tank* didn't change any of that. The reality of pitching to any investors, whether it's on *Shark Tank* or someone on Sand Hill Road in Silicon Valley, is you hear lots of opinions about why the business will never work. One thing you have to learn as an entrepreneur is that feedback is a gift. You get to choose whether you accept the gift or not. You have to develop a thick skin. Everyone has a different opinion, and you can't let it change what you've set out to do.

Who do you consider your biggest competitors, and what sets you apart?

Our biggest competitor is probably Calm, which is an app on your phone that helps people calm down. A lot of people use it to help them sleep. They've really managed to create an interesting brand and product experience around falling asleep, so we consider them a competitor because our products—Restore, specifically—help people fall asleep. The reason we consider ourselves better is because we help you fall asleep, help you stay asleep, and help you wake up feeling rested. We are doing more to take care of you all night long. We're also doing it without relying on your phone, which sleep science says is a really bad thing to have next to your bed when you sleep.

How do you address diversity and environmental justice in your company?

Being socially conscious is an especially important part of being a company these days and a really wonderful change. It used to be that most companies only cared about shareholder value. The beautiful thing is your generation is pushing corporate America to really think more about things like diversity and environmental justice. We know that if we are not smart about doing the right thing early on, as we become bigger, we are only going to compound our problems. From an early stage, we are trying to think about how we can create an environment within our company that is reflective of the things that are important in the world. I am a woman CEO, so just by virtue of who I am, we attract a more diverse talent pool than normal corporate America does. Oftentimes, when women see a woman in charge, they think, "I could be in a place like this." We are less naturally good when it comes to racial diversity. We try to make a coordinated effort to recruit a workforce that looks like America. We try to post our jobs in places where we think we will get diverse candidates. We try to make sure that when we do have diverse candidates who work for us that we provide the right support for everyone to feel included and like they belong.

Do you use your own products?

I have a Restore that's at my bedside that I use every night. I also have a nine-year-old son who uses Rest every night. I have two teenagers who also use Restore. The feature that they care about most is that they can set a ton of alarms with many different sounds because they are both sleepyheads and have a hard time getting out of bed in the morning.

How do your personal beliefs carry over into your work?

In today's corporate world, there is much more of an understanding that we have to bring our whole selves to work. We need to think about how we can nourish and really take care of people as their whole selves. The way my personal beliefs affect how I run our company is I have done a ton of work on myself. I've been to individual therapy, couples therapy, I've done workshops—all designed to help me live a more authentic life for myself and for my family. The personal beliefs I have around taking care of oneself affect who I am as a leader. We talk to our company regularly about the importance of being kind to yourself, taking care of your mental health, and exercising. We try to back it up by giving people real time off to take care of themselves. I believe in being straightforward with people. I try to be direct in a tactful way about how I'm feeling, where they stand with me, and ask for feedback on where I stand with them.

What personality traits do you value most in a friend? An employee? Yourself?

In an employee, it is a "get it done" attitude. In a friend, I like a good listener. And in myself, I value most that I am determined.

 # Key Takeaways:

- ➲ Be straightforward in your communication.
- ➲ Bring your whole self to your work.
- ➲ Be true to yourself and your ideas.
- ➲ Do things that scare you.
- ➲ Be determined.

The Creator

JENI BRITTON BAUER (she/her)
Founder and CEO, Jeni's Splendid Ice Creams

#JenisIceCreams

On life: All the answers are inside you.

On business: Push yourself and allow yourself to be scared and vulnerable.

On social: It has brought people together and connected us with movements we might never have been connected to without it. But it can be dangerous. It's important to pay attention to who you really are IN REAL LIFE. You must nurture that first and deeply.

Jeni Britton Bauer is the founder and CEO of Jeni's Splendid Ice Creams, an Ohio-based artisan ice cream company that uses fresh ingredients from local farmers to create imaginative flavors such as Brambleberry Crisp, Brown Butter Almond Brittle, Texas Sheet Cake, Lemon Bar, and Watermelon Taffy (to name a few!). Jeni started making ice cream when she was twenty-two years old, and draws inspiration from books, people, and art. She moved frequently as a child, which taught her resilience and forced her to blaze her own path, characteristics that sustained her during challenges with her business. Now with sixty-five scoop shops around the United States, Jeni's has grown a devoted customer fan base through its fun vibe, commitment to fair trade, and mouth-watering taste. She has paid homage to other fan faves through limited-edition collabs with the TV show *Ted Lasso* (Biscuits with the Boss) and icon Dolly Parton (Strawberry Pretzel Pie). In this conversation (for which we prepared with a lot of taste testing), we discover how Jeni inherited creativity and tenacity from her grandmothers, and how she listens to her intuition and feelings. By staying true to herself, she not only succeeded, but revolutionized an industry.

What is your creative process in developing your unique flavors that are so different from most brands' generic strawberry or chocolate?

I read a lot, gather experiences, talk to people, listen to people, and then I get ideas that I send to the test kitchen team. I am

> "No one has success without many deep, hard fails, so make it a point to get good at failure and getting knocked down. The most successful people are good at getting back up over and over."

not just a whole-brain thinker but a whole-body thinker. I feel things deeply. Of course, my heart and gut have reactions to the world, but even my arms and legs can feel a sense of urgency and delight. When we hit on a perfect flavor, my shoulders go up and down and I almost dance with excitement. If it's good, but not perfect, it stays only in my brain being analyzed. When it makes your whole self feel good, that's when we know it's right.

If you were to meet the CEO of Baskin-Robbins, what would you tell him about how your brand is better and more unique? (Which it is.)

I'd probably want to reminisce about the early days of Baskin-Robbins—they were very unique and wonderful in their time. Quite frankly, I'd want to ask how to prevent my own brand from losing its essential character. I think it's sad when brands lose their creative spirit and spark. I blame too much data thinking.

What is a business problem right now you are trying to tackle?

How can a founder stay relevant in a company for the long term?

How can you stay competitive in a market with much cheaper ice cream?

By making better ice cream even if it costs more.

What is the most important thing you accomplished over the pandemic?

The importance of a good friend and of being a good friend.

What types of people do you like to hire, and why?

I like to hire self-starters and team players. I admire people who bring their unique perspective and whole selves in, so I like to hire people who are different from me.

Who is your biggest mentor, and what did they teach you?

My grandmothers each taught me different things. Enid was an artist and art teacher; she taught me insatiable curiosity. Betty was a scrappy doer, and she taught me that I can do or be anything I wanted. They both exist inside me.

What type of art form do you like the best and how does it influence your work?

I like painting and illustration. I'm very influenced by color and the flavors and emotions we perceive when we view color. And I don't go a day without drawing. I use my whole body to think, and drawing helps me move my thoughts from my brain through my body.

What can your story teach kids about resilience?

I have lost everything three times. The first time was when I was fourteen when my family exploded. I was all but on my own, living in a damp basement in a small old town house with my mom and sister and taking care of my new baby brother because my mom was sick. We each were too preoccupied with our own survival to matter much to each other. I lost my first business and had to start over in 2000. Now I think of it as my "practice business." And in 2015, I nearly lost Jeni's and built it back from less than nothing.

The most important thing is to push yourself. Allow yourself to be scared and vulnerable. The more you do that, the better you get at surviving it. It doesn't take long to get better than others. Many people are very afraid of risk. Getting strong is about how good you are at recovery and how much you can rely on yourself and your skills to recover. No one has success without many deep, hard fails, so make it a point to get good at failure and getting knocked down. The most successful people are good at getting back up over and over.

Did you do well in school? What was the best/worst thing that teachers said about you?

No. I was/am a daydreamer. Every teacher I ever had called me kind and patient. It's because I was quiet. They didn't see that I was boiling over with ideas as I sat in their boring-to-me classes, full of energy to do something awesome when I got home. At worst, I was called lazy—and of course, I was to them! I didn't do what they wanted. I was busy with other things, like starting a business or raising money for a local charity.

Did you worry about tests when you were a kid?

No, and even though I didn't do my homework, I managed to do okay on tests.

Were you ever bullied?

Yes, I moved every year, so I was always the new kid. New kids are often an easy target.

> "You will not always be right, but if you are intentional about it, you will always learn and that becomes you."

One school was so bad that I stopped going. I tried to fit in, but it felt as if the entire school was against me. My dad would drive me to the bus stop, wait until the bus was almost there before heading to work, and I'd just walk home anyway.

What movie character are you most like?

Frodo some days, Aragorn on other days.

What's one thing that exists today that you never would have imagined existed when you were a kid?

I grew up watching *Star Trek*. I definitely thought we'd have FaceTime and video watches, etc. In fact, I'm disappointed we don't have the transporters. Sometimes I'm in my car and I actually think about it—I thought we'd have much faster transportation by now. Maybe hyperloop will still happen in my lifetime, and that'll help. In other words, I'm not amazed by any of it—thought we'd be further. Ha ha!

If you were to come up with a flavor for Harry Potter, what would it be?

I'd want it to be served on the train to Hogwarts. Maybe an ice cream drumstick-like novelty that stays frozen and doesn't melt until you eat it. But you can put it back in the wrapper and save it for later and it'll be frozen again. That way, it can be stocked on the cart as they sell the goodies in the train cars. I think it would be neat if it could change flavors, so you'd always get what you wanted.

What do you do when you are really stressed?

I try to breathe. And I reach out to a friend.

What's one habit that you wish you could break?

Going it alone.

 # Key Takeaways:

> ➔ Push yourself.
> ➔ Do what feels right rather than what others tell you is right.
> ➔ Be intentional.
> ➔ Bring your whole self to what you do.
> ➔ Allow yourself to be vulnerable.

Sebastian Martinez (he/him) and
Brandon Martinez (he/him)
CEO and Director of Sales, Are You Kidding Socks

#KidEntrepreneurs

On life: If you're passionate about something, do not let anyone get in the way of your dreams. If you think you can do it, go for it.

On social: It's both good and bad. Good because you can grow your company so much faster through social media, but also bad because someone could ruin your reputation for no reason.

On college: School is always priority number one. You've gotta educate yourself.

When **Brandon and Sebastian Martinez** tell people they own their own company, the response is invariably "Are you kidding?" Hence the name of their brand, Are You Kidding Socks. The teen brothers started selling custom socks eight years ago when they were just eight and six years old, respectively, as a way to combine their love for socks with their passion for design. Their mission? To help other kids and give back to the community. They have partnered with more than twenty charities, including Autism Speaks, Make-A-Wish, Cowboys Who Care, Big Brothers Big Sisters, American Cancer Society, and others to raise money for their causes, and they have donated more than $350,000 of their earnings. While currently prioritizing their education, they still have big dreams for their company: sell at bigger retail stores and expand their line of apparel beyond socks. The Martinez brothers prove that age doesn't define entrepreneurial talent or the passion to make a difference.

How did you come up with the idea for Are You Kidding Socks?

Sebastian was obsessed with socks as a little kid. He had a collection with over one hundred pairs of crazy, funky socks. Because of his passion for socks, our mom asked him if he wanted to design his own socks, and he ran to the table and started drawing designs that he loved. A year later we launched our brand.

What did the early days of your business look like?

In the beginning years we didn't have a warehouse, so we had to stack all our boxes of socks in our house. We turned our house into our own warehouse. That was our first showroom. We had to get rid of our living space for our workspace. It was kind of hard to manage.

What made you so passionate to start a business with the purpose of giving back to the community?

We always wanted to give back because we've got to do our part in the world, because you never know what someone's going through. We just love putting smiles on other people's faces.

How do you show that your entrepreneurial skills aren't limited by your age?

People think just because we're kids, we can't own a business because we don't know what we're doing, but we actually take the time to learn and practice what to do. When we sell socks, people say, "Wow, you're just a kid! Are you kidding?" That's how we got the name. When you see kids running their own business, it's something you don't see every day.

What is your creative process?

New ideas for us are new designs. When we are thinking about a new design, we think about what people might want. For example, we have race car socks because a lot of people are into cars and racing, so we decided to make a race car design. That's how we get most of the designs, but some of

> "We're doing it because we actually love what we're doing."

our designs are made from the charities and the people impacted by charities; we get them to design it for us. It's their own special sock that we sell.

Many businesses were forced online during the pandemic. How did you benefit from your existing e-commerce presence?

It actually hurt us. We do sell our socks online, but we also work a lot with schools to sell our charity socks. We have sock hops the last Friday of the month, where everyone goes to the gym or cafeteria or wherever the school wants and they all dance in their socks together. That's where a majority of our sales came from, and we also go to events to sell, so the pandemic impacted us badly.

What advice would you give to young entrepreneurs who have unique ideas but don't know how to get started?

If you're passionate about something, do not let anyone get in the way of your dreams. If you think you can do it, go for it.

If you could go back and start over, what would you do differently?

We didn't think about a worst-case scenario: a pandemic hitting. We didn't have to prepare for that. I think going back in time, we would have a little fail-safe, because most of our sales came from schools and events. We needed more of an online presence and a bigger social media presence as well. That's what we would focus on if we went back in time.

What qualities do you see in a great leader?

I think a good leader is someone who speaks up, someone who actually asks for help, because some people are scared to ask for help and that's why they fail. People who ask for help from other people, from people who are bigger and better than them, so they can grow. I think that's where we are. We're not scared to ask for help.

What advantages or disadvantages has it brought to your company as small business owners?

We've been on some big news channels like *Good Morning America* and the *Today* show and that itself has brought us many orders. Just being on a two-minute interview on the news has grown our company so much. So I also feel like it can help other companies raise their visibility to get on these news channels so they can grow their companies as well.

How do you balance your business, school, and just having fun?

School is always priority number one. You've got to educate yourself. We go to school, do our homework, and we obviously have sports, too. I have a girlfriend, so I have to make time for her as well. When we have that little slim free time in the day, an hour or so, that's where we get to work.

What are your plans for the future of your business?

We want to get into some bigger retail stores, like Nordstrom and Target, so we can expand our company more. We also want to expand our apparel to make shirts, shorts, and shoes, of course, because socks and shoes go together like peanut butter and jelly.

What are your plans for yourselves in the future?

Keep educating ourselves, go to college, and continue with the business.

Is there any other advice that you think would be important to give?

Don't give up. At first, it's gonna be a struggle. You're not gonna know what to do. You're not gonna get that many orders. It's gonna be tough. But if you don't give up and keep striving for greatness, it's gonna go great.

 Key Takeaways:

➔ Cultivate empathy for others.
➔ Ask for help.
➔ Speak up.
➔ Never give up.
➔ Find balance.

TARA BOSCH (she/her)
Founder and CEO, SmartSweets

#FeelingTheFearAnd
DoingItAnyway

 On business: Everything that feels like a challenge at the time is truly an opportunity hidden in disguise.

 On social: It's an incredibly powerful tool that we have in our belt as entrepreneurs, but it takes a lot of intentionality to not get lost in the noise.

 On college: Everyone's journey is different.

Tara Bosch is creating a candy revolution. She has turned her obsession with sweets into a multimillion-dollar candy empire and is on a mission to give people their beloved sweet treats without the sugar. Tara started SmartSweets after realizing her relationship with sugar was growing unhealthy, and asking a radical question: "Why can't you kick the sugar, but keep the candy?" While still in college, she decided to take the matter into her own hands and began experimenting in the kitchen, creating recipes using plant-based fibers and sweeteners instead of sugar, and inventing a brand-new product that removes 99 percent of sugar, the main ingredient in most candy. Today, SmartSweets's versions of popular treats such as gummy bears, licorice, and Swedish Fish are sold in massive chain stores like Target and Whole Foods and have helped people kick billions of grams of sugar. Despite making it big while still only in her twenties, Tara says she's just getting started. She talks with us about following your own path, trusting your intuition, and learning as you go.

You've said that you once had a sugar addiction, which was a reason you created SmartSweets. Can you tell us more about your motivation and inspiration for creating the company?

Growing up, I was obsessed with candy. It brought me so much joy. As I got older, I realized that it didn't make me feel good about myself, so I stopped eating candy. Then I had a conversation with my grandmother, and she shared with me that she regretted having so much sugar over the years as well. She had a lot of that excess sugar from candy, which we enjoyed together. That really made me pause and ask myself, "Why can't you feel good about candy?" That inspired me to start recipe testing in my kitchen.

You started selling SmartSweets from your car, and now you're in more than 130,000 stores, including big-box stores like Whole Foods and Target. What were the biggest highs and lows from where you started until now?

The challenge of creating something new in the world that hasn't existed before is just the roller coaster of the highs and the lows, but I truly believe that if you're creating something that is going to positively impact others in the world, that the universe is going to support you on your journey. At SmartSweets, every single day was full of highs and lows where it felt like the world was crashing down and that the company could fail at any moment. A few in particular stand out. One was two weeks before our initial launch on shelves, my manufacturer called and said that they were going to increase the minimum, so I could no longer afford the first run, and I thought I was going to have to try to raise money. I started scraping on LinkedIn and calling people who might be interested in investing in the company. At that time, the company's name was Stevi-Sweets, and nobody wanted to try the product because— they said—of the negative connotation associated with stevia. That made me pause and change the company's name from Stevi-Sweets to SmartSweets. I like that example in particular because everything that feels like a challenge at the time is truly an opportunity hidden in disguise. If you hold that view, I think it really gives you a lot of grit and wherewithal in all the countless daily challenges you're facing in creating something that has never existed.

The SmartSweets brand has licorice, gummy bears and worms, and sour rings and lollipops, among other candy varieties. How did you decide on each one as you added to your product line?

Since day one, I've been really intentional about taking the candy that you know and love and reinventing it without sugar. We started with gummy bears because it's a classic. From there, we just began re-creating other classic favorites that people grew up with and have nostalgic memories of but stopped eating because of all the sugar content. The vision with SmartSweets is to be the global leader in revolutionizing candy so you can go to any grocery store or wherever you buy candy and choose your favorite candy, and SmartSweets can deliver a kick-sugar version you can feel good about.

You have been upfront about how you started without a background in entrepreneurship. What is the single most powerful thing you have learned in building SmartSweets?

I always thought that people who were successful in creating what they set out to do had something figured out or that they had an unwavering confidence. What I've learned in building Smart-Sweets is that nobody really knows what they're doing. It's those who have the courage to confront the fear that can feel so overwhelming at times and move forward who figure it out along the way. That has been incredibly powerful. Once you realize that everyone is just figuring it out along the way, it really gives you the ability to continue venturing into the unknown, knowing that you may not know what to do or

> *"Have the courage in yourself to think big. Once you've thought big, pause, and think big again."*

how to do it now, but that if you just keep moving forward every single day, you will figure it out.

What have you learned as a woman founder that would be helpful for other young women entering the field?

I think for young women, and for young guys as well, but especially young women, with all the statistics around women and entrepreneurship and the percentage of capital that goes to women still being so low, it is important to really have the courage in yourself to think big. Once you've thought big, pause, and think big again. Know that you are capable and know the power that lies in all the amazing qualities that you have. You don't have to try to be tough or to put on a serious or more masculine front. You can be just who you are, and that is going to be exactly who you need to be to get you to where you need to go. For example, I was always a quirky and kind of awkward person, and for many years at Smart-Sweets, I felt like I had to hide the quirkiness. I thought I wouldn't be taken as seriously if I showed up to a meeting in my ball cap and my high-waisted jeans with my crop top. But that was just who I was, and it represented the playfulness of the brand. Once I embraced that, I very quickly learned anyone who didn't take me seriously was not worth being part of SmartSweets's journey, and that it helps to weed out those people.

You're also a very young founder. Did you ever have trouble with people taking you seriously because of your age?

I think there's a lot of power in being a young founder. When

I was starting, I would research people who had built something like I aspired to build, and when I reached out to them and they would respond, I was always so grateful and so shocked that they were giving me a couple of minutes of their time. I realized that people who have been there and have done it before are seeing their younger self in you, and it gives them so much energy and inspiration to be able to support someone who is younger in their journey and trying to figure it out. Embrace the fact that you don't have to feel like you have anything figured out. There's a lot of power in just showing up with the energy, enthusiasm, and passion for your vision that other people who have been down the path before will be attracted to and excited to help you build.

You left college early to focus on SmartSweets. Do you still believe that was the right decision?

For me, going to college gave me the greatest gift of learning what I was not passionate about. I went to college for three years, and in that time, it was abundantly clear to me that I was not passionate about anything that I had studied. Knowing that I wasn't passionate about that really gave me the time and space to think about what else I could try that I might be passionate about. My first start-up failed and that was a huge blessing, because it led me to my next idea, SmartSweets, while I was in college.

What skills do you think will prove most critical for young entrepreneurs?

It's those soft skills that are going to be the most powerful. It's the things that you don't learn in school. It's the ability to pick up the phone and cold-call someone, the ability to be resourceful and scrappy, and learn a new skill that you may not have had before by watching YouTube videos.

"You can be just who you are, and that is going to be exactly who you need to be to get you to where you need to go."

What is one last takeaway from your experiences in business?

I think what's so powerful is never underestimating the unique power of your own ideas and thoughts. If you have an idea, or you have something that you want to try, view it as something that is being brought to your mind uniquely by the universe, and that it's something that the world needs, and lean in and try it. With SmartSweets, I always felt an immense sense of responsibility that somehow the universe or God, or whatever it is that someone believes in, gave me the idea and entrusted me with the idea to act on. Viewing the thoughts and ideas you have as something that's a unique-to-you gift from the world is really powerful.

 Key Takeaways:

→ Trust your intuition.
→ Be intentional.
→ Always be yourself.
→ Hone your soft skills.
→ Teach yourself something new.

ZLATA FILIPOVIĆ (she/her)

Filmmaker and Author

#Storyteller #Eclectic #Activist

On life: Try to feel good at the end of the day about the work that you've done and be able to know that you gave it your best and treated people well.

On social: It can be really good in mobilizing and connecting people. But it can also incite violence and be very harmful for individuals.

On college: I met fantastic people at Oxford and Trinity. The exposure to this new environment, people, subjects, libraries, and everything else is all going to feed into more holistic growth of you as a person. You define yourself, get a little lost, and find yourself.

Zlata Filipović was just eleven in 1992 when war broke out in her hometown of Sarajevo, Bosnia-Herzegovina. For two years she survived multiple bombings a day and then chronicled her life in the bestselling book *Zlata's Diary.* Through her writing, Zlata helped people around the world better understand the conflict, and her work prompted the media to call her a modern-day Anne Frank. While she will always carry stories of the war with her, she hasn't let the experience define her. Today, Zlata stands on the other side of the camera as an award-winning filmmaker and advocate focused on social justice issues, including LGBTQ+ rights and anti-bullying in schools. She speaks to students worldwide about children in conflict and tells us about the lessons of kindness, adaptability, and resilience she has learned through her life and work.

You experienced the horrors of war when you were only eleven. How has that experience shaped you?

It's a massively defining experience of my life, having gone through a very sudden change when my life flipped from being a peaceful childhood to a war childhood, and everything that came with it, which included surviving, then moving from Bosnia to France, then to Ireland. It was two years of living in war, having bombs fall on our city, living without water or electricity, and with constant possibility of being shot or somebody that you care for being hurt. One of the big things that I learned through all that, which has shaped me, is adaptability. It taught me that humans can adapt to all sorts of circumstances and changes in our life; then we can harness that adaptability in our future endeavors.

What was it like starting your new life in France and then Ireland?

Moving to France, I didn't speak French, but I was in a French school, so I didn't know what was going on for the first six months, but then suddenly the French language started emerging. I think your brain is more primed for languages when you're thirteen than when you're in your forties. It required a lot of adaptability to new languages, new environments, new schools, new friends, but I'm quite an adaptable person. I'm very curious, and nosy. After having to adapt to living without school, water, food, a sense of safety and shelter, and pervasive danger, adapting to living in Paris or Dublin was not so bad.

You captured what it was like living day-to-day in a war zone in your book, *Zlata's Diary*. Did this experience create your drive for activism through filmmaking, and influence the topics you choose to work on today?

Both the topics I choose and the way in which I approach my work have been very much influenced by my early experiences during the war. There were so many journalists in Sarajevo dur-ing the siege, and I became one of the people that they reported on, and that has certainly fed

"Everything can change in a second. Nothing is guaranteed."

into how I approach my work as a filmmaker now, because I'm reporting on other people. The way I noticed how my story was told, and how people approached me when they were reporting on me or filming with me, I have carried on to being on the other side of the camera and how I behave toward people that I film with. I want them to feel like they're still owners of their own stories, that they feel empowered by the experience, that it isn't something that's being taken away from them, but that they're very much actively involved in their own storytelling. Because I've gone through a war and I've seen firsthand the challenges to human rights, or social issues, and young people's issues, a lot of the films that I have been involved in have had an activist, human rights, social issues angle.

How did you stay positive during the war?

I'm an only child, and I was very close to a lot of my friends. When the siege began, some of my friends left the city and moved to safer countries, and I couldn't see the friends that stayed behind because we couldn't leave our houses; we were all very isolated. I was very much at home with this pervasive danger outside, and so my world turned inward, into my house and toward my parents who I'm very close with. We got to know the neighbors very well. These were people we usually would have just nodded to and said a quick hello to in the street, but now suddenly we were sharing all our time with them, our food, our happiness, our sadness, everything. That little community was something very positive and powerful that came out of the experience. We all helped each other. One of the apartments next door got a cat, and that cat was suddenly everybody's cat and brought so much joy and positivity. Writing and reading were very helpful to me. Obviously, with reading, there's an escapism, and with writing, especially writing what is happening to you, is an opportunity to process what's going on, and help you deal with it a little bit better. There was a lovely community, and there were books and a piano and a cat.

What can your experience teach kids today about politics, history, human nature, and hate?

One of the things that I've discovered through my diary, and then later when I worked on another book called *Stolen Voices,* which is a collection of other young people's diaries written during various conflicts throughout the twentieth century, is how much people responded to some really small human things like the cat or a piano or a favorite book. That helped people connect with something that otherwise would feel quite abstract, like a conflict or living under a siege. I think there's a way in which people can connect with other people which brings a level of compassion. It's like putting a bit of flesh on something that's otherwise abstract, historical, or political. That human dimension is important and makes us see that something like war can happen to any of us, and that it does happen to people who are exactly like us. It doesn't happen in some faraway places to people who are completely different from us. It happens, and can happen to us, unfortunately, and as a result, we need to mind peace and protect and preserve it. I think that sort of human dimension is really important.

When did you first discover your passion for filmmaking and why did you decide to combine it with activism?

"Everything that I've lived, studied, experienced, and carry in me comes into a project."

My first degree was human sciences, which was a mixture of natural and social sciences—human genetics, demography, statistics, social anthropology, child psychology. It was all about understanding humans. My master's was in international relations and conflict prevention, and that was very much sparked by my own experience. Then I worked on *Stolen Voices.* Working on books was a very solitary experience, and I wanted to work more with other people. I also wanted to stay in the nonfiction world, which is what I'm quite passionate about. That's how I got into documentary filmmaking. I could see that documentary work can make people think about things in a different way. You can chisel away at making slight changes in society.

How do you pick what documentary to work on?

I'm very intrigued by the topics I work on, but that's possibly also my curiosity, because an awful lot of topics can be very interesting to me. It's also the people that I work with. I know that with certain people, the experience will be positive. There have been documentaries that I've worked on that were about marriage equality, mental health, the Cuban missile crisis, the Voyager spacecraft. I find that everything that I've lived, studied, experienced, and carried in me comes into a project, even when they don't seem obvious.

What personality traits do successful entrepreneurs possess?

In terms of my own work, you have to be collaborative, tenacious, good, just, fair, and compassionate. Put yourself in another person's shoes.

What personality traits do you value most in a friend, colleagues, and yourself?

Justice, honesty, empathy, and giving it your best.

What was the best piece of advice you got from your parents growing up?

They always told me to do what I love. Do what you enjoy, what you love, and you will be good at it. That was uttered to me many times.

What was your favorite moment during your childhood?

I loved going skiing to the mountains outside of Sarajevo and to the seaside in Croatia. Those carefree winter days and carefree summer days in beautiful locations. When you're asked to imagine a place where you feel happy, it would be those.

What is the most important lesson you've learned in your lifetime?

Everything can change in a second. Nothing is guaranteed. You have to be adaptable. You should be kind. You should understand others and relate to others. You should try to feel good at the end of the day about the work that you've done and put your hand on your heart and know you have treated people well, and that you gave it your best. Those are the lessons I've learned and what I try to do every night when I go to bed.

 Key Takeaways:

- ➔ Do something you love.
- ➔ Be adaptable.
- ➔ Be kind.
- ➔ Be tenacious.
- ➔ Have empathy and compassion, and put yourself in others' shoes.

DANIELLE VINCENT (she/her)
Cofounder and CEO, Outlaw Soaps

#LiveOutlaw

On life: Your life will always have some crisis, but you've always got to try to be a bigger person than the size of the crisis.

On business: You have to believe that you're able to do it even if a lot of people tell you it's crazy.

On social: People connecting directly and authentically can be magic, but it comes at a very dear cost. There's a lot about targeting, marketing, and behavior analysis that people would be shocked and devastated to learn.

On college: If you want to be an entrepreneur, there's no experience more important than humble real-world experience.

Danielle Vincent plays by her own rules. She's the cofounder of Outlaw Soaps, an online indie soap company with scents such as leather, gunpowder, and campfire that are designed to be the "scent soundtrack of your inner cowboy or cowgirl." Outlaw also makes cologne, lotion, beard oil, and body wash with names like Calamity Jane, Home on the Range, and Blazing Saddles. Danielle left her job at the Oprah Winfrey Network to become a soap entrepreneur, with stops at Microsoft and Mozilla along the way. She's a lot like her customers, whom she calls the "Outlaw Gang" and whom she describes as some of the most complex, interesting, enthusiastic, rad, cool people she's ever met. She shares with us adventures from her bootstrapping beginnings, turning crisis into opportunity, and living life on the edge.

Why did you start Outlaw Soaps?

I just had an idea that I wanted to make stuff that smelled like camping and not like lilacs. That was the only thing guiding me. I didn't know the difference between handmade soap and milled soap. I didn't know anything about the industry. That's where I started.

Where does Outlaw Soaps stand in the competitor landscape?

I have an unpopular view of competitors, which is that I believe if you're doing your business well, you don't have competitors. You should be better. You should be in a completely different world than other people who are doing similar things. Some people say that Dr. Squatch is a competitor, but I don't think they are. They're focused on natural products, and we have natural products, but it's not our sole focus. They're focused on bar soap, and we're focused on everything. Our cologne sales outpaced our soap sales last year, so are we even in the same industry?

You based your company around seven "Magnificent Outlaw Values": kindness, best customer service, incredible products, ethical production, responsible employers, conscious commerce, and made in the USA, supporting real people in local jobs. Which of these values is the most significant for success?

Without a doubt, kindness is the most important across the board forever and ever. I follow a lot of Gen Z marketing influencers. Why would I follow a bunch of old people's marketing stuff? I think authenticity and kindness go hand in hand. You can't be authentic without being kind and compassionate. That's the most important. That's why we start with it.

What advice would you give to young entrepreneurs looking to start small businesses?

I can't think of any reason why anybody of any age couldn't start a business. That said, not every business is going to be one that you'll want to stay on with forever. I don't know of any businesses that truly fail. I only know of founders who don't bleed enough. A lot of businesses just don't make sense to continue, and smart founders know when they're more interested in something else. I see it as a puppy running through a field and rolling in things that smell interesting. Sometimes, the thing smells interesting for a long time, and sometimes it smells interesting for not much time at all. Then you keep running. That's how I think about business and about jobs in general. Do something you're really interested in with enthusiasm and keep going for as long as it makes you happy.

Is soapmaking something you would recommend?

When we were thinking about starting the business, we didn't have any start-up funding. We weren't well connected. We didn't know venture capitalists. I think we had twenty dollars, so we went to the grocery store and the hardware store and bought the first supplies that we needed to make the soap. If I was going to start all over, I would definitely focus on products that are scalable, because if you get popular, you don't want your most popular product to take a long time to produce. Soap has to cure for thirty days, but also it has to be hand poured and hand mixed by humans, which is really slow. It's difficult to scale. I don't think I would recommend this industry as super-high growth, unless you're super passionate about handmade soap, and there are people who are all about that.

How did your talent for writing come in handy when creating Outlaw Soaps?

You have to be a good writer to sell scent online. Nobody is going to buy scent without smelling it unless you're a good writer, so I'm very glad that I was given the ability to write. That came through a lot of practice. That is really the foundation for Outlaw. I still write every single thing that comes out of the company, including every blog post, newsletter, social media post, and ad. It is a lot of writing. It's a very specialized skill to be able to write well enough to sell scented products.

You had a digital tech background. Would having a business background have been better when you started?

If you're just bootstrapping, which we were doing, your mistakes can only be so catastrophic, which is a great blessing in the early days, because business mistakes abound. I still don't know what I don't know. I'm still learning.

What qualities does our generation possess that will help us succeed in business?

Energy, buoyant enthusiasm, and optimism to make it through the darkest times. You don't give up. You trust your vision and you don't give up. That's terrific, and that's not common at all, by the way. You have to be so confident that your business is going to survive. You have to think it is worth it even if a hundred people are telling you your idea is stupid. That's the kind of attitude that people need to have.

What is the most important lesson you have learned through your business?

Every disaster is an opportunity waiting to happen. When the pandemic hit, I was in an existential crisis, as I think every person was, and then I thought, "Oh, wait, this is really good for us! We sell soap online that reminds people of the outdoors and concerts! This is our time; we are going to rule this year!" That's how you have to approach every crisis, because you will never have a life free of crisis, but you have to be a bigger person when you encounter it than the crisis itself.

"You've got to get out there and make your own awesomeness."

What was the best piece of advice you got from your parents growing up?

My dad is a fountain of wisdom. He said that every contract that you're negotiating is like putting frogs in a box. You put frogs in the box over and over until more frogs jump out than you can put in, and then you close the box and sign the contract. That is so important because you'll never work out every detail of everything. Sometimes you just have to think, "This is good enough. We agree on enough. I don't want to lose everything that we've achieved so far. Let's just sign the contract." That's a hard time to know. You're never going to be perfect. You have to decide when you're losing more ground than you're gaining.

What personality traits do you value most in a friend? In an employee?

In a friend, thoughtful honesty. In an employee, it is people who believe that the best way to solve problems is by bringing them to light. You want people who identify the problem and respond quickly and dedicatedly. I really value that attitude.

 Key Takeaways:

- ➔ Learn to write.
- ➔ Be a participant, not a spectator.
- ➔ Practice kindness and authenticity.
- ➔ Bring a great attitude to everything.
- ➔ Trust your vision and don't give up.

JENNIFER DOLLANDER (she/her)

Founder, Alumni Cookie Dough

#LifeIsShort
#EatTheDough

On life: Go after your goals and don't take any day for granted.

On business: No idea is a bad idea, and it's never too late to start a business.

On social: Social media is a good platform for a business to expand and advertise but has negative effects on young people.

On college: College proves to others you can start and finish something. If you have a passion and believe in something, definitely go to school for that. If you don't have an idea of what to do and are going just because your friends are, it's not a good reason.

Jennifer Dollander has loved cookie dough for as long as she can remember. After experiencing her first cookie dough café in New York City, she left a secure job as a teacher and started her second career as an entrepreneur. In January 2019, she and her husband launched Alumni Cookie Dough in the college town of Athens, Georgia. Less than a year later, they had a second storefront and their sights on more. Alumni Cookie Dough has grown beyond their wildest expectations, and their focus now is helping other families achieve similar success through franchising. Jennifer believes that, for our generation, the sky's the limit, and encourages us to surround ourselves with positive people and ignore doubters. She proves it's never too late to follow your dreams, or your taste buds.

How did you come up with the idea of edible cookie dough?

I took my daughter to New York for her eighteenth birthday, and I happened upon an edible cookie dough café in Greenwich Village. It struck me that this would really do well in Athens, Georgia, where we live, which is a college town and home of the Georgia Bulldogs. I called my husband and told him about where we were, and my idea about bringing it to Athens, and he did a little research and realized that it was a good business idea. Before our plane landed in Atlanta, he had already secured the limited liability company (LLC) structure. We hit the ground running.

How do you come up with your unique flavors and their names?

We've had a really good time with the flavors. It's something that I think about all the time. I truly do love the experience in the kitchen, making these different flavors. I literally think about it all the time. I've had dreams about different flavors of cookie dough. We have been creative with the names, like our Freshman Fifteen; that is a name that my husband actually came up with after he tasted the dough. It's a salted caramel chocolate chip.

What is your favorite flavor?

My favorite flavor is Cookies & Cream and has been since day one.

Where do you stand in the competitor landscape?

Less than 4 percent of the cities around the United States have cookie dough cafés. We've hit this market at a really great time. There's not a lot of competition. We've had the benefit of trying out a lot of cookie dough cafés around the country, in San Francisco, Las Vegas, Phoenix, and New York. One of the great things about our dough is that it's edible and bakeable. That makes us unique.

What mistakes have you made in your journey to open this business?

I've made a lot. We've definitely grown from one of the mistakes that we made in the very beginning. We opened with lines out the door and down the street. We really did not have any experience in the restaurant business. The first four to five months doubled the staff that we needed. It was a costly mistake, but we learned from it.

> *"If you're going to start a business, if you're going to be an entrepreneur, you've literally got to eat, breathe, and sleep it, because that is what you're going to be doing, hopefully for a very long time."*

What value do you place on customer satisfaction?

Customer satisfaction is number one. I want people to feel important, and I want people to feel very satisfied when they leave our establishment. We will do whatever it takes within reasonable boundaries to make them have a great experience. Customer service and the quality of the dough are equally important, and they are absolutely number one.

Have you changed anything based on customer reviews or ideas?

We've changed our menu a little bit because of people's suggestions. We added a smaller, mini scoop to the menu, and families with small kids have appreciated that. We've also made a smaller size of the Dream Creme, and now we have a Jr. Dream Creme. That was a customer suggestion. We also listen to their suggestions for future flavors.

What advice would you give to our generation that you wish you knew as a kid?

Don't let anyone tell you that something is not a good idea. You will have so many naysayers and you've just got to believe in your-self and keep pushing. If you believe in something, your goal should always be to surround yourself with people who are better than you. If you do that, you will always strive to be better.

Who is your biggest mentor?

My biggest mentor by far is my dad. He always pushed me to the limit. And he's always repeatedly said to me, "What's the worst thing that can happen?" Whenever I wanted to try something new or do anything, he would always encourage me. That's what I've always tried to do with my children as well.

What do you think will be the biggest problems our generation will have to tackle?

Having close relationships with people tends to be a little bit of a challenge because you are surrounded by technology. You need to have some communication and that personal face-to-face with people.

What is the biggest item on your bucket list?

I want to grow this business through franchising so it can change other people's lives like it's changed ours. My bucket list number is twenty. If I can get twenty franchises, I would be happy with that.

How have you changed over the course of your lifetime?

Life is really short, so you've got to go after your goals and surround yourself with people who are important and positive. In

2012, I had open heart surgery, and that was very life-changing for me. I feel very lucky to be here, and I don't take any day for granted. Even bad days are not so bad, and that experience really showed me that.

 Key Takeaways:

- Think outside the box.
- Don't be afraid to try new things.
- Believe in yourself.
- Don't take anything for granted.
- Don't listen to the naysayers.

The Investor

SERGIO MONSALVE (he/him)
Venture Capitalist and Founding Partner,
Roble Ventures

#Hustle

On life: Never think you cannot do something.

On business: Work hard for yourself and the benefit of other people.

On social: It can be positive and negative. There should be checks and balances. One entity shouldn't make all the calls, especially an entity that doesn't necessarily have all the stakeholders in mind.

On college: College can be transformational. You learn as much from dorm room conversations as the classroom. You build connections.

How do you predict the next Apple or Amazon? That's the formula **Sergio Monsalve** is always trying to perfect. He's a venture capitalist who invests in companies with potential for positive social impact, in recent years focusing on education tech platforms like Kahoot! and Udemy. A graduate of Harvard and Stanford (where he now teaches), Sergio says he listens carefully to ideas and trends from young people, and believes our generation has the resilience and strength to create the next industry giants. We talk about the role of the investor in supporting entrepreneurs with more than money, surviving setbacks, intellectual honesty, and diversity. He shows us the joy he takes in lifelong learning and helping to bring the best new products and ideas to the world.

There is no shortage of venture capitalists or investors, so what sets your business and personal investments apart?

There's a lot of money out there and there's a lot of investors and venture capitalists. What sets apart an investor is the ability to help the entrepreneur that they're funding really be successful. The most important thing is to make sure that as a venture capital investor, you know where to help and know where not to hurt. You have to be really self-aware and have an ability to help mentor the entrepreneur, offering value-added services to get their company up and running, offer the right advice when it's needed, and step away when they don't need it. I've decided that the best way I can help is being thematically focused on one area of expertise, which is what I call human-enablement technologies or technologies that help you

> *"The most important thing is getting people to buy into your dream and be part of the dream."*

get ahead as a human. I also focus on building a board from the seed stage that is very diverse, equitable, and inclusive because that creates better debates, dynamics, and culture. Start-ups often fail not because of the technology; they fail because of people. If you get the people and chemistry right, and you are betting in a good market, you're going to be in great shape. It's a very competitive game. You have to work very hard, and you cannot let the entrepreneur do all the work.

How hard is it to predict the next Amazon or Apple?

Extremely hard. That's why there are only two of them at that size. In your generation there's going to be a lot more successes. The trajectory of how fast the acceleration of technology is going and entrepreneurship and big companies—you've seen bigger companies get big faster than before. That bodes well for your generation that there will be many Amazons and Apples that have yet to be created. It's very hard to identify them early. It requires a little bit of luck, too. For example, we're using Zoom right now. It's unfortunate that COVID-19 happened, but Zoom itself has been a big beneficiary. You've got to be a little lucky and you have to pick the right team, the right solution, and the right big problem to solve. Usually, the best companies solve big, big problems.

Besides simply having a growth mindset, what skills, motivation, or life perspectives make the best start-up entrepreneur?

The best entrepreneurs are the ones who try bold things, don't get discouraged, have growth mindsets, and learn from those mistakes. The biggest difference between a great entrepreneur and just a great operator is resilience, risk tolerance, and the ability to think big and not get bummed out by failures. It requires stamina, self-confidence, drive, and passion to get it done, but you can't do it by yourself. Even though you're starting the company, maybe by yourself, the most important thing is getting people to buy into your dream and be part of the dream. Hiring the right people and partnering with the right people who believe in your vision is super important.

How much of entrepreneurship can be taught, and what qualities make the best businesspeople?

Are you born with it, or can you build it? It's a little bit of both. You're going to need many hours of practice to get good at it. If you put yourself in a place where you're surrounded by entrepreneurs and entrepreneurial thinking, then you're going to iterate through those hours a lot more quickly because you're going to be sleeping, eating, and breathing it. Having an entrepreneurial mindset helps in general in life because it makes you more resilient, makes you have a growth mindset, and become a lifelong learner. That's a big skill, but not everybody can be an actual entrepreneur, because you do need to tolerate suffering through the stumbles.

How do you determine whether a company fits with your beliefs before investing in it, and how big of an impact do your personal beliefs have on what businesses you invest in?

The impact component is important. I've gotten to a place in my career where I want to do good, and I want to do well. I want to do well economically and generate returns for my investors, but I also want to think about the side effects of the company that I'm building. For example, I'll never do a cigarette company or harmful food company. I'll never do anything that affects humans in a negative way. In terms of education, there's subtleties. For example, I don't want to do educational technology investments that just favor rich people because it's a price point that's too high for everybody to access. I prefer investments where everybody can get access to education so that we don't create this bifurcation in society where people with money can get more education so they can get richer, and they can make more money. That whole cycle needs to get broken, and technology can help. I put a lot of thought into whether I want to invest in a company not just because it is going to make money but because it is going to do good for society, too.

Do you buy products from the businesses your company invests in?

Definitely. If you get serious about a company, the first thing you want to do is be a customer yourself. I am looking at investing in a company that teaches you how to play better golf by using coaches around the world and using text and videos. I'm very excited. I tried it, and it helped me play better golf. It's a simple app where you take a video of your swing and then you submit it to a coach. My coach happened to be in Australia. He came back and said all the things that I was doing wrong. I fixed it, and I sent him another video. That cost me thirty dollars instead of going to a range and paying two hundred dollars.

What qualities in a business reassure you that they have the potential for success and are therefore worth investing in?

"You have to pick the right team, the right solution, and the right big problem to solve."

It depends on the stage because the signals come in different forms. The ultimate signal of success from a monetary standpoint is your ability to generate free cash flow, generate net income. You don't get there for a long time. If you do it in a way that's helping society, has a diverse set of people around the table, and has a full sense of what they can do to help their community, that's great. Those companies are very rare. You start from the beginning having a very empathetic—but driven—founder with a great vision for their company. They have an ability to navigate through challenges, either pound through the wall, or go around the wall. They're malleable, driven, and adaptable to their conditions. They're also very intellectually honest. You have to be very convinced that your solution is going to work, but you don't fall in love with your solution if it's not working. You have to pivot when you need to, but don't lose faith if you hit a soft patch. Your ability to have emotional intelligence, intellectual curiosity, and the ability to analyze a lot of inputs are key.

What is your favorite fictional world, and what could our society learn from it?

I always wondered about the whole city around the Jedi Temple and knowing more about how that Jedi Temple and Star Wars really worked. That Star Wars set of worlds is amazing to me. What I learned from those movies is that you can't have one group leading and you have to have the good guys winning. The good guys are all based on your ability to do good for society and for the world.

What personality trait do you value most in a friend?

Honesty is the most important thing.

What is the most important lesson you have learned in your lifetime?

You should never think you cannot do something. It's always empowering to think that you can work to solve a problem if you put your mind to it. That has helped me incredibly well in my career. When people have said things that I cannot do and I've been able to do them, I had the attitude that I would be able to attack the problem and do it, as long as I have a plan and approach. Have a can-do attitude, be a lifelong learner, and always learn from other people.

 Key Takeaways:

➔ Be bold.
➔ Create your own path.
➔ Be intellectually honest.
➔ Try things that are hard and uncomfortable.
➔ Think beyond yourself.

ALISON ROSENTHAL (she/her)
Founder and Managing Partner, Leadout Capital

#ProudlyGenX
#OutdoorsIsFree
#FamilyFirst

 On business: I've always thought of success as a group thing. It's really hard to do big things alone.

On social: Social media has driven connections and social discourse at scale, which has had positive and negative consequences. And here are good cases for some oversight.

On college: Currently, there are questions about whether the gap in premium is worth what the product promises to deliver. That said, my college experience was really good.

Alison Rosenthal is the founder and managing partner of Leadout Capital, an early-stage software investor with a focus on "non-obvious" resilient founders who are building purpose-driven companies to solve problems in overlooked and underserved markets. In creating Leadout Capital, Alison's idea was to be the change she wants to see in the world, and she utilizes her business to personally fulfill her goal of increasing diversity in leadership positions—including more women, persons of color, and historically underrepresented groups. She's invested in a range of companies that includes a mobile platform to connect barbers and their clients, a business-to-government (B2G) marketplace product for public procurement, and an Earth-imaging lab on a mission to "democratize geospatial intelligence." Before launching Leadout Capital, Alison was an early Facebook (Meta) employee and helped launch the "Share" button. She also spent time on Wall Street and was appointed ambassador for global entrepreneurship under President Obama, and was formerly a professional cyclist. In addition to running Leadout, she teaches at Stanford University Graduate School of Business, where she earned her MBA, and says she learns from the next generation as much as she helps guide them.

How did working at Facebook (Meta) and on Wall Street prepare you to launch Leadout Capital?

The operating experience during a hyper growth phase at Facebook (Meta) was an invaluable experience. The team was building and creating a next-generation technology business; we were an organization and a product that defined a new market. I helped develop and utilize business tools and skills for operational efficiency, growth, and value creation. This experience, combined with my investing and educational background, helped to prepare me to create an investment platform to invest in technology-driven businesses. And, given the early stage of building at Facebook, I learned how to recognize the early signals of product-market fit in businesses. At Leadout the strongest signal is in the founders and the early team who can execute on their vision and build product into a viable business.

"Diversity wins in nature."

Did you start Leadout Capital purely because you thought most venture capital firms were missing some crucial piece?

Systems change is really hard and systems, especially at scale, can do harm. At the time I started Leadout, there was a lot of discussion happening about the imbalance of power between those with and those without systemic power across industries and in technology, in particular. This discussion started to drive some incremental change at the general partner (GP) level of decision-making investment teams. That said, the numbers still aren't great. As a new entrant, as Leadout, I wanted to push change faster and in the ways I wanted to see for the world.

What gaps does Leadout Capital fill in the industry?

We fill a gap with respect to who gets access to capital at the earliest stages. Software-driven solutions for **pain points** that exist in large-end markets that have not

Pain points: Pain points refer to roadblocks that obstruct the flow of a system or process, hindering optimal performance and customer satisfaction.

been addressed with modern solutions—whether it's **Cloud compute**–driven, or mobile computer-driven—those are the

> Cloud computing: Cloud computing is an integrated platform of remote, internet-based severs to collect, store, and analyze data.

solutions that we get excited about backing because the founders can identify real pain points in the community that is looking for a solution and are closing the gap in that problem space with software.

How do you define non-obvious groups, and how does focusing on them give you a business advantage and help the business world?

Generally speaking, talent is equally distributed, but access to opportunity is not. Power begets power, and the notion of pattern recognition tends to give those who come from systems of power more of the benefit of the doubt. As someone who is underrepresented in positions of power, in my view, you qualify as non-obvious. You can also be non-obvious in your approach to solving problems for markets and for customers, assuming you really understand a customer pain point. You can be someone who is not inherently diverse but who, through character, born of empathy, and a desire to have a positive impact on someone's life, can build an understanding of a customer need in a marketplace that enables you, with the talents that you've developed, to be non-obvious. In the case of Leadout, it is building great software-driven solutions to a problem you've identified.

What advantages does a diverse company bring to the table? Do you look for diversity internally as well as externally?

We look for diversity internally as well as externally at Leadout. In founding the firm, I never wanted to be an arbiter of what constitutes diversity. Diversity is a function of numbers. Diversity wins in nature. The way we look at diversity is both through objective metrics as a way of providing context to the broader ecosystem of investors and founders of the sector we play in, but also subjective. Do you have cognitive diversity on your team? Do you have intellectual diversity on your team? Is your lived experience diverse to that of your colleagues, especially at an early stage when important strategic decisions are being made? We look for founders who have traits of what has been defined as moral leadership: leading by modeling, defining a purpose for an organization, building a diverse team so as to unleash innovation and creativity and understand problems through an empathetic lens that we think will define the next generation of leaders, successful companies, and organizations. We value economic success, especially when there's a positive impact on society, whether it is in addressing our climate crisis or improving the way we detect and treat threats to our health and wellness.

How are the businesses you invest in making waves in their industries?

One example of a business making waves is a company we backed that was founded by two Black founders who are serving Black barbershops in urban settings, and helping them find, identify, book, and take payment from their clients, using mobile phones. The barber can manage their whole business on their phone and reach their community with technology, which helps them continue to serve their community so effectively, and the business has seen a real impact made on the lives of these barbershop owners and their clients.

How did your education prepare you to become a venture capitalist?

I went to Brown University, where I majored in history. I learned to study and analyze the past: understanding trends, causes, and consequences. I learned to think and write analytically, which is useful in evaluating and helping a company with its narrative, its market, and its strategy to win in that market. I earned my MBA at Stanford, which introduced me more in depth to the types of organizations and leadership management that can be characterized as early-stage and entrepreneurial. Stanford excels at that. Some of it was contextual, and some of it was certainly skills learning.

> *"Moral leadership and building diverse teams—defined in both subjective and objective ways—are vital to unlocking the value that the world needs from the next generation of founders."*

Is entrepreneurship nature or nurture?

Probably nurture. There is a movie about Alex Honnold, who climbed the face of El Capitan in Yosemite without ropes. Doctors proved that Honnold has a smaller amygdala (the part of the brain that senses fear). Maybe there's some of that with respect to who might be more biologically or neurologically a better entrepreneur, but I think a lot of it is nurture because entrepreneurship requires so much resilience and grit. I don't think you're born with grit. I think you develop grit. I don't think you're born with a passion for something; I think you hear a song or see a piece of art, or you are inspired by someone or a story that you learn and understand and want to use as inspiration.

In your career, do you value enjoying the work or good people more?

It's both. I'm inspired by people and work is inextricably linked to people. The stories we tell each other that inspire, and the way we communicate using all the senses, is innately human and creates this experience that can be elevated. As you develop your character and what is important to you, hopefully you hone the ability to keep great company with other human beings. I've always thought of success as a group thing. It's really hard to do big, big things alone. That starts with good people.

You were a presidential-appointed global ambassador for entrepreneurship. How is the United States doing in terms of entrepreneurship compared to other countries?

The United States is still second to none with respect to its ability to innovate and foster great entrepreneurs. We have a lot to improve in our systems, but I still think we're pretty good.

 Key Takeaways:

➔ Develop resilience and inspiration.
➔ Keep great company with other human beings.
➔ Push for the change you want to see in the world.
➔ Be empathetic.
➔ Create diverse environments.

NITIN PACHISIA (he/him)
Founding Partner, Unshackled Ventures

#ImmiGreat

On business: Find reliable sources of information, and don't take no for an answer.

On social: It's intended to be good, but everything that's intended to be good also has unintended bad outcomes. People have taken advantage of social media to spread misinformation, to create chaos and distrust.

Nitin Pachisia is the founding partner of Unshackled Ventures, a mission-driven venture capitalist firm that helps immigrants succeed faster as entrepreneurs. Nitin, an immigrant from India, says he has "found his true north" by helping others navigate their path in the world of US business. Once he landed a job in a large consulting firm, and then started his own business, he realized the problem that needed solving: as an immigrant, starting a business had far too many hurdles, including navigating a mountain of information (and misinformation). He is steadfast in his belief that immigrants create jobs—not take them, as many claim—and bring a fresh perspective to the world of business by never being satisfied by the status quo. Unshackled Ventures has invested in dozens of new companies that are solving ambitious problems and creating products—everything from plant-based protein and health care for seniors to logistics software, cell towers in space, data platforms, enterprise software, and consumer digital products. Nitin's unique take on the venture capitalist industry is allowing newcomers to seize the American Dream—which had previously been, indeed, just a dream—and level the playing field for immigrant entrepreneurs.

What made you want to start a business to help immigrant entrepreneurs?

I came to the United States in 2005, and by 2012, I was ready to start my first business, Trymbl (a "try before you buy" beauty products company). In the process I was told by many that I should not do it because I'm on an H-1B visa, which is the permit to be in the country and work. However, that visa did not allow me to start a business, which is when I started looking at venture capitalists who could help me do that, and I found that there weren't any. It is a widespread problem because we have about fifteen million immigrants who have come from all over the world to the United States to build their lives here, and, with their work, they're creating American jobs. That was my prompt to take on this problem that nobody else was taking on, and the form of that became venture capital, and the firm that we started is Unshackled Ventures.

How has your experience as an immigrant made you more knowledgeable in helping your clients?

When you go through an experience yourself, you understand the nitty-gritty and the nuances of what's involved in that journey. When I came to the United States as an employee of Deloitte, there were other people taking care of my visa, because Deloitte is a big firm. But when you're starting your own business, you're responsible for everything. In that process, I learned that for entrepreneurs to spend that much time taking care of immigration, which they are not experts at, is a time sink. It would be the equivalent of you asking LeBron James to play football. He would still be good at it because he's a great athlete, but he would not be what he is on a basketball court. To allow founders to do what they are great at, VCs provide specific resources that amplify a founder's time. The one resource that almost any immigrant who's on a visa needs when they're starting a company is for someone to take care of immigration, and if there is not someone, then the founders have to do it themselves. If they're doing it themselves and not building the business, that becomes a bottleneck because the entrepreneur's time gets distributed into other things. That's where we focus. That focus is also very well aligned with value creation because entrepreneurship is the path to long-term value creation, not just for the founders but the employees they hire, and its value creation for their customers whose problem they're solving.

What kind of person do you look for when you are investing in their company or idea?

We're looking for the immigrant ethos: hard work, not giving up, and grit and tenacity. The children of those immigrants see how hard their parents work and feel the duty to emulate them. They know that attitude and approach should not take a problem for granted. If there's a problem, we should try to solve it, not just whine about it. That ethos gets built into the children. At an early age, we see that a lot of the children of immigrants start taking an interest in business and especially technology and the interdisciplinary educational approach of science, technology, engineering, and mathematics (STEM).

What is your leadership style?

My partner and I are the two people who started this company. He grew up here in America; I grew up in India and then came to America. We have different analytical frameworks on how we analyze a situation, but whichever way we do it, we are working toward a common goal, and that goal is the guiding light, which helps us apply our leadership styles. We believe in enablement, by putting people in a position to succeed and providing the training and resources necessary to achieve their full potential. We lead by example. And we are continuous learners ourselves. We learn from our team members and founders around us.

What kind of people do you hire, and what characteristics do you look for?

We hire people who are smarter than us, and people who may disagree with us on certain things, because if we are only hiring for agreement, we're not bringing new viewpoints into the firm. We're learning from them, and they're learning from us.

Is there a false narrative out there about how immigrants can start a business?

The biggest challenge for immigrant entrepreneurs is not immigration. It's misinformation. Things get oversimplified, and immigration is not a topic that should get overly simplified. One of the biggest challenges that we must address ourselves to, and as a country, is providing better information when immigrant entrepreneurs or immigrants in general are seeking information on their pathways. Because of the misinformation, a lot of entrepreneurs end up not starting their entrepreneurial journey because they're confused and scared. They decide to wait in the employment of other companies until they receive their permanent residency or citizenship, which is a loss for the country because the sooner these entrepreneurs start businesses, the

> *"When I see a problem, I can see an opportunity in solving that problem, because I've learned from so many people along the way."*

sooner they'll begin to create jobs. Solving for that information flow for the entrepreneurs themselves is one piece of it. The broader part is the narrative that is being painted about immigrants. The story should always be that immigrants who are coming here within our policy framework are good for the economy.

Are there better policies for immigrant entrepreneurs elsewhere in the world?

Some people have advocated for a start-up visa, which is a visa that would allow foreigners to come to the United States and start companies, but that never got converted into policy. Other countries use start-up visas to attract entrepreneurs. Canada, Singapore, and Australia are great examples of countries that are using that approach to attract entrepreneurs. If that continues to happen, we will lose our edge as the most entrepreneur-friendly country. Should we have a policy that makes it easier for foreigners to start businesses? Sure. Are we going to have that? I don't know. But I do know that foreigners who come to the United States come with a dream, and if they want to pursue starting their own business as the way to accomplish that dream, there are ways for them to do it within our current policy framework. They just have to find the right answers and the right partners to work with, not taking no for an answer. Ultimately, entrepreneurs are not interested in loopholes or misusing the system. Entrepreneurs want to solve big problems. And when they do that, they create American jobs. It's a win-win for everybody. It's not an immigrant versus American issue. It is just an American issue.

How did growing up in another culture lead to your success in the United States?

It makes me look at problems not as given problems. As kids growing up here in the United States, there are certain things that you may just accept as how things always are. But then a kid your same age comes from somewhere else, and they look at that and say, "You know, it wasn't like this back home. Why is it like this here?" They ask questions that lead to root cause problems versus symptom problems. That's a core advantage that immigrants have: a different vantage point of looking at things that are just culturally accepted to be. That advantage allows us to come up with solutions that sometimes get overlooked because you just assume this is how it's always been. It is a true innovative vantage point advantage of immigrants. Our backgrounds enable us to analyze things in a slightly different way.

What was your greatest challenge in school? What is your greatest challenge today? Are they related in any way?

I was an introvert in school, and so my greatest challenge was not being perceived as cool, which may be my challenge today as well. I've had to adapt because when you start a business, you have to step out of your comfort zone. You have to go out and talk to people. You have to be extroverted. You have to be okay with rejection because a lot of people you're trying to sell a product to or sell a dream to are going to say no. I think that's opened me to be less of an introvert now. But sometimes I'm in a situation and I choose to stay quiet instead of speaking up and later I regret that I took that path.

Who was your first friend from another culture, and what did you learn from them?

One of my childhood friends' respect for his parents was something that I thought was just beyond normal, and it still stands out to me. I look for what I can learn from every person I come across. That's been one of the biggest reasons I was able to build up this repository. When I see a problem, I can see an opportunity in solving that problem, because I've learned from so many people along the way.

Our generation has grown up with modern conveniences such as smartphones. What lessons did you learn by approaching problems without using technology?

I have more of a contrarian view on that. I didn't have an internet connection until I was in college. It brings about a different way of approaching the world. You're getting information from books, newspapers, magazines, and the people you have direct access to. With the internet you're getting information from anyone anywhere in the world. It makes it faster and easier. I can't change the past, but I can change the future. Where it helps in the future is understanding that things are changing all the time.

What movie character are you most like?

Neo from *The Matrix*.

 Key Takeaways:

- ➔ Learn to adapt.
- ➔ Step out of your comfort zone.
- ➔ Don't believe everything you read.
- ➔ Think of problems as opportunities.
- ➔ Value different perspectives.

LARRY KRAMER (he/him)
President, William and Flora Hewlett Foundation

#Listening

On life: Make your voices heard.

On business: Help people in a sustainable way and don't exaggerate your importance or impact.

On social: There is incredible misinformation, disinformation, and stoking of division.

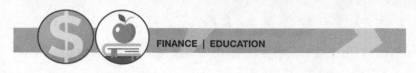

What role do foundations play in solving the world's problems? And which causes deserve the most attention? For **Larry Kramer**, president of the charitable William and Flora Hewlett Foundation, these questions are always top of mind. He believes the real power of foundations is not just in giving away billions of dollars, but in leveraging the public and private sectors to do more. After leading Stanford Law School for nearly a decade and helping teach some of the world's best and brightest students to solve the toughest of challenges, he is now doing the same at Hewlett, focusing on issues like climate change, education, and the arts, and trying to make the world a better place. He talks with us about his views on education, technology, and using your voice for positive change.

What role do foundations play in tackling huge societal challenges?

People in philanthropy often like to exaggerate our importance, as if foundations and philanthropy are singlehandedly bending the arc of history toward justice, but that's actually not remotely true. The scale of resources we have are minuscule compared to the scale of the problems. For instance, last year, the big foundations—organized philanthropy—gave away a total of about $90 billion globally. The K–12 budget for California schools alone is $120 billion a year. To make things happen in the world, government and the private sector are vastly more important. At the same time, even though our resources are tiny, philanthropy can play an important role in nudging those sectors to do things that they might not otherwise do. If we deploy our money smartly, we can find ways to move the private sector or move the public sector to address problems differently and more effectively than they would otherwise. It's all about leverage. That's the most we can do. And seen in that light, we do a reasonable amount of good. In terms of what we could do better, the more we work together, the more we get done. But cooperation and collaboration in philanthropy are still less robust than they should be because we're so decentralized.

What can individual philanthropists do?

Individual philanthropists, especially the new ones who bring a lot of new wealth into the field, could make a big difference. So far, most of them, even the ones who have pledged to spend, are not following through. They're just sitting on their wealth and letting it grow even more for reasons I don't understand. And when they do spend, they haven't yet shown much interest in learning how to do philanthropy well. I think they just assume it is easy and anyone can give away money well. So they do what they do without much sense of how much it actually contributes to solutions and no one tells them otherwise. It would be better if everybody were more willing to sit down and work together to figure out the best things we can do.

You were the dean of Stanford Law School. What did you look for in admitting students?

There was a baseline level of academic success, reflected in grades and test scores. Those screens still left a pool of potential students vastly larger than the number we could admit, even discounting for the fact that not everyone we admit chooses to come. Within that large pool, we kept an eye on diversity—not just racial and gender and ethnic diversity, but also diversity of interests and background experiences and geography, and so on. But we also looked for people who showed two things: originality and passion. So we looked at what people did—which is why it's a good idea to take some time off after college before applying to law or graduate school. We looked for people who had some experience in life. What did that tell us about them? What kind of people were they? We were looking for genuine interests and passions, as opposed to people who do things because they thought that's what we wanted to see them do. You can usually spot people who are building their résumé because they want achievements, not because they're passionate about doing the thing that produces the achievements. We wanted people who seemed genuine. We also looked for people who showed some capacity for leadership and demonstrated that they were capable of thinking for themselves.

What did it take to thrive in an environment like Stanford?

Work hard and learn from mistakes. Don't have a thin skin, because law school is very much about arguing with people and batting around ideas. Pursue ideas and the chance to develop your skills so you can make a bigger difference in the world outside the academy when you get there.

What are the most important skills we need to develop as we start to enter the workforce?

The ability to listen to people with whom you disagree fundamentally and hear and understand how something that seems so obviously wrong to you can seem reasonable and right to them. You need to get past dismissing views because of who someone is. You need to understand that it's not that they know you are right but have some bad motive for pretending otherwise. That doesn't require changing your mind or giving up anything you regard as important. But it's necessary if you want to live in a society as complex as ours and essential if you want that society to remain a democracy.

We believe that climate change is the most pressing issue of our time, so that it renders many other causes moot. We were happy to learn that you share that belief. How do you educate young people on this topic?

You can't educate people who aren't interested in learning. I don't think it's a lack of information. The question is, how do you engage people who are either apathetic or only thinking about the next week to recognize that there's a bigger, long-term problem? That's what teachers and parents are for. It is their responsibility to make sure their kids see it. When it comes to climate, though, the opposite is happening. That is, we see young people who actually do know and understand what's going on, who care about their futures, trying to educate their parents, who seem bizarrely comfortable not doing anything about this. I don't think educating young people is our problem. Acting to protect their futures is our problem.

Then how can you educate everyone who needs to act on climate?

It's a global problem that's different in different parts of the world, which means what people need to do is different. In the United States, first, we need everybody to vote—and I mean especially young people, whose turnout remains low. Then we need them to vote against people who want to deny or minimize the climate problem. Not because it's bigger than every problem but because it is every other problem. Whatever you care about will be made worse by the cascading effects of global warming. So people in this country need to vote, need to make their voices heard, collectively. Your voice matters if you express it. And not just through voting. Make your voice heard about the need to do something on climate in your schools and in whatever other organizations you are part of. And especially teach your parents to care about it and make them realize what their indifference will do to you and your children.

Racial justice is a central topic of discussion in society today. Many companies are making changes to achieve greater diversity. What are you doing to help?

Achieving diversity is the easy part, though you might not know that from where things are. We began making concerted efforts to make the foundation more diverse a decade ago, and we've succeeded in that respect. But it's not enough just to add diverse voices. You need also to ensure that those voices are able to speak and are heard (which is not the same thing). You need to recognize all the subtle and non-obvious ways in which structures and practices and customs exist that get in the way and make concerted efforts to dismantle them. But you also need to do that in a way that brings everyone along, including the people who are skeptical. And you need buy-in and active involvement from everyone in the organization—it needs to be something everyone feels responsible for addressing, as opposed to something they look for someone else to address, for someone else to tell them what to do. We've been working on all those things. And as we change internally, our work has changed with it—but in a way that feels natural and right, as opposed to forced or explicitly reparative. As such, I hope and believe the changes will be more enduring.

What is the most important lesson everyone should learn from this moment in history?

I think everyone needs to acknowledge that there really are forms of discrimination and effects of discrimination that run through our whole society. That is, to some extent, always true everywhere. No complex society has a single culture. There is, rather, always a dominant culture and subordinate cultures, and dominant cultures take an unfair share of whatever society offers as well as inherently pressuring subordinate cultures to conform. In the United States, though, there is a unique history when it comes to race. That unique history—a product of slavery and the entirely inadequate way we dealt with its consequences—creates a different kind of problem that requires a different kind of response. People need to face up to this. To say that if African Americans are doing less well, it has nothing to do with racism is crazy. It has everything to do with racism, with racism that doesn't require conscious effort because it's so thoroughly institutionalized. Recognizing that we have to address this is important lesson number one. Important lesson number two, though, is that we need to do this in ways that are enduring. That means approaching change pragmatically, recognizing that people still need to be persuaded, and that they have their own problems that cannot be ignored—not if you want their support. As strange as this sounds, just being right is seldom enough. That's something you learn fast in any leadership position. You need to act in ways that build support and consensus. No loaf really isn't better than a half. It's more important to make progress and get something done in a way that's lasting.

What lessons did you learn by approaching problems without technology?

I think the benefits of your generation's technology are mixed at best. It's really fun to have all that information instantly at hand and to be able to answer any question, though it's taken a lot of the fun out of arguing. We used to argue for hours about things, silly and unimportant things (like who wrote what song), and we would just have fun doing it. Now there's no point in arguing. You just look it up on Google, and you get your answer right away. And, of course, as we all now know, these devices are addictive. That said, there's nothing really all that new here. There are always new technologies, and people are people. People tend to shape technology as much or more than the reverse. At the end of the day, we're all still people. We all figure out our problems and find our answers to them with our brains, regardless of what kind of technology we have enabling us.

What movie, TV, or literary character are you most like?

I don't know. I can tell you who I'd like to be like: Oliver Queen from *Arrow*, in the later seasons. Atticus Finch from *To Kill a Mockingbird*, Darcy from *Pride and Prejudice*, Rick Blaine from *Casablanca*, or Hermione Granger.

 # Key Takeaways:

- ➔ Don't do things just for your résumé.
- ➔ Listen to people you disagree with.
- ➔ Be genuine.
- ➔ Develop a thick skin.
- ➔ Vote (when you are old enough).

The Strategist

ANNABEL CHANG (she/her)

Head of State Policy and Government Relations, Waymo

#MakeItHappen

On life: Speak up on behalf of people who might not be in the room or at the table.

On business: Ask the right questions and think of yourself as a leader.

On social: We have a responsibility to understand the information we have access to, and to ask questions, look at the sources, and be thoughtful about it.

On college: Your friends and classmates from college or university will become one of your lifelong networks and have an impact beyond the few short years when you attend.

Annabel Chang has spent the last decade at the intersection of innovation and transportation. As the head of state policy and government relations at Waymo, she is helping lead the world into the era of self-driving cars. She was one of the leading advocates for ride-sharing before it even existed, and she navigated Lyft through its early days of government regulation. She then became the top California executive for Alaska Airlines and was brought in to ensure its smooth acquisition of Virgin America, right before COVID-19 grounded the airline industry and handed her a whole new host of responsibilities. She has used her experience as a prosecutor and Capitol Hill staffer in all of her transportation industry jobs and talks to us about how her training in debate club and Model UN gave her a foundation for public speaking and critical thinking that helped her in college and beyond. We also talk to her about the importance of reputation and building confidence as the youngest person—and/or only woman—in the room. Annabel believes that frequent travel and understanding other cultures are critical business skills and explains that growing up in an immigrant family has given her a competitive advantage in life, and helped her grow into a compassionate, empathetic leader.

People have talked about self-driving cars for a long time, but you are actually at the vanguard of the industry. What is the most exciting thing you are working on?

Autonomous driving technology is already here! You can already hail a fully autonomous ride as a member of the public on the

> *"Traveling and experiencing new places and new cultures and going there with an open mind and a sense of curiosity is one of the most critical skills of any business leader, especially if you have a business that you imagined to be all over the world."*

Waymo app in Chandler, Arizona, and if you're one of our beta testers, you can catch fully autonomous rides in San Francisco and Phoenix. And when I say fully autonomous, it means there is no one at all in the front row. You can be sitting in the back seat and relaxing in your chauffeured ride. The first time I rode with a Waymo it was a thrilling and surreal experience, and I realized that this technology is going to change the world as we know it in the near future.

As head of state policy and government relations at Waymo, what is your main focus?

I oversee our legislative, political, and government relations strategy for all fifty states in the United States. Since self-driving cars are a new and little-known technology, most states are grappling with creating brand-new and untested regulatory frameworks for the deployment of this technology. In response, our state policy team works closely with policymakers and regulators to help educate and inform these regulations, which we believe may one day set the foundation for autonomous vehicle regulations around the world.

What lessons have you learned working in the travel industry?

I think travel is one of the most important opportunities that anyone can have—particularly if you can travel abroad—to see another culture, another lifestyle, a totally different experience, and really get a sense of the common humanity of us all, but also how different we can be. How is a government structured? How is media structured? How is an economy structured? In some countries, for example, women can't drive and can't vote. How does that impact their economy? In some places, like Cuba, mega US corporations aren't allowed to operate, so most of the businesses you will see are small businesses, but in the Philippines, you see KFC. Traveling and experiencing new places and new cultures and going there with an open mind and a sense of curiosity is one of the most critical skills of any business leader, especially if you have a business that you imagined to be all over the world. Whether you become a Google or an Apple or a Netflix, you have to have a global view and global understanding.

What challenges did you face because of COVID-19, and how did you innovate to overcome these barriers?

COVID-19 devastated the airline industry. Many airlines have gone under and haven't been able to survive. Airlines are unique because they connect people and supplies all over the country. For example, Alaska Airlines connects some of the most rural communities in northern Alaska. Those people who are living in northern Alaska would not be able to get supplies like toilet paper or milk without Alaska Airlines. They provide a critical "essential service" to these communities, and because the government recognized that they played this essential service, they provided this loan and grants. They have to really reduce the size of the airline, lay people off, and reduce the number of planes, but also look for creative ways to get people to feel comfortable flying again.

What lessons did you learn in law or politics that would apply to your current career?

Reputation really matters. Establishing a good reputation early on, and really following through in how you treat people, how you treat your teammates, how you treat the people below you and above you. That is something you learn in politics because in politics, everything is personal. Your reputation is what people know you by. It is the same thing in law. You establish your reputation as a good ethical attorney who works hard and represents the interests of your client, or you're a good and fair judge. I think those elements are all super critical. I would say the number one lesson from both law and politics is to guard your reputation and make sure that you cultivate it, and that you recognize that it is something to be built. You want to establish a reputation of integrity and hard work, and if possible, kindness.

How has your law degree helped you in life?

The law degree has transformed the way that I think about, view, and perceive the world. Law trains you to be highly analytical and ask the right questions; it also equips you with the tools to navigate very complex systems like the justice system. I don't think it's a coincidence that many of our former US presidents or current governors and US senators are lawyers. It teaches you high-level communication and high-level analytical thinking. On the downside, it doesn't teach you entrepreneurship, for example, or resourcefulness, necessarily, or an understanding of how to run a business.

What lessons such as empathy or determination have you learned from being brought up in an immigrant family that

have been invaluable to you in your lifetime? Have these traits given you a competitive advantage?

I was born in the West, but I grew up at home speaking Taiwanese and went to Chinese school as a young kid, and the community that I grew up in was very heavily immigrant. But when I went to Washington, DC, it was not diverse. Capitol Hill is very homogenous, and you very rarely saw women or people of color as elected officials. It was an eye-opening experience for me. Growing up in an immigrant family, I learned to be empathetic. If I'm in a meeting, and see that three or four people consistently aren't talking, part of my responsibility as a leader is to help bring those perspectives in. I understand that the room can be very intimidating. It can be very scary to be in a room where no one looks like you, and you don't feel like you have the right to speak, but there's a reason you were invited. I also recognize that I'm often a younger Asian female in the room, and maybe there's no one else that looks like me. Part of my job is to speak up on behalf of people who look like me or may have my same interests. Maybe it's millennial. Maybe it's California. Maybe it's being a woman. Maybe it's being a mother. I have an obligation to speak up. Thanks for asking that question; I've never heard it framed that way, and I think it is a benefit.

How did politics play a role in your education and childhood?

My family fled Taiwan to go to Singapore when they were young because they thought that there was going to be a communist takeover of Taiwan, so politics and government have a profound impact on my family's background. I think a core value that has lasted is to be an active and engaged citizen, that you should be informed about what's happening not only in the United States, but around the world, especially if you are going to be a business leader who has factories, offices, or customers all around the world. The second is that people fought and died for the right to vote. There are women around the world who do not have the right to vote. We need to take advantage of that and make sure to vote. If you haven't worked on a campaign, or haven't volunteered to work on a campaign, I strongly encourage it because it's an incredible insight into the power of being a citizen.

Do you think our society is too reliant on technology?

I'm a firm believer that technology has transformed the world for the better, and it will continue to transform the way we live. I believe in self-driving cars. I was a prosecutor before, so I actually prosecuted a lot of people who were drunk driving and put other people at risk by making a stupid decision, such as having a couple of beers and then getting behind the wheel. Self-driving cars could take away that harm, that human behavior that puts others at risk.

 Key Takeaways:

- ➔ Be a global citizen.
- ➔ Work on a political campaign.
- ➔ Establish a good reputation.
- ➔ Be kind to everyone.
- ➔ Speak with conviction.

KEN STERN (he/him)

Founder and CEO, Palisades Media Ventures; former CEO, NPR

#BigIdeas

On life: Things will often look better after you take a little bit of time away.

On business: Stay nimble.

On social: There is value, but I think by far it's been terribly destructive of public conversation. It has divided us enormously as a people.

Ken Stern once ran one of the largest twenty-four-hour news stations in the world, but he doesn't believe in working around the clock. The former CEO of NPR values balance in all things: family, media, and politics. He gives us the inside scoop on today's news industry and underscores the importance of consuming a wide variety of news sources. He believes our generation is growing up with a polarizing and politicized view of the media that is very different from the media landscape he grew up with—and he doesn't think that's a good thing. We learn his strong opinions about social media and introduce him to Instagram. After leaving NPR, Ken started his own media company and is using his news-sleuthing skills on a new endeavor—discovering what it means to age. As CEO of the Longevity Project, Ken and his partners at the Stanford Center on Longevity are studying the implications of longer life spans for health care, the economy, and caregiving. His natural curiosity has also led him to write several books. As a lifelong Democrat, he wanted to better understand the Republican party and traveled the country talking to ordinary people about their beliefs. The result was *Republican Like Me,* a book that proves people are more alike than the media or political parties might have you believe.

At a time when the news is so polarized, where do you get your news?

I'm a news consumer. I go to NPR, the *New York Times,* the *Washington Post,* CNN. I also get my information from places that

I think are less interested in being "objective" and having more point-of-view journalism. On the left, that might be places like the *Atlantic* or *Vox* or *Slate.* On the right, I spend time with the *National Review, Daily Wire,* and *Daily Signal.* I try to get a lot of different perspectives on what's going on in the world.

Do you find that most news radio stations consist of more opinions or facts?

News on radio falls into three categories, one of which is NPR, sort of a category itself, which is mainstream, traditional reporting. You can challenge it—and I have from time to time—but they try hard to be objective. Then there is local news you can use, traffic and weather on the eights, places like that. That's also trying very hard to be straightforward and objective. Then there's conservative talk, which is probably the most listened-to form of news on the radio. That is very opinionated. By and large, they'll tell you that they are opinionated.

How can political beliefs and biases leak into reporting and news?

Faith in the media has been going down for about forty straight years, in part because people keep getting told the media is full of fake news. It's also because people don't think they're being represented in the news. News organizations would do better to diversify their perspectives of people and have people with different political views involved.

> *"Part of the challenge in life is trying to embrace and learn the things that don't come easy for you."*

You can do all the truthful reporting you want, but even how you choose a story or what the story is that you are covering reflects political biases. It's a very hard thing and part of why we're such a divided country.

Do you think our generation will be more or less skeptical of the media as we get older?

Gen Z is being raised in two ways that I fundamentally disagree with, one of which is to be inherently distrustful of the media, and second is to think of the media as being right or wrong. Being right or wrong is essentially being whether they reflect my views or not. I think of the media as being a tool of the political process, or the political parties. That's where the media is definitely going, and Gen Z will likely take it to the next step. I am fairly bleak on the topic.

What is the most important thing you have accomplished in the last year?

I now have my own company. I had two business partners who decided to divest, so I bought them out. We launched the company as my own and put it on a new path with some risk that it wouldn't work, but it's worked pretty well. That's a big, exciting change.

What is a business problem right now that you're trying to tackle?

My company does a lot of events, and events were difficult during COVID-19. Developing thought-leadership ideas and public conversations in the absence of that has been hard, but we've been doing things virtually that we've done in person before. That's been actually kind of fun.

Who is your biggest mentor, and what did they teach you?

The fellow who I spent the most time working with and learning about leadership was a guy named Kevin Klose. He was my boss at a couple different places, but ultimately at NPR, where I succeeded him. I learned lessons about the role of leadership, which was not necessarily making the right decision, but was trying to inspire others to make the right decision. He was always focused on inspiring and empowering others rather than on the details of decision-making.

What is one habit that you wish you could break?

I often regret getting frustrated with others who maybe have less experience than I do and getting frustrated with their work rather than asking how I can help them do better. That's a challenge I wrestle with a lot.

What was your greatest challenge in school, and what is your greatest challenge today?

I was very good at some things and less good at others. In my case, that was science. Part of the challenge in life is trying to embrace and learn the things that don't come easy for you. The work we do, some of it comes very naturally and easily. The challenge is trying to figure out what you're less good at and get better at it, either by doing it yourself or finding people to be partners. The hardest thing in business is finding good people. The company is only as good as people who work for it. Figuring out who those people are and convincing them to come work for you and keeping them there is super hard and super important.

What is one thing that exists today that you never would have imagined when you were a kid?

So much. So much good and bad. The obvious answer and the true answer is the availability of instant information. The idea that you have a question that you can have answered instantly is an idea that would have been foreign to me when I was a kid. I remember you had encyclopedias to find out something. If it was there, you were lucky to find the answer, and if you didn't, you were basically out of luck. The idea that you have instant access to the collective wisdom of the entire world is astonishing.

What Instagram filter would you use to motivate your employees?

I have no idea what an Instagram filter is.

It's like a camera filter that may change your face, add ears or whatever, can be anything you want. It's a selfie filter.

A good leader is inspiring. I'm sort of tempted to think of horns like the devil to scare people, but that's not the right frame for a leader. What would make me look inspiring? I might want to get one of them.

Key Takeaways:

➔ Learn the things that don't come naturally.

➔ Be nice to your friends.

➔ Listen to others.

➔ Respect other viewpoints.

➔ Inspire others to make good decisions.

ANDREA CLARKE (she/her)
Founder and CEO, FutureFitCo

#FutureFit

On life: If you're committed to deliberate learning, you can achieve anything, even in high-pressure situations.

On business: Originality is the last competitive advantage that we really have.

On social: Social media has had a seismic impact on the way society functions, but like anything, it needs regulation.

On college: I value street smarts over book smarts and worked around a system that often stifled innovation and failed to reward originality. School is not for everyone, but as long as business values it as a credential, we should be part of it.

Andrea Clarke is the founder of FutureFitCo, a company devoted to preparing business leaders to stay relevant in a rapidly evolving world. In training hundreds of CEOs each year, she has found that the most successful leaders are willing to listen to others' opinions and never assume they are right. She wrote a book fittingly called *Future Fit: How to Stay Relevant and Competitive in the Future of Work,* in which she outlines the eight human skills that she says everyone should invest in for work, school, and everyday life: personal brand, adaptability, communication, networking, creativity, problem-solving, leadership, and lifelong learning. Andrea talks to us about how she applied her theory to her own career in moving from journalism to entrepreneur and coach, street smarts versus book smarts, the timeless nature of her business model, and her plans for helping our generation become future fit.

How did you first learn the lessons you teach at FutureFitCo?

I learned everything by trial and error. I was not a good student at school or at college; I repeatedly failed subjects because I was so anxious and enthusiastic about getting into the real world, where I could demonstrate my street smarts. Learning on the job for me, particularly as a TV reporter, was far more important than learning journalism in the classroom. Even though I was quite young, probably seventeen, I was at college. What I found was that I failed journalism subjects at college, but as soon as I got into a newsroom, where I could get my hands on what was really happening, I picked up lessons quickly, in great part because of two mentors who taught me the ropes, like how to write a high-impact script and how to communicate on camera. I felt like the best version of myself when I got into a newsroom because I could actually get into the work, deliver, and have an impact as a professional. I had great mentors that helped me every step of the way. I believe that we all need mentors. We don't know what best practice looks like until we have someone in front of us showing us what it is. We can interpret that in our own way and deliver it in a way that's authentic to who we are.

How can adaptability and relevance, two lessons you teach, be useful to young people?

Adaptability is a key trait that is useful regardless of where we are in life, and regardless of how old we are. An ability to adapt is really about a flexible mindset and a growth mindset. We cannot adapt to change if we don't see it coming, and when we see it coming, we have to have the courage to take whatever action is required to stay relevant, whether that's personally or for work. Let me give you an example. In 2008, I was a reporter and producer for the Al Jazeera English network. I was walking to work, and for the first time in my career, I did not pick up a newspaper. I was reading the front page of the *New York Times* on my phone. In that moment, I realized that my own consumer habits were changing. I was in the business of creating content for news, but here I was, as a consumer, not prepared to pay for it. That very same day, I decided to leave journalism because I could see that the business model of news was failing right in front of me. I made a decision at the time that was very unpopular with my friends and family, but I knew that if I'd stayed in that job, I would probably have lost that job in three to five years, and I would be three to five years behind in developing a different skill set that was going to keep me future fit in my own career.

> "We need Gen Z more than we need any other generation. You're strong, you're opinionated, you connect so easily with communities around the world. That's a force for real change."

Since part of adapting is always looking forward, what do you predict will hold relevance in the coming years?

When economic historians talk about the impact of technology and the impact of disruption, they always land on the same point: that it's not the technology or the disruption that drives social change and that drives our behavior; it's very simply the way we respond to it. My advice when it comes to staying relevant is all about developing our own skills and upgrading our own real skills and soft skills because they will land differently in new environments. Staying relevant is about staying committed to active learning and staying committed to upgrading our own skill set, mindset, and behaviors.

Considering our generation is more likely to support businesses with similar views to ours, how is supporting social causes important for adaptability?

I think it's critical that businesses recognize the shared purpose between what they deliver and the consumers that they deliver for. That shared purpose is becoming much more relevant now. I think it's important that businesses demonstrate they are in step with what's happening socially, and in step with the reform that has been called for by different groups. I'm a small business, and I

> *"You only have blue sky in front of you as far as what you want to do with your lives, careers, and the change that you want to see happen in the world."*

am taking this opportunity now to consider how I can contribute to the future-fit education of Gen Z, and the generations that are going to follow. I think it will look like a pro bono program for younger generations to understand and develop the soft skills that are needed to be a continuous success in the workplace. That's an idea that's been percolating with me.

If you were to predict, how many of the eight skills you discuss in your book will be relevant when we reach our thirties and forties?

All of them. These are skills that have helped many generations transition through major change. I think these skills will stand firm as required skills for your generation as you get into the workplace, into your mid-career, and into senior leadership positions, because these are the skills that help us stay connected and networked. They are the theory of mind skills, the relational skills, because we all want to work with people that we like and respect. That means getting along with people is really important. Communication, reputation capital, understanding your brand, networking, creativity, being an adaptive leader—these are all things that will have real longevity throughout your careers.

You worked in journalism before coming to your current work. Were the lessons you learned in journalism helpful when you started FutureFitCo, or did they require you to remold your mindset to fit your new sector?

Personally, there could have been no greater grounding to start a business than working in journalism, because I was required to move fast, get along with people well, communicate a shared purpose with my news crew, be creative in finding solutions, and work as part of a high-performance team, often remotely. When I started creating a business, all of those factors were critical, and I was able to apply all of those skills to new content, new people, and a new industry.

What are the biggest mistakes CEOs make, and what areas do they usually excel in?

That ability to communicate directly with their audience. If we want to be truly connected to our community, our constituents, or our clients, we are obligated to communicate actively and frequently to our audience. Otherwise, how are we going to expect people to trust us if something goes wrong? I think the greatest opportunity that lies in front of leadership is that ability to connect, and that means investing more in communication skills, and being bolder in the way we want to communicate with our customers.

Do you value work you enjoy or good people more?

I feel like there's nothing more important than being part of a high-performance team and being surrounded by people who really bring out the best in you. I can do any kind of work, but I want to be able to work with people who challenge me, inspire me, educate me, and help me see a different side of the story.

How do you define your personal brand?

"What is the conversation I want to start in my career?" This is the question I asked myself before I started my business. The conversation I wanted to start was about the skills that will keep you engaged, employed, and contributing to the world. I wanted to talk about the mindset, skill set, and behaviors that will keep us all living a life that role models both confidence and competence to those around us.

What is the most important lesson you have learned in your lifetime or career?

Adaptability and the ability to not just forecast change coming your way, but actively engage with it and respond to it is the greatest lesson that I've learned. Adaptability is the standout lesson, and being committed to being adaptable. That doesn't come naturally to a lot of people, but that is what's going to keep us relevant, current, and competitive in the marketplace.

What was the best piece of advice you got from your parents growing up?

My mother said to me one day on the way to school, "Why be the passenger when you can be the pilot?" That stuck with me. There is nothing stopping you from going after what you want to achieve.

What personality trait do you value most in a friend and employee?

It's really important to have people around you that don't agree with you all the time. Otherwise, how can we be exposed to different ideas or go down a path of finding different solutions? We all make decisions with our own bias in mind, not even knowing that we're biased. People confirm our bias all the time, but what we need around us are people that respectfully disagree with us.

What about for yourself?

I value the ability to really question certain belief systems. It's important that you're always anchored in your values because that will help you make decisions faster and give order to chaos around you. But what's important is being constantly aware that sometimes our behaviors and mindsets are out of date. It's a wonderful thing to rethink problems and to put a different lens over ideas that we've had for a long time.

What literary character helped shape your leadership style?

Kermit the Frog! Kermie found his tribe and always led through communicating a shared purpose. He always managed to get so many unruly characters to work together.

 Key Takeaways:

- ➡ Rethink problems applying a different lens.
- ➡ Surround yourself with people who challenge and inspire you.
- ➡ Learn communication skills.
- ➡ Adopt a growth mindset.
- ➡ Chase your ideas.

DAN FRANK (he/him)
Former CEO, Three Wire Systems, LLC

#MilitaryVeterans

On business: Invest every penny of your profits that you don't need for yourself back into your business.

On social: It is not black and white, but I don't like what I see in society with social media. I don't think it is healthy. I'm concerned that we've created a society that looks down and misses other things in the world.

What can the navy teach you about entrepreneurship? For **Dan Frank**, a naval aviator turned businessman, spending his early career in the military instilled certain habits and characteristics that he still carries: teamwork, accountability, and responsibility. However, it took running his own business for Dan to truly understand what it takes to be a leader and full-fledged entrepreneur. After working in the technology sector for more than a decade, he took a gamble on a mental health-care start-up and has now come full circle as the CEO of Three Wire Systems, which uses technology in service of veterans' health.

You were once in the navy, but now you are an entrepreneur. What crucial lessons or skills had you learned in the navy that would apply to business?

I went to college and graduated. I went into the navy as an officer and flew airplanes, so I was an aviator, and I did that for eight years. The military teaches many things, such as leadership, accountability, responsibility, and motivation. Some of these key buzzwords that you hear about, you get to put into practice. Additionally, you are with people from all walks of life. You get to meet people from all over the United States and work with them in a very intense environment. You work with people all over the country with different backgrounds, but you are oriented in a similar mindset. That's good, but it is also not so good

> *"You've got to bring your own motivation to the game."*

because sometimes you get a bit too homogeneous in your thinking, and you don't have new ideas brought up by people who aren't interested in the military and, of course, didn't join the military. There are pros and cons, but overall, the experience of being in the military and having this intense training, work, and tempo created an excellent base for me to jump into the business world.

It seems like not as many kids in this generation are enlisting in the military. Do you think this is a mistake?

It is a lack of awareness about what the military can offer. We have about 380 million citizens in America. Less than 1 percent of American citizens serve in the military. We have something called the soldier citizen divide. Since so few serve, it is hard for the general population to understand what the whole military is about. If you are not around people who can be role models, then many young people that seem to go into the military today are kids that don't have any other opportunities. As a veteran, I would love to see more people interested in the military and understanding what it is all about, but I do understand the reasons why they don't. There are stereotypical movies about what the military is about, the yelling, the screaming, the killing. That is not for everybody.

How can schools integrate business skills and other useful knowledge into regular classes like math and science?

My eldest son did a personal finance course during his last year of high school, and learned about bank accounts, mortgages, and things like that, which was terrific. From what I can tell, our public schools, they do a crappy job of building business skills, self-reliance skills, personal finance skills, and financial acumen skills. Ultimately, they could do better at incorporating it.

> *"The experience of being in the military and having this intense training, work, and tempo created an excellent base for me to jump into the business world."*

Is entrepreneurship nature or nurture?

I don't think you can teach entrepreneurship. You can expose people to the concept, but I don't think you can teach it. After the military, when I was working for software companies, I thought I understood business. It wasn't until I started my own business that I realized I didn't know anything. Over time, through trial and error, I got the experience for everything from bank loans to tax returns, accounting systems, human resource regulations, sales, and marketing.

How would you advise our generation to use their profits from starting a small business?

My advice is to take every penny of your profit that you don't need for yourself and invest it back in the business. That's going to be your catalyst, your driver to hopefully have a better return over time in the stock market. You are building your wealth with your equity in your business, and the more money that you can keep in the business to grow it, the better.

What Instagram filter would you use to motivate your employees?

I wore a Chewbacca mask to a meeting the other day. I would probably do something like that.

What do you do to deal with stress?

I have moved twenty or twenty-five times over my career. I have moved internationally, and I have been at sea for months at a time. I work out, usually at the same time every day. I watch what I eat. I go to bed at the same time and get up at the same time. I am into routines and discipline. I find that by doing those types of things, I can accomplish more, and I feel good because I know what I'm going to do and when I'm going to do it.

 Key Takeaways:

→ Learn basic finance skills.
→ Balance innovation with market demand.
→ Invest back into your business.
→ Be disciplined.
→ Be accountable.

SEAN PENG (he/him)
CEO, Taishan Sports

#Lifestyle

On life: Never be arrogant.

On business: Don't be satisfied with the status quo.

On social: Social media does a great job of targeting the right content for you, but if you're not selective, you get distracted trying to read everything.

On college: It helps give you the edge and the ability to think outside the box. No matter what kind of college you go to, you have to think outside the box. Break through the ceiling; then you can best utilize what college has to offer.

As a shy child growing up in rural Inner Mongolia, **Sean Peng** never imagined he would one day lead the top sports equipment manufacturer in the world. But with tough competition and limited job opportunities in China, he was determined to create a different path for himself and came to America twenty years ago in search of the American Dream. Sean learned the value of hard work from his father, a farmer turned bank manager, and lives by the philosophy that you can learn something from everyone. A strong believer in networking, he sought the advice of the best minds in his industry, built connections, and turned himself into the definition of a self-made entrepreneur. From his college entrance exams to building his career from the ground up, we learn about the tenacious drive behind Sean's journey to success.

What are the top five skills needed to be a successful entrepreneur?

The very first one is the curiosity to learn. I think that's very important for all entrepreneurs, no matter your age. The second one is learning ability, the third one is execution, the fourth one is leadership, and the fifth one is the ability to resolve challenges.

Do you think you had any of these at a young age, or were they developed over time?

Some of them I did have at a young age, but some of them I didn't. I was a very good student. I was always curious, asking all kinds of questions, trying to learn. I was the president of the student board when I was in high school. I credit much of my success today to back then. Running for leadership positions helped me strengthen my-

> *"It's crucial for a young entrepreneur to be very mindful that you could learn anything from every person that you meet."*

self with experience and the ability to resolve challenges.

Could you share some tips about how to overcome the language and cultural barriers to be an effective leader?

To learn a second language, you must have genuine interest in learning the other culture as well. If you're only interested in learning the language, it can be boring. When I was young, I volunteered to be an interpreter working to learn English. I learned a lot more about the United States than I could learn on my own. In the process of doing it, I met people with different perspectives of the world, and that inspired me.

Many students from other countries come to America to seek a better education and future. What inspired you to come to the United States?

I came to the United States more than twenty years ago. Back then, the biggest difference between China and the United States was the political system. The path to success in China was very limited due to job mobility, job opportunities, the political system, a very conservative culture, and a barrier to entry. China has over a billion people. Every single job has thousands of people competing for the same position. You feel like you need to be a genius to advance in society. At a young age, I felt it was a little depressing. Even though I wanted to learn, I didn't have a place to learn like in the United States, where you can go to college. In China, for a decent college, you have to go through an extremely difficult college entrance exam. America sounded like heaven.

Entrepreneurship can be a 24/7 job. What is your philosophy on making the work manageable?

For young entrepreneurs, I would suggest asking yourself an essential question: "What kind of entrepreneur do you want to become?" There are two kinds. The first kind is you're going to profit 100 percent in your own pocket. You don't share, and you become a slave to your business because you do everything yourself. That's the extreme case, but there are many people like this. They try to pocket everything, and they have a hard time growing their business. The second type is you are willing to share your profit, and you are eager to spend time to develop your team and build your staff so they can in turn be successful and grow your business. If that's the case, then you can increase the market, and you can liberate yourself from a lot of the tasks of the business. Your business can become bigger quickly. I chose the second one.

Who do you turn to for advice?

The first thing is you always want to establish a relationship with the best minds in the field. You're not going to have all the connections that you need, so reach out. People are very receptive if you have a good idea. When I was work-

"You have to brainstorm, come up with your plan, finalize your strategy, and then execute it. If you have the right planning strategy, then you will not be far from success. If you don't, and you occupy yourself with just doing, that's pretty dangerous."

ing in San Francisco on my fashion, e-commerce business, I convinced a lot of people to become my advisers, like Simon Ungless, executive director at Academy of Art University School of Fashion in San Francisco. He contributed the whole graduate class to my project. Twenty-five designers were working for one semester for our company. The second thing is, in daily life, never be arrogant. It's crucial for a young entrepreneur to be very mindful that you could learn anything from every person that you meet. If you go on a fishing trip, the fishing captain might look like he only knows about fishing, but you might find that he knows Wall Street, or Bitcoin, or the financial world, or how to protect yourself in the pandemic. I will always have a good conversation with people that I meet.

What types of people do you like to hire?

I think the person needs to have two essential traits. One is the ability to have consideration for others, and the other is to be driven. If a person is considerate, whatever task they're going to do, they're going to think about the team as well. They are going to think from your perspective and respect your situation and environment. That's a good team player. The other thing is being driven. You can teach things to anyone, but only those people who are driven can learn and develop. If they are driven, it's much easier for you to hire and train them.

How did your educational environment affect your personal development as a business leader?

I failed the college entrance exam, and I ended up going into a less desirable university. It was one of the worst-ranked colleges in

China. As a result, I also ended up spending less time than average studying. I thought I was hitting rock bottom, but I realized I could graduate in three years, and go to work and start making money, so I finished college a year earlier. Back then, I didn't realize the value of college, and I also didn't know the value of a good education. When I started working and attending business meetings, I met people from all over the country and realized they were all smarter than me! They had more knowledge. When you think that college is not essential, and have thoughts of skipping college, you better reconsider as you might regret it. College prepares you for life. There is a small percentage of people like Steve Jobs, but he did not get where he was because of college; he was very driven, inspired, and smart. Those qualities make successful business leaders. But for the vast majority of people, a college education is critical.

 Key Takeaways:

- Be considerate.
- Think outside the box.
- Ask the right questions.
- Network.
- Experiment.

JULIE SKAFF (she/her)
COO, Viz.ai

#JourneyOfLearning

 **On business:** To get your message across, use fewer words.

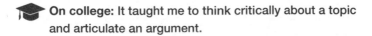 **On social:** It allows you to connect with people in your life that you wouldn't be as able to otherwise, but it can lead people to say things that they wouldn't if they were talking to somebody face to face. That trend is dangerous.

On college: It taught me to think critically about a topic and articulate an argument.

Julie Skaff always thought she would be a sports journalist and believes the values she learned as the only girl on her youth baseball team have helped her navigate the male-dominated tech industry. As the chief operating officer of Viz.ai, an artificial intelligence company that helps patients get access to lifesaving treatments, she is always learning more about the health and technology industries, and how they work together. Julie's growth mindset has helped her thrive where others might feel overwhelmed or discouraged. She is incredibly enthusiastic about what AI can accomplish in the medical field and talks about how her industry will continue to grow and improve.

What drew you to the health-care technology field?

I have a real interest in public policy and dealing with complexities that are big issues for society. After business school, health care was a natural fit for me. I love it because it's fast-paced, and we get to work on things that really help people. There's a bigger purpose to what we do.

Your company uses artificial intelligence to help patients get the care they need quicker. Can you explain how you use AI to do that?

We build software that detects diseases—for example, an algorithm that is cleared to detect suspected large vessel occlusions, a form of stroke—in order to dramatically reduce the time to treatment for patients, leading to better outcomes. In the United States there are seven hundred thousand or eight hundred thousand strokes every year, and roughly a third of them are large-vessel occlusions. Studies have shown that Viz helps providers reduce time to treatment and, as a result, reduce the mortality and disability caused by stroke.

Could you use actual machine robots to help in your sector?

It's hard to imagine robots performing procedures on a mass scale—though there are some examples. We measure our algorithm based on sensitivity and specificity. It's statistics. The higher the sensitivity and specificity, the better. We also want to err on the side of caution. We naturally toggle the algorithm to be more sensitive, and importantly, we're helping optimize workflow; we're not replacing it.

What can AI do to help stop climate change?

I think more broadly, AI has applications in transportation, energy, infrastructure, and in general around the energy grid that have impacts on carbon emissions and climate change. I think there are massive applications for AI in smarter systems. Even things like self-driving cars—fewer traffic jams can result in much higher fuel economy. In health care, one of the best things that we could do is help improve outcomes and reduce the cost to society, because in the United States, we spend over $4 trillion a year, about 18 percent of gross domestic product (GDP). Those high expenditures crowd out the federal budget for other advancements that could deal with climate change. One of the things that we could do is to make health care more sustainable for society.

Are people or machines better equipped to solve big problems such as climate change and racial justice?

I think we need both. When writing a program or an algorithm, if there is implicit bias behind that code, then the AI itself is going to project discrimination. For example, if you had AI looking at résumés, and something about the algorithm it was based on conveyed an implicit bias against certain groups, then the AI could have the negative effect of increasing discrimination or increasing bias. There have been a couple of cases where large tech companies have had trouble realizing that if you feed the wrong things into a chat bot, you could get negative results. I think in both climate change and racial justice, we need both humans and AI.

There are far fewer women in the technology sector than men. Why is that?

It depends on the sector that you're in. I do think that there tend to be more women in health care than there might be in other parts of technology. Some of it has to do with really being comfortable being different from the other people in the room. All of us have reasons why we might feel out of place or unique in a situation. I've just been used to that. I've also been lucky to work with a lot of companies that really value diversity. In my experience, there are lots of people with different backgrounds in the room and that makes for a richer experience for everyone.

What traits do you have that have helped you succeed in the field?

I played a lot of sports growing up. The confidence that we get from team sports and working together is an important foundation for women in their professional lives. It doesn't mean that you must be a star athlete, but to be part of a team—whether it is chess or basketball—is meaningful. When I played baseball as a little girl, I was the only girl on the team and the only girl in the league. I don't know if that would be the case now, but I do think it made me prepared to be okay if I'm the only woman in the room.

What was your greatest challenge in school, and what is your greatest challenge today?

I find it hard to focus, and I get easily distracted. That was hard for me in school, and in my job now because I'm the chief operating officer of a company, and there are lots of things that come across my desk. Being able to focus and accomplish things is a real challenge. I come up with little tricks like blocking out an hour or two here or there for deep work time.

Do you think you would have the occupation you did when you were our age?

I wanted to be a sports journalist. I used to write a magazine about baseball when I was about ten. I would write it on the typewriter, print it at a copy shop, and friends would subscribe to it.

How did your college experience shape who you are today?

I went to Northwestern University, and I loved my college experience. What it really taught me was to think critically about a topic and articulate an argument. I don't think everyone needs an in-person, four-year education, though. There are great vocational programs, and learning can and will change. I also lived in Europe for a year while I was in college. Learning a new language and living in a foreign country was certainly huge for my self-reliance and independence.

If you were to start your career over again, what would you change?

This is my fifth health technology start-up, and the amount of learning that I've had is motivating and exciting. Our CEO often says: "I always like to think about how much I've learned in the last week." Essentially, he's saying: "I was unaware of these other things, and two weeks later, look how far we've come." That sort of learning and growth mindset is important in life, and especially to your generation. I don't know that I would do anything differently, because everywhere that I have been and every relationship that I've built has led to the next chapter. I think if you're reflecting on it, it doesn't become a regret so much as what you can take away from the experience and how you can apply it in the future.

Who is your biggest mentor and what did they teach you?

One of my managers had a saying around getting your message across. He said, "If you can use three words, use three words." In other words, be concise. Really practical advice. It isn't overarching like "follow your dreams"—which is true, you should.

Key Takeaways:

- ➔ Have a growth mindset.
- ➔ Be mission driven.
- ➔ Apply yourself to a passion.
- ➔ Be part of a team.
- ➔ Set aside focused work time.

LEE BRENNER (he/him)

Head of Public Policy, Digital Assets,
Goldman Sachs

#CuttingEdge

On life: Even if you have a vision of the way things are going to go, they may not always go that way, and you need to be adaptable to whatever external forces may come at you.

On business: Make sure the problem you are trying to solve is not just interesting to you, but that it solves a problem for other people.

On social: Everything in moderation.

On college: It's not just about the diploma. It is about the experience you have and the people you meet.

Imagine transferring money as fast and efficiently as sending a text. Media and tech entrepreneur **Lee Brenner** is working on new blockchain and digital-assets technology to accomplish that very thing. Lee has spent his career at the cutting edge of technology, media, public affairs, and politics, and now works in the public policy sector to help digital currency become as stable as the traditional dollar and build trust in the system. Before his current job at Goldman Sachs, Lee worked at Facebook (Meta) trying to find a way to move the US dollar quicker than ever before. Before that, he founded HyperVocal to capture trending news topics and make them attractive to young audiences, as automated and factual doses of the internet. He launched a luxury baby bag company shortly after earning his master's degree in Hong Kong, and he traveled the world making deals and learned the intricacies of entrepreneurship. He has worked at CNN, Myspace, and Microsoft, where he first became interested in blockchain technology. In all his positions, Lee's goal has been to use technology and innovation to help people. He talks to us about wearing multiple hats, thinking on your feet, and surrounding yourself with inspiring colleagues.

What is your goal as Goldman Sachs's first ever head of public policy for digital assets?

My goal is to be as helpful as possible as this new ecosystem is developed and as regulations and public policies are explored to make sure innovation can flourish and the ecosystem is as safe as possible for the businesses, governments, and people who use it.

Many people are incredibly skeptical of the volatility and legitimacy of cryptocurrency and non-fungible tokens (NFTs), since they only exist digitally. What is something you wish more people understood?

The technology is still in its early days, so don't make conclusions yet. There will be things that work and some things that don't. And the "killer app" probably isn't created yet. The companies on the cutting edge need to constantly be educating others and themselves. Always be learning.

Many people know Facebook (Meta) only as a social media platform for expressing their political views and sharing family photos. You worked on a piece of it that many don't know about. Can you explain the blockchain technology project you worked on, and what the goals were?

I worked on a public policy team, which deals with governments, regulators, and third-party groups like think tanks, academics, and trade associations who influence policy decisions. The reason behind this project was that if you think about the speed at which people can communicate with text messages, email, or videos right now, it's instantaneous. What hasn't kept up is the speed at which people can send one dollar. Right now, if you want to send money from Washington, DC, to somewhere in Africa or the Philippines, it's costly, and it often takes more than a day to get there, but it is imperative for people around the world who need that money and are sending it to their friends and family. People who might not have access to financial services often have access to a phone, so we were building a wallet app for your phone to be able to send money as easy as it is to send a text message.

What is the problem you were trying to address with blockchain technology?

Blockchain technology has the potential to be transformative for all different areas of people's lives. Technology has not, to this point, kept up with people's needs in financial services, so the goal was to provide a service that was really useful for people. There are almost two billion people around the world who don't have access to basic financial services, so the goal was to help move that needle a little bit.

How do you plan to change the scene of digital currency? Do you think it will be hard to do?

It will not be easy. Part of the challenge of digital currencies up to this point has been because of the volatility of Bitcoin and other cryptocurrencies. It moves up and down so quickly, and the value of it goes up and down. It hasn't been beneficial for people to use it to buy a soda at the market, right? People don't want to do that, because one day it could be worth one dollar, the next day it could be worth ten dollars. The Facebook project was trying to build a system that allows more people around the world to be comfortable with digital currency. A digital currency that has the backing of real traditional currencies like the dollar lets people know that the value of it will be the same today as it will be tomorrow, and people can use it to buy the things that they need on a day-to-day basis. The more people have access to something stable like that, the more comfortable people around the world will be with the concept of digital currency.

How did your career and work at CNN prepare you for your work at HyperVocal and Facebook (Meta)?

CNN teaches you how to think on your feet and be reactive to different scenarios. When you're working in a newsroom during breaking news, you learn about what decisions need to be made in a moment, such as who the best people are who are influencing policies, so that you can bring those people on and interview them. Decisions are made in the actual newsroom about which cameras you want to go to, which places around the world, and where the reporters should be to tell the story to make sure that the viewers are getting the most facts. Working in the news, you learn how to wear multiple hats. That's an essential skill set that I think has been applicable in every job I've had.

As a serial entrepreneur, how would you describe yourself and your skills?

Being able to juggle multiple things, but also being adaptable. In the news world, especially, you learn to understand many different things. One of the most essential skills that I have is relationship building and making sure that I can listen to other people, understand their concerns, and potentially try to find the solution. That applies to anywhere you are in any role. I've been

> *"When you start something from scratch, it forces you to learn all different aspects of the business. That's the best part of being an entrepreneur."*

fortunate to work in some exciting companies and surround myself with brilliant and interesting people. The most crucial part is making sure that you're in a place surrounded by people who are intellectually stimulating and, hopefully, smarter than you.

What skills are most important for our generation as they enter the workforce, especially if they want to work in tech and finance?

Learn to listen, be excited by trying something new, and don't be afraid to fail.

What is the best business advice you would give to young entrepreneurs?

Try to be solving a problem. Make sure that it's not something that is interesting just to you, but that it's something that solves a problem for other people. And if it does that, then there's probably value in it, and if you can solve that problem, that should be the core of the business model.

Who is your most significant mentor, and what did they teach you?

I've been fortunate to have a bunch of mentors from growing up with a family of entrepreneurs—I learned quite a bit from them. In all my jobs, though, I've tried to find at least one person to help guide me, but everyone has something to teach you.

What movie, TV, or literary character are you most like?

Have you ever seen the movie *The Goonies*? It's one of my favorite movies from my childhood. I think going on adventures and having a sense of humor about things are the two things that I identify with.

 Key Takeaways:

➔ Learn to juggle multiple things.
➔ Don't be afraid to fail.
➔ Learn to listen.
➔ Be adaptable to external forces.
➔ Surround yourself with people smarter than you.

STEVE DOUTY (he/him)

Cofounder and CEO, Octopus Software,
Smaarts Inc., Scayl Inc.

#Opportunist

On business: Be persistent in your ultimate goal, but flexible in how you get to that goal.

On social: At its core, it is a good thing that allows people to interact with others in real time, but it has become politicized and what's considered acceptable has become very fuzzy.

On college: You can't virtualize the kinds of bonds you build when you're having a true shared experience, like at college or graduate school. It follows you for your whole career.

Before there was Gmail or Outlook, there was Hotmail—considered the first web-based email service, launched in 1996 and sold to Microsoft for $400 million a year and a half later. Technology entrepreneur **Steve Douty** not only watched the meteoric rise of the company as one of the first four employees and the vice president of product, sales, and marketing, he was also helping make it all happen. Lessons from those exhilarating early days of email shaped his business philosophy throughout his career, which has included management positions at such tech giants as Microsoft and Yahoo!, as well as founding and leading several successful software start-ups. Steve predicts that coding will become as common as speaking English, believes that technology companies should stay out of social justice issues, and guarantees that social media will never replace human interaction.

You were one of the first employees at Hotmail. What was it like to help launch such an iconic company and the first email company?

They call companies that get huge really quickly "unicorns." Back then, there was no such notion as a unicorn. When I joined, we had a hundred users in beta, and eventually ended up with 380 million users. I was thirty-five at the time. I summoned everything I'd ever learned about business, marketing, sales, and technology, and pulled it together and applied it. I was responsible for product, sales, and marketing—essentially everything except engineering and the data center. Every day, we would look at the number of people who had signed up, and within about three months, we hit one hundred thousand. You have to multiply those numbers by ten because there were one tenth the number of people on the internet as there are now. It grew exponentially. It was truly a geometric curve. One of the cofounders wanted to put more ads on the home page and get more money, and my instinct was not to touch it. If something is working, don't change it. We were trying to resist the temptation to do more.

What were the biggest challenges?

There were a lot of copycats. There were email services with crazy names that completely copied our user interface (UI) pixel for pixel. We had the traction. We had to be really present in the marketplace. As things got bigger over time, we started talking to some of the big companies that we thought might acquire us, like Microsoft and Yahoo. We were getting on their radar. It was so cool and fun, and we couldn't really believe what we had. At the same time, we were always on the edge because we wanted to make sure the trend continued. It was exciting, but also nerve-racking at the same time.

How did each step of your career prepare you for the next?

When I was in college, I planned my career. I read an article about a guy who started a billion-dollar computer company. He described his career path, and I planned to do the same thing. I was in sales, then marketing, then engineering. I had a computer

> *"To be a successful entrepreneur, you have to be willing to live in a gray area and deal with ambiguity and uncertainty."*

science degree, but I'm not a coder. I wanted to have experience across the board. I wanted to understand how to raise money, how to run a company, and how to finance it. I had this crazy career path that was jumping from one discipline to another, so that when I became CEO, I would know about all these different areas. I chose this well-rounded approach as opposed to the linear approach. Every job I picked was a stepping stone for me to continue to the next job. It was very deliberate.

Since you mentioned coding, how important do you think learning coding languages will be in the sector?

I think it will become as common as speaking English. Today's executive has to have a lot of knowledge about the way things are working, and an understanding of what's possible. There was an expression we used to use: "It's just a simple matter of coding," or SMOC. Of course, it's not as easy as it looks. To understand that, you have to at least know one of the languages, like Python or JavaScript. To have any sort of appreciation, and a sense of your limits, you absolutely need to know what sandbox you are playing in, and how the stuff is actually built.

What skills will our generation have to learn to succeed in business?

If you want to start a company, you've got to raise money and be able to speak that language. The technology changes, but the way businesses work has not changed. You've got to have some understanding either through your own experience or through education. If someone has a dual major in computer science and business, they will be best equipped to go out into the world. Then you can code, but always know the business underneath it. If you want to be successful, you also have to understand social media. You have to understand how to apply social media to get your name and company out there. Branding is a big skill. YouTubers, with all of their followers, are a brand. They want to understand how to build and maintain their brand.

What are the most important personality traits for an entrepreneur?

You've got to be extremely persistent. You have to be receptive to the fact that some of your ideas might not be exactly right. You've got to be able to change directions. You're always tweaking. You've got to be persistent in your ultimate goal, but flexible in how you get to that goal. You have to be willing to live in a gray area and deal with ambiguity and uncertainty. If that freaks you out, you won't be successful.

What is your most unique personality trait, and does it relate to business in any way?

The ability to describe and communicate very complicated things in a way that everybody can understand. It's why I went from being a computer science major in college to sales. In sales, you've got to be able to sell technical products to people who aren't technical. I'm lucky to have had the ability to explain what's really happening in a way people understand and take something complicated and break it down into something more digestible.

What is your greatest passion outside of work?

Computers and music. I think they're intertwined. Music has structure, melody, and meaning. Music gets you emotional, creates moods, and can influence how you feel. I think if you write great applications, and you have great products, it's a similar experience. I get the same kind of high from business that I do from playing music.

 ## Key Takeaways:

- ➡ Stick to your plan, but be flexible.
- ➡ Learn to be comfortable with ambiguity.
- ➡ Be persistent.
- ➡ Make an effort to be with other people.
- ➡ Learn to communicate complex ideas.

JENNIFER SILBERMAN (she/her)
Chief Sustainability Officer, Dollar Tree

#PassionateChangemaker

On business: Thinking about the long-term environmental and social impact can lead to different kinds of disruption and design innovation.

On social: It is a great way for entrepreneurs to showcase their products, but the vitriol and the hate allowed on these platforms is very dangerous.

On college: It's a valuable time in a young person's life, to open your horizons and your eyes to new things to study. One of the most important and intangible ways you learn are the social experiences and the softer skills.

How do you create a brand that is both good for business and good for the world? That's the problem **Jennifer Silberman** tackled when she was creating strategy for brands such as Hilton, Target, and YETI. As an expert in corporate responsibility and global sustainability—and the current CSO of Dollar Tree—her job is to make sure companies balance profit with environmental and social impact. That goal is becoming more important as customers become increasingly savvy and call out companies if they aren't honest, transparent, and action forward. Younger consumers are demanding more transparency and accountability from businesses, and Jennifer is helping them deliver. She talks to us about being true to your brand, employee buy-in, sourcing, supply chain accountability, and product design.

How can you help large corporations focus their impact on the community and environment?

While lots of companies might have the right intentions, they often lack the connection to the business and aligning it to both market and business incentives with societal good. They often think it's a trade-off—either be profitable or socially and environmentally responsible. It's about helping companies expand their thinking that environmental and social impact and benefits can lead to greater innovation in product development, cost savings, greater efficiencies, and more engaged employees who feel that they're working for a place that has a higher sense of purpose. Companies can realize different benefits by creating the right incentives internally. Rewarding only for driving costs down or looking for the cheapest labor or materials won't incentivize companies to continue to push for greater innovation and greater integration between profit and environmental and social impact.

The current events impacting our generation, such as COVID-19, climate change, and racial inequality, are becoming more and more significant concerns. How do you have to consider these things when helping companies make the right move while still maintaining the brand and core values?

That's the million-dollar question. Customers want to give business to and shop with organizations that align with their values and what they believe in. There are some nonnegotiables. Obviously, racial inequality and injustice, violence, police brutality—most companies are on the right side of those issues. If not, they're definitely called out and boycotted. We've seen what's happening to social media platforms for being seen as more of an enabler of hate speech than working to stop it. Target is a mass merchant serving 80 to 90 percent of America. The retailer has a diversity of consumers across the country with different values and beliefs. You're weighing these complex social and environmental issues and trying to understand where you step in and what the expectations of your consumers are. While you may have consumers who want you to be more proactive and outspoken on certain issues, there may be others who feel very strongly that it is not your role. It's really important to know who you are as a brand, what your values are, and what you stand for. What is your North Star? You have to be very specific about why you're engaging and why it makes sense for you.

YETI has become a popular "cult" brand with over $450 million dollars in sales. What have you learned from helping YETI that is different from other brands you have worked on?

What attracted me to a company YETI's size and where they are on their growth cycle is being able to be disruptive, innovative, and nimble. Working for large companies has benefits, but often, moving fast and being disruptive are not among them. Being able to support the overall growth of YETI and understanding how sustainability can help is exciting. How does it dimensionalize the brand? How does it expand our product offerings? It is also exciting to have a diverse consumer base. YETI's customers include fishermen, hunters, rock climbers, foodies, beachgoers. The environmental movement has felt exclusive to some people, or very left of center, and with YETI, there's a lot more in common on issues of conservation, healthy habitat, and the natural resources that we depend on, where can you find common ground across different segments of the population who agree on a lot of the same things. They might have different approaches or solutions for that; for example, one may believe in the power of regulation or a price on carbon, and one may believe in the power of individual conservation actions. How can you work with groups and bring more of a common framework together that can ensure that we support and protect the wild that we're all dependent on?

"It's like that Nike slogan—there is no finish line."

What types of people do you like to hire?

The most important thing in people is a little fire in the belly. That can come out in different ways, like being able to try new things, being passionate about learning, being curious, asking a lot of questions. A lot of times we say, we can teach you how to do the job, what we can't teach you is to be a good team player, a good thought partner. We can't teach you to have empathy for your coworkers. We can't teach you to be inquisitive and curious. We can't teach you to learn how to have cognitive dissonance and be comfortable with respectfully discussing and debating ideas. All those things are really important. Are you teachable? Do you take feedback well? Are you coachable? Do you listen to constructive criticism and feedback to continuously improve?

Many in Gen Z grew up with modern conveniences such as a smartphone and the internet. How has your experience been without these tools, and what lessons did you learn by approaching problems a different way?

The instant gratification aspect of technology has not been good for society and the environment. As beneficial as it has been to order everything on your phone or be able to get into an Uber, we do know that there are elements within this gig economy that have negative impacts on social and environmental considerations. There are labor issues, how workers are treated and how they are compensated. The tension between receiving a product immediately that we didn't really need obviously has huge environmental impacts like transportation and packaging. Did you really need to order that, and do you really need it within twelve hours? The toll that it places on the whole ecosystem because of that one click to buy in that moment is huge.

Who was your first friend from another culture, and what did you learn from them?

My mother is Argentine, so I always have had a deep connection to Argentina and South America through my family. I met a lot of other Latins when I was young who were friends of my parents. That is something that is very important to me. I've always had friends from all over the world. I went to an international studies graduate program, and I have very close friends from that program who live everywhere. At Hilton, I worked for a global hospitality company and traveled to more than seventy countries over seven years. That's always been very important to me to get to know other cultures and experience food, travel, art, and politics and to really get immersed in where I am.

 Key Takeaways:

➡ Get to know people from other cultures.
➡ Find common frameworks.
➡ Look at the whole picture.
➡ Be a team player.
➡ Be transparent.

ALAN TURLEY (he/him)

Minister-Counselor for Commercial Affairs, US Embassy, Tokyo

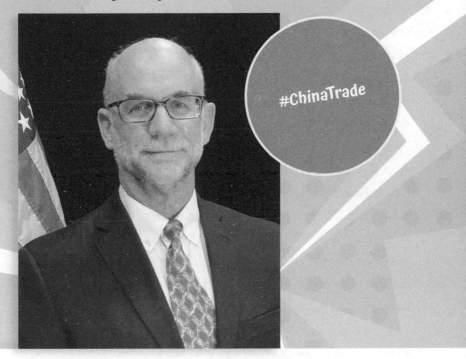

#ChinaTrade

On business: Do what you say you are going to do.

On social: It's a tool that can be used for both good and bad.

On college: It is very important for intellectual and social development. College made me realize I wasn't as smart as I thought I was.

POLITICS & POLICY

What can working in a completely different cultural and overseas environment teach you about business? Turns out many of the same things it can teach about life. Be humble, seek to understand context, and be ready for the unpredictable. **Alan Turley** grew up in a small Connecticut town but has spent his professional life working overseas, which has given him a whole new way of looking at the world. An expert in international trade and commerce, Alan has headed operations for FedEx in East Asia, served in the US embassies in Beijing and Tokyo, and worked in the US Commerce Department, leading to a post as deputy assistant secretary of commerce for China and Mongolia. He shares with us his experiences doing business with and leading people from different cultures, and says the United States has plenty to learn from other societies.

What business problems are you trying to tackle right now?

In a large sense, how does the United States coexist with China in a way that creates maximum benefits for both countries? In a narrower context, my job is export promotion, so the thing I'm struggling with now is the ongoing trade war with China. How do we help American companies sell their goods and services to China, and what is the best way to do that?

How do you think your experiences overseas have changed your perspective and values?

I have spent more of my life overseas than I have in the United

370

States. That experience has changed me profoundly. I don't think it has changed my basic values, but it made me understand and accept different ways of expressing those values in different cultures. For example, how families operate in different cultures is very different from how families operate in the United States. It doesn't mean that people in the culture I am most familiar with, China, have less family feeling, but they express that family feeling in a different way. As much as I love the United States and Americans, there is a lot we can learn from other cultures and other societies. We have this feeling that everything in the United States has to be the best way of doing things, and I certainly feel we would have a lot to learn by borrowing experience from other countries.

Do you need to tailor your management styles for different cultures to be more effective?

Yes. My experience is limited to East Asia and the United States, but to give an example, when I was working in Japan, very often you would have to talk to senior people in the office before you discuss a decision and give them a chance to air their views to help you to shape the discussion. In China, criticism is very hard. People do not like to be questioned in public, even gently. You must be careful about how you tell someone they have made a mistake and that we need to fix that mistake. You can be a little more direct with Americans. One of the things I found back in the United States that I had forgotten is that Americans love to be told what a great job they are doing. It's sort of a management custom here to always tell everyone how fantastic things are going, and what a great team they are. There is less need for that in the other places I've worked.

What types of people do you like to hire and be around, and why?

I like to hire people who are hardworking, diligent, and smart, probably in that order of importance. I have worked with many smart people, but they weren't very reliable. Tell them you need something done by Thursday, and on Friday they say I have all these reasons not to do it. That's intensely frustrating. I'd rather work with someone who is not as smart but who gets the job done on time and does what they say they are going to do. Similarly, those kinds of people are most fun to be around. They mean what they say and do what they say, and they are also smart and engaged in their work and in their lives.

Who is your biggest mentor and what did they teach you?

My biggest mentor was a woman named Ying Ye, who was my boss in Taiwan and then in Beijing. I learned a lot from her about being a manager in a Chinese context, about how to focus on the things that were really important. I appreciated that it reinforced my belief that it is important to make good decisions. I have had bosses before Ying who would think over a decision for a week and then not really decide on what to do. What I really liked about her was she would usually decide something right away. If she wanted to think about it, she would say, "I need to think about it overnight," and always come back with an answer. I also learned an enormous amount about operating in-

> *"There are many things in the world that are unpredictable and long-term trends that you can't foresee. There are other things that happen that change the world that are entirely predictable, and you have to be ready for those as well."*

terculturally. She was a fascinating woman who was born in Beijing, raised in Taiwan, worked in the American system, and had a tremendous understanding of all sides of the culture.

Many people in our generation are questioning the value of college. How did your educational environment affect your personal development as a leader?

I think that college was very important in terms of intellectual development and social development. It impacted me in a couple of important ways. First, because I had always been a good student, it made me realize I wasn't as smart as I thought I was. That's an important lesson to learn. You aren't always the smartest guy in the room. You don't always know more than anyone else. The other thing I would say about college is my experience gave me a broad look into a lot of different fields of education and learning. I took courses in history and religion. I also took courses in accounting and science. I think it was a fantastic experience to understand the breadth of opportunities that were out there and what it would take to be academically successful in any one of those fields.

What one habit do you wish you could break?

Procrastination.

What type of art do you like best? How does it influence your work?

I am a huge fan of poetry. It makes me very careful of the words I write and appreciative of people who can express their thoughts elegantly and clearly. It reminds me of the power of words.

What movie character do you think you are most like?

Kermit the Frog. Sometimes I feel I am like Kermit trying to hold everything together.

 **Key Takeaways:**

- ➔ Be decisive.
- ➔ Be humble.
- ➔ Express yourself clearly.
- ➔ Appreciate the power of words.
- ➔ Expand your horizons.

RICHARD BIRD (he/him)
Chief Product Officer, SecZetta

#TheGuyWithTheBowTie

📊 **On business:** There are no free rides. There is no easy path to success. To be successful, you have to put in the effort.

📱💬 **On social:** A hammer, when it's used for its intended purpose to drive a nail, is a great tool. A hammer, when used to commit a crime by attacking somebody, is a weapon. Social media is exactly like that.

🎓 **On college:** The education doesn't become the thing that determines whether you're going to be successful or not—you do.

As the chief product officer for cybersecurity firm SecZetta, **Richard Bird** spends his days fighting to protect information and personal identities. He says companies must do much more to invest in protection against cyberattacks and identify theft because the bad guys are always two steps ahead. But cybersecurity isn't just a one-way street, and individuals need to use the same precautions in the digital world that they do in the physical world. Richard travels the globe to evangelize the need for better digital security. He gives us the ins and outs of hacking, teaches us how to think like the enemy, and tells us about the big role our generation has to play in moving the field forward. He also shares life lessons such as the importance of recognizing that success is a team effort, not getting too full of yourself, and being the best at whatever you choose to do.

What can we all do as individuals to keep our identities and information safe?

You need to expect better from companies. The vast majority of companies want all of your information because they get paid for it. They monetize it and create products from it. At a very minimum, they use that information to sell you more stuff with targeted marketing, but they don't protect it like they should. Even though there's money being spent on cybersecurity, it is being spent to protect information in a way that hasn't changed much in thirty years. We have to start thinking differently about how to protect people, because what we've been doing is protecting data.

What can companies do better?

If all I am required to do as a company is protect your stuff, all I have to do is be you and I get your stuff. That is the best explanation for hacking: it is somebody trying to be someone they're not to get something that they shouldn't have or do something that they shouldn't be allowed to do. That's what needs to change.

How is cybersecurity different at the corporate level versus the individual level?

At the corporate level, cybersecurity is challenging because as soon as there is any new way to protect a company, data, applications, and information, the bad actors are figuring out a way to get around it. In cybersecurity, you have to think like the enemy to have a chance at the corporate level. At the personal level, human beings are extremely predictable with rituals and habits. We tend to do the same things in the same order. Every morning, I get up, drink coffee, eat toast and jam, and work out. It's the same every single morning. If a bad guy was following me, he'd know my pattern. That's the problem with cybersecurity. The bad guys know humans have patterns, and that we're very strict about keeping those patterns. When you combine that with the other part of personal cybersecurity, which is that most people believe that companies, organizations, and governments are protecting them when they're really not, it becomes relatively easy for the bad guys to take advantage of the situation.

On the flip side, what do individuals need to do better?

Cybersecurity is more about human behavior than it is about technology. In order to protect yourself, you have to start thinking like you do in the physical world. You don't leave your doors un-locked, you don't leave your keys lying on the table, you don't put all of your medical records out in the dining room, but we do that all the time in the digital world. Most people are willing to give away the right to protect themselves for a 20 percent discount. Does a company that I'm buying shirts from really need to text me? Do they need my cell phone number? The real challenge with personal cyber-security is that it's super hard to change human behavior.

What will the future of cybersecurity look like?

The future of cybersecurity is always unknown, but I think that we're going to see a very important change in the creation of digital identities that we have some power over. Right now, gaming com-panies, news companies, and browsers tell you what your identity is; they actually create a digital version of you that's incomplete, because it serves their purposes. Facebook (Meta) collects a tre-mendous amount of data about you and turns it into a digital you, but it's not an accurate representation. It is always the good side of you—where you travel, your pets, your kids. It doesn't include the times you are late or the things that frustrate you. The work going on right now will have a massive impact on cybersecurity in the future and give people the power to prove that they are who they say they are. In identity cybersecurity-speak, that's called authen-tication. The reason that we can do that now is because the devices we own are becoming ubiquitous. Phones are very personal to us now. The future of cybersecurity

> *"Your success in life comes when you are surrounded by people who see more potential in you than you see in yourself."*

is definitely going to be oriented toward more personalized security and devices, and the bad guys will try to figure out how to get around that. That is where we need to see changes in attitudes and for people to understand that the first obligation for your personal security is yours.

Considering the impact of keeping data safe, how important do you think learning coding languages will be in the future?

I think the future is going to be a lot less language based and more microservices, application programming interface (API), and low code, no code based. The cool thing about that is it allows people to be creative. It knocks down barriers to entry for entrepreneurs and creative minds. It doesn't necessarily mean that we will leave all of those languages behind; there will always be a need for enterprise-grade programming languages. Python has been a great example of that because it has been around for a long time, and it's critical. C++ , COBOL, and Fortran are almost as old as me, but they are still here. There will always be a need for people who have a formal interest in computer sciences and want to learn those languages, but I think we're going to see a change in how technology gets developed that's going to be significantly different than it is today and means that you don't necessarily need to be a master in a particular language to be successful in building technology solutions.

If you could choose three key skills you've developed from traveling and speaking around the world, what would they be?

The first is recognizing that my career is not about my effort exclusively. I have a lot of people working hard to put me out front.

I have public relations, marketing, and media people. Many entrepreneurs are dependent on other people for their success. Second, when I travel, I walk everywhere and explore. I've made friends all over the world. Third is that your success in life comes when you are surrounded by people who see more potential in you than you see in yourself.

What are the most common personality traits of successful entrepreneurs?

They really don't understand "no." Entrepreneurs will get the answer no a lot when they're seeking funding or trying to create a new market. Every great entrepreneur has never heard that word when shared with them. The other characteristic is that they recognize that being an entrepreneur is a very personal investment. That's why so many companies are a reflection of their founders— Steve Jobs, Steve Wozniak, Elon Musk. They've invested themselves so much that it's hard to tell the difference between the person and what they've developed. Every successful entrepreneur knows that it is a tremendous amount of work.

What is the most important lesson you have learned in your lifetime?

The most important lessons I learned from my father. My dad owned his own business. I started working for him when I was twelve, until I was twenty-three. I worked with my father every day, a hundred days a year, as a fishing boat guide and first mate. My dad taught me not to believe your own advertising.

Don't ever get so full of yourself that you think you have all the answers or that your ideas are the best, because the instant that you

begin to behave like that is the instant that you will begin to fail. He also taught me that no matter what you do in life, be the best at it. If you're a garbage collector, be the best. That advice has had a huge amount of influence on my career, and I think it applies to entrepreneurs.

What else can entrepreneurs learn from this advice?

You have to have an attitude that, when you find your passion, you are going to be the best at it. But remember, don't believe your own advertising, because if you believe that your success as an entrepreneur, or as a human being, is all about you, you're missing it. If you're going to be an entrepreneur just to become wealthy, you're focused on the wrong things. You also have a responsibility to pave your way to success by aligning with others. You have to have other people come along with you on your journey. If you don't, you won't get there.

What personality traits do you value most in leaders?

The most important characteristic of people who are successful is self-awareness. You understand your weaknesses and strengths, and you understand situations that are developing around and in front of you. I have never met an entrepreneur or successful executive who wasn't self-aware. They know what they love, what they don't, what they stand for. Self-awareness is the single most important characteristic that I look for in everybody, including myself.

 **Key Takeaways:**

➔ Take the same precautions in the digital world as you do in the real world.
➔ Know your strengths, weaknesses, and passions.
➔ Acknowledge the contributions of others.
➔ Don't believe that you have all the answers.
➔ Make friends everywhere you go.

TIMOTHY KIGHT (he/him)
Founder and CEO, Focus 3

#DoTheWork

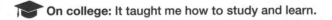 **On business:** Take advantage of modern innovation, but make sure you get the fundamentals right first.

On social: You have to be able to cut through the noise and find the signal. Just because something gets your attention doesn't mean it deserves your attention.

On college: It taught me how to study and learn.

Tim Kight is a public speaker and the founder and CEO of Focus 3, an organization that has taught leadership, culture, and teamwork to hundreds of other companies and organizations, including the Ohio State Buckeyes and ABC News. Tim's leading principle is *E + R = O,* which stands for *Event + Response = Outcome.* The meaning behind his concept is that someone's reaction to any situation influences the outcome, and he teaches us how thinking about your reaction first can positively change the outcome of any situation. He shares with us the meaning of the name Focus 3 and the six factors that are necessary to consider in order to achieve his formula for success. Beyond business, he also discusses with us his positive outlook on his cancer diagnosis, his perspective on diversity when hiring, and his unconventional approach to technology.

What mistakes have you made along your entrepreneurial journey, and how did you learn from them?

I'm a big believer that experience is a great teacher if you reflect on it. Mistakes are simply feedback, an opportunity to do something over again, with greater insight. What would I do differently from the very beginning? I would have focused earlier, hired people earlier, rather than try to do it all myself, and moved from California to Ohio earlier. The Midwest was a better business environment overall.

"Know your market and have a laser focus."

What are two or three principles you know now that you would love to tell your younger self?

The way you treat employees in your business matters enormously because your employees will never treat customers or clients any better than the way you treat your employees. I always believed that, and I always behaved and acted that way. I love the people on my team. I've always respected, valued, and honored my employees. I treat them very well and as a result they treat our clients very well. Culture is also really important when it comes to company performance. Strategy is important, but culture eats strategy for lunch. If you want to have a great company, you have to build a great culture as well as a great strategy.

You work with hundreds of organizations and your core philosophy is $E + R = O$, or event plus response equals outcome. What factors are most critical to getting that right?

The notion is you don't control events, but you do control how you choose to respond, and how you respond is what produces an outcome. We have identified six disciplines that you must have to consistently manage the art in that equation. Number one is press pause. Number two is get your mind right. Number three is step up. Four is adjust and adapt. Five is make a difference. Six is build skill.

Can you unpack that?

The purpose of pressing pause is clarity. You want to be clear about the $E + R = O$. Be clear about the event you have, that's the E. Be clear about the O that you want, that's the outcome, and then

> *"Mistakes are simply feedback, an opportunity to do something over again with greater insight."*

be clear about the *R* that will get you there. If you don't press pause, you become very susceptible to mismanaging things. Number two is get your mind right. That is, manage your mindset, make sure you have the skill to put yourself into a productive emotional state. Number three is step up, which is to take disciplined action and do what needs to be done. What does this situation require of me? For every situation you're in, there's an effective response available; go find it and do it. Adjust and adapt. The purpose of that is flexibility. Sometimes the *R* that you chose doesn't work very well, so go choose a different one. That's being flexible. Five is make a difference, which is that your *R* is an *E* for others. The way you manage the *R* has an impact on the people around you. So manage your *R* to give other people a great experience. Number six is build skills. Always be growing and getting better. Always be developing yourself. Never get satisfied or stuck. Always be improving in everything that you do.

What values must an organization have to be successful?

Every organization has to be very intentional about choosing values and be careful that they don't borrow some other company's values because they sound good. We help organizations create their cultures by choosing the values that they want to follow. Every company must decide what beliefs they need to create an environment where their people are fully engaged and energized to execute strategy.

What business advice would you give to young entrepreneurs?

Build your business on timeless truth and be innovative. Take advantage of what modern things are happening, but make sure you get the fundamentals right. Build a great culture, have a focused strategy, hire the right people, and behave with discipline every day. Love your people, serve your people, support your people. Make sure that the clients are well served.

Do you think college is necessary today?

I think it is likely that the four-year college is going to become almost obsolete. We're going to find new ways to get educated. If you want to learn accounting, there will be accounting schools. If you want to learn how to sell, there will be sales schools. If you want to learn to be an entrepreneurial business starter, there will be entrepreneurial schools.

What is one bad event in your life that led to something good?

This isn't my normal hair. This is my hair because I had cancer and I'm going through chemo treatment. Having cancer is a pretty bad thing, and here's the really great thing: I get to use $E + R = O$, and I get to have a great attitude. I'm high energy. I'm positive. The side effects of chemo are awful. I can't change that. So my attitude is "Let's fight this cancer. Let's win this battle." It's an opportunity for me to practice what I preach.

Key Takeaways:

➡ Be laser focused.
➡ Choose values you want to follow.
➡ Respect others.
➡ Control how you respond.
➡ Bring energy to all you do.

RESOURCES

Now that you've read the book, here are a few more resources we've put together to get you started on your entrepreneurial journey.

These are some of the camps and programs that have helped us hone our entrepreneurial skills. Some are dedicated to business, and others have entrepreneurship programs within a larger structure. Two that have been particularly awesome are the Acton Children's Business Fair, which has grown to a global movement of kid entrepreneurs turning ideas into legitimate businesses. If you don't see a fair in your city, start your own! The other is DECA Inc., which offers learning plans in many high schools and colleges. DECA challenges emerging leaders to take on real-life business scenarios in global competitions, helping them develop presentation and networking skills.

Entrepreneurship Camps, Programs, and Fairs

Acton Children's Business Fair: childrensbusinessfair.org

Baltimore Children's Business Fair's Launch Business Camp: baltimorechildrensbusinessfair.org

BETA Camp: beta.camp

Bizzy Boys: bizzyboys.com

Bizzy Girls: bizzygirls.com

DECA Inc.: deca.org

Johns Hopkins Center for Talented Youth: cty.jhu.edu

Jr. CEO: jr-ceo.com

Juni Learning: junilearning.com

Junior Achievement USA: jausa.ja.org

KidBiz, Inc.: kidbizinc.com/expo

Lead Camp: leadcamp.org

Spark Business Academy: sparkbusinessacademy.com

Stanford Pre-Collegiate Summer Institutes:
summerinstitutes.spcs.stanford.edu

TIC Camp: ticcamp.com

Entrepreneurship Competitions

There are many high school entrepreneurship competitions. Here are a few that we've competed in or that are offered by our schools:

Blue Ocean Competition: blueoceancompetition.org

Conrad Challenge: conradchallenge.org

DECA Corporate Challenges: deca.org/complete

Diamond Challenge: diamondchallenge.org

Wharton Global High School Investment Competition:
globalyouth.wharton.upenn.edu/investment-competition

Entrepreneurship Books

Read as much as you can! We read the news religiously, as well as magazines like *Entrepreneur,* which often features teen entrepreneurs. There are also many business books for teens, college students, and adults. Here are a few to start with:

Founders at Work: Stories of Startups' Early Days by Jessica Livingston

Good to Great: Why Some Companies Make the Leap . . . and Others Don't by Jim Collins

The Secrets of Sand Hill Road: Venture Capital and How to Get It by Scott Kupor

Steve Jobs by Walter Isaacson

ACKNOWLEDGMENTS

We'd like to thank the following people:

Our editor, Sara Sargent, at Random House, for taking a chance on two teenagers, guiding us through the world of book publishing, welcoming us onto a real team, and giving us the opportunity of a lifetime. Wendy Guarisco, for sharing enthusiasm for our project and for introducing us to our agent. Pamela Harty and the Knight Literary Agency, for being the first to see our vision, teaching us how to write a book proposal, and encouraging us to be patient.

All the business leaders who said yes to our interview requests, treated us like professionals, and took time from their busy schedules to share their wisdom: Semhar Araia, Jeni Britton Bauer, Richard Bird, Tara Bosch, Lee Brenner, Emma Butler, Annabel Chang, Andrea Clarke, Claire Coder, Gary Cox, Jennifer Dollander, Steve Douty, Zlata Filipovic, Dan Frank, Deepa Gandhi, Casey Georgeson, Mark Hanis, Rebecca Hu, Michael Jacoby, Ariel Kaye, Timothy Kight, Michael Krakaris, Larry Kramer, Lou Lauria, Eyal Levy, Wonya Lucas, Brandon Martinez, Sebastian Martinez, Ava McDonald, Charles Miller, Sergio Monsalve, Marissa Morin, Alina

Morse, Nitin Pachisia, Jane Park, Sean Peng, Sophie Pinkard, Dejan Pralica, Eric Rapprich, Aaron Rasmussen, Rich Riley, Travis Rosbach, Alison Rosenthal, Daniel Scharff, Gerry Sepe, Vivien Shen, Jennifer Silberman, Julie Skaff, Davis Smith, Cindy Soo, Ken Stern, Laurie Strongin, Yen Tan, Stelleo Tolda, Alan Turley, Danielle Vincent, Ann Crady Weiss, Helen Wu, Albert Xie, Mei Xu, and Karl Zottl.

The public relations professionals, schedulers, assistants, agents, and friends who helped make our interviews happen and showed us how to network: Catherine and Scott Ballenger, Allison Bennett, Jennifer Pifer Bixler, Jessica Botero, Klinton Briney, Heda Burdzovic, Katherine Campbell, Aria Keming Cao, David Clinch, Ashley Corwin, Michelle Cumbo, Ben Dalton, Collin Dennis, Beth Elliott, Yasser El-Shimy, Alison Fairbrother, Cassie Flores, Rainey Foster, Heather Frank, Courtney Froemming, Andrea Fuller, Holly Furner, Jussie Gamache, Joan Garretson, Betsy Goldman, Elisa Goldstein, Jennifer Gootman, Alex Guinand, William Gunn, Joe Hixson, Andrea Hong, Annie Howell, Stephanie Huynh, Silvia Iorgova, Sami Jenkin, Ashley Johnson, Lorelei Kelly, Mat Kestle, Andy Kill, Ken Kohan, Amy Kramer, Daniel Labin, Danielle Lane, Jackie Lange, Lindsay Lassman, Drew Lederman, Jennifer Lee, Mason Liffmann, Melissa Long, Jessica Loss, Daniela Maron, Rachel Martinez, Ted Matthews, Laura and Paul McGeary, Maria Mesina, Aaron Morehouse, Ryan Morgan, Heather Palladino, Camille Pareto, Emily Prechtl, Adi and Pooja Raval, Linda Roth, Xanthe Scharff, Abbie Steckler, Amy Stewart, Susan Toffler, My Ton, Amanda Turner, Sheilah Watts, Mitch Waxman, Becky White, Jennifer Zweben, and many others.

Kate Blackwell, for her beautiful illustrations in our book proposal, and Ashley Davis for her design.

Our friends and family who were the first to read the book and give us feedback: the Ballenger family, the Crisp family, the Norris family, the Poirier family, and the Soin family.

Our friends and family who answered surveys and questions for our market research: Leo Basso, Evan and Ray Davis, Rory Denman, Mariyah Espinoza, Derin Goktepe, Karoline Gonzalez, Lida Mann, Charlotte McGeary, Patrick and Jake Scurlock, Finn Thornhill, and Nikhil Vaish.

Fen's Personal Thanks

Acton Children's Business Fair of Washington, DC, for igniting my interest in entrepreneurship when I was seven. Takoma Park Children's Business Fair, Baltimore Children's Business Fair, Frederick Children's Business Fair, Chevy Chase Children's Business Fair, Alexandria Children's Business Fair, Montgomery County Children's Business Fair, Olney Farmers and Artists Market, Telluride Wine Festival, Leisure World, and KidBiz, Inc., for giving me the opportunity to sell my products and practice pitching, marketing, and negotiation; Spark Business Academy, Juni Learning, and Montgomery County Public Libraries, for their entrepreneurship classes.

My mentor, Zach Lasko, for modeling what it takes to run a small business; teaching me how to write a business plan, build a website, and edit video; and generally guiding me in life.

My English teachers Tara Barnhart, Dana Smith, Lesley Stanford, Dr. Hanna Janiszewska, and Dr. Kathleen Washburn for teaching me to be a close reader and deeply analyze texts, exposing me to new literary works, and pushing me to write shorter sentences. My history teachers Dr. Elyse Banks and Dr. Adrienne Chudzinski, for teaching me to look for knowledge for the present within the past; my philosophy instructors Dr. Heather Walker-Dale, Dr. Jonathan Weil, and Dr. Morgan Wallhagen, for teaching me to question everything; my Chinese and Latin instructors Lauren Bickart and Dr. Michael DeVinne, for expanding my world; and my Juni coding instructors, for teaching me what I believe is a fundamental business skill.

My parents, grandparents, extended family, coaches, and mentors for their fierce and unconditional love and for being my biggest fans in everything I do.

Jason's Personal Thanks

Mom, for always putting my well-being first and guiding me to be a better leader. Dad, for inspiring me every day to think like an entrepreneur and being my first teacher in business. My aunt, for training me to read more books and get out of my comfort zone. My grandparents living in America, for keeping culture forever close to home, and my grandparents living abroad, for widening my perspective of the world. The American Chinese School, for immersing me in Chinese culture and literature for ten years and sparking my passion for cross-cultural understanding. President of the Asian Pacific American Chamber of Commerce Stuart Rutchik, who believed in me and helped me get my first web development job at twelve. The Chinese American Museum in Washington, DC, for inspiring me to write about diverse perspectives. DECA, for building my competitor mindset and preparing me to tackle real-world business scenarios.